Shale Energy Revolution

Binlei Gong

Shale Energy Revolution

The Rise and Fall of Global Oil and Gas Industry

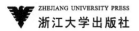

Binlei Gong
Zhejiang University
Hangzhou, Zhejiang, China

ISBN 978-981-15-4854-3   ISBN 978-981-15-4855-0   (eBook)
https://doi.org/10.1007/978-981-15-4855-0

Jointly published with Zhejiang University Press
The print edition is not for sale in China (Mainland). Customers from China (Mainland) please order the
print book from: Zhejiang University Press.

This Springer imprint is published by the registered company Springer Nature Singapore Pte Ltd.
The registered company address is: 152 Beach Road, #21-01/04 Gateway East, Singapore 189721,
Singapore

Dedicated to my family, Zhanguo Gong, Fengjuan Chen, Guanhua Zhong, Wei Li, Cuihua Gong, Lu Zhong, and Qizhen Gong, for their love and support!

Foreword by Yuzhu Kang

Energy is an important resource that guarantees the economic development of a nation. In recent years, the United States has launched the "shale energy revolution" through new technologies such as horizontal drilling and hydraulic fracturing to effectively exploit unconventional oil and gas resources. China's conventional oil and gas exploration, especially in the eastern areas, has entered the middle and late stage of exploration and production, which makes it difficult to maintain the overall domestic supply. Therefore, it is urgent to strengthen the exploration and production of unconventional oil and gas resources to make up for the declining production in the old oilfields.

What is encouraging is that China has made major breakthroughs in unconventional oil and gas exploration and production. In particular, the output of unconventional natural gas such as tight gas, shale gas and coal-bed methane has exceeded one-third of the overall domestic natural gas output. Among them, shale gas is the unconventional variety with the greatest development potential in China in the near future, and will become the main driving force of natural gas production growth in the next 5–10 years. Tight gas and coal-bed methane will also achieve steady development. At the same time, tight oil exploration and production have begun to take shape, shale oil and oil shale resources have great potential and will become an important alternative resource.

However, there are still some deficiencies in the exploration and production of unconventional oil and gas in China, such as insufficient understanding of the importance and potential of shale resource, the lack of establishment of the industrialization system of unconventional oil and gas, and the gap between China and the United States in technical theory and basic pipeline network construction. In this context, learning from the advanced experience of the "shale energy revolution" in the United States, and carrying out independent research and development (R&D) and technological improvement based on the characteristics of unconventional oil and gas resources in China are the keys to achieve the "shale energy revolution" in China as soon as possible.

Dr. Binlei Gong's book entitled *Shale Energy Revolution: The Rise and Fall of the Global Oil and Gas Industry and its Changes* uses a lot of data and cases to generate high-quality research on important subjects, such as how will the global oil and gas market change over the next decade? How did the United States become the world's No. 1 oil and gas producer? What is the future of China's shale industry and energy security? Are hydraulic fracturing and horizontal drilling technologies cheered or feared? Is energy production economically or environmentally driven? Who are the major players and competitors in the global oilfield market?

In this clear-cut and logical book, the author presents the rise and fall of the global oil and gas industry from both macro-and micro-perspectives. The macro-part first introduces the structural changes in the global oil and gas industry and its trend in the next decade, then analyzes the rise & fall as well as the change of the natural gas market and the oil markets, respectively, and finally studies the current situation of unconventional oil and gas development in China. The micro-part focuses on the micro-level behavior and performance of the upstream oilfield service firms and the petroleum enterprises that have footprints in the whole industry chain, including the spillovers of new technologies and technical efficiency, the impact of ownership on economic performance, and the competition and cooperation among enterprises. If you want to know what will happen to the energy markets in the future due to the Shale Revolution, this is a great book to read.

November 2019   Dr. Yuzhu Kang
                          Academician of Chinese Academy of Engineering
                                                           Beijing, China

Foreword by Bi Fan

Since the 1950s, oil and gas have gradually replaced coal as the dominant force in global supply of primary energy. During the Cold War, many countries raise their energy security to the height of national security because of experiencing the "oil crises" twice. In the twenty-first century, shale energy revolution has succeeded in the United States. As a result, the United States, which originally had a high degree of dependence on foreign energy, achieved "energy independence" in a short period of time.

How did the United States make this achievement? How will the US "energy independence" affect international relations and geopolitics? What is the position of oil and gas in the future energy landscape? Can China replicate the successful model of the US shale energy revolution? These questions lead to the universal concern by many in China's energy industry.

Shale Energy Revolution: The Rise and Fall of Global Oil & Gas Industry written by Dr. Binlei Gong is a monograph on the comprehensive study of the U.S. shale energy revolution. Dr. Gong has studied and worked in U.S. universities, energy companies, and energy public policy research institutions for a long period, and he currently works for the School of Public Affairs at Zhejiang University. During his studying and working in Houston, which was precisely the time when the U.S. shale energy production grew rapidly, he acutely witnessed this historic change in the field of energy. Persistence is the key to success, and he finally compiled his close observation and experience into this book.

The book is divided into two parts, and the impact of the shale energy revolution is discussed from both macro- and micro-perspectives. At the macro-level, the author investigates the changing trends of the global oil and gas industry structure, the role of natural gas in the future energy structure, as well as the challenges shale oil and gas industry in China will face, and draws a series of valuable conclusions. At the micro-level, this book involves issues such as large oil and gas companies and the development of shale technologies. As a public policy researcher, the author has a solid academic background in both energy technology and economics. Not only does his research give us a deeper understanding of the shale energy revolution, but also puts forward a series of valuable policy suggestions.

I believe that the publication of this book can provide many referable opinions for researchers and practitioners in the energy industry, and help readers to expand a global perspective of energy issues. I hope that the author will have more research outcomes and make greater contributions to China's energy industry.

November 2019   Dr. Bi Fan
China Center for International Economic Exchanges
Beijing, China

Introduction

Human civilization requires energy to function. Due to environmental pressure, China is trying to reduce the consumption of coal. In the context of slow development of renewable energy, oil and gas resources, especially natural gas, are still an important guarantee for the sustainable development of China in the coming decades due to their relative cleanliness compared with coal. However, China's oil and gas production cannot meet domestic demand. In 2018, China's dependence of oil and gas on foreign countries was 70% and 45%, respectively, reaching a record high. Therefore, how to better develop and utilize oil and gas resources is of great significance to energy security, economic development and environmental protection in China.

Since the earliest shale gas wells were discovered in New York State in 1821, people gradually realized the fact that a large amount of oil and natural gas were buried in shale. Many efforts have been made since then to extract crude oil and natural gas from shale. The key issue is how to fracture the rocks effectively. The basic concept of fracturing was born in 1860s. In 1930s, acid fracturing was applied to create fissures in oil-bearing limestone. Gel solution was used to allow oil to flow from limestone in 1950s. However, gel solution was thwarted by dense shale becoming clogged with fracking gels in 1990s. In 1998, Nick Steinsberger in Mitchell Energy developed a new method using high pressure water solution, which revolutionized modern frack industry and was regarded as the beginning of technical revolution. In 2001, Devon Energy perfected horizontal drilling allowing multiple fracking jobs using a single well. The joint utilization of hydraulic fracturing and horizontal drilling, along with other new techniques, unlocked shale resources and led a new energy revolution, which promotes energy market revival and economic boom.

The shale energy revolution triggered the energy renaissance in the United States. First, in terms of natural gas, thanks to the large-scale exploitation of shale gas, the United States replaced Russia as the world's largest natural gas producer in 2009. Subsequently, shale technology was applied to the petroleum industry, and the U.S. oil production doubled from 5 million barrels per day in 2009 to 10 million barrels per day in 2017, surpassing Saudi Arabia as the world's largest oil producer.

Its foreign dependence degree of crude oil decreased from 61% in 2008 to 24% in 2015. In recent years, it has begun to export a large amount of crude oil. Oil and gas companies represented by Mitchell and Devon Energy use technological innovation to help the United States seize the opportunity to change the international energy market and have a profound impact on geopolitics, socioeconomics, and climate issues, which provides important implications for the development of China's energy industry.

From 2009 to 2011, I studied at Michigan State University for master's degree, focusing on the investigation and evaluation of a renew energy policy entitled Renewable Portfolio Standards in the United States. After two years of research, I find that there are still many obstacles and challenges in the development of renewable energy, making it unable to replace hydrocarbon energy and become the main energy source to support the development of human society in a short period. At the same time, the shale energy revolution which is sweeping the United States has shown me how technological innovation can overwhelmingly reshape the oil and gas industry, changing it from a "sunset industry" into a "sunrise industry" after the 2007–2009 financial crisis. Therefore, after getting my master's degree, I chose to enter Rice University for my Ph.D. training, studying energy economics and focusing my research on the oil and gas industry.

From 2011 to 2016, I studied, worked, and lived in Houston, Texas, known as the Energy Capital of the World. In addition to studying in the Department of Economics at Rice University, I also observed and analyzed this energy revolution through other channels, taking advantage of the strong energy industry in Houston. In August 2014, I started working at Weatherford International, one of the world's largest oil service companies. I mainly engaged in macro-analysis and financial analysis of the energy market. Since the fourth quarter of 2014, oil prices began to plummet and the market changed dramatically. This work experience gave me the opportunity to closely observe the competitions among nations as well as the competitions among new and old enterprises. Moreover, it also allowed me to recognize the strong competitiveness of the shale technology revolution. A year later, I entered the Energy Center of Baker Institute for Public Policy. In this world's No. 1 energy think tank, I focused on the rise and fall of the entire oil and gas market. The Baker Institute for Public Policy was founded by James A. Baker III, who served as White House Chief of Staff and the United States Secretary of the Treasury under President Ronald Reagan, and as the U.S. Secretary of State and White House Chief of Staff under President George H. W. Bush. Mr. Baker arranged the Plaza Accord the Baker Plan, and played an important role in events such as the dissolution of the Soviet Union and the Gulf War. Baker Institute for Public Policy attracted politicians and scholars from all around the world to visit and give lectures. This also gave me many opportunities for communications and discussions, especially the opportunity to discuss energy policies and energy strategies with dignitaries of various countries. For example, Steven Chu, former U. S. Secretary of Energy and Nobel Laureate, gave me many suggestions on my Ph. D. dissertation. This dissertation studied competitiveness analysis of global oilfield companies and won the Outstanding Economics Dissertation Award at Rice

University. The results of the study also provided important information on merger and acquisition strategy of the oilfield market.

This book is based on my Ph.D. dissertation and subsequent research results published in academic journals *Energy Economics* and *Energy Policy*. It consists of two parts: one analyzes global oil and gas markets at macro-level and the other at micro-level. The first part is a macro-analysis of the oil and gas market, consisting of four chapters: Chap. 1 is the overall analysis of the global oil and gas industry; Chaps. 2 and 3 introduce how Shale Revolution changed the natural gas market and the crude oil market, respectively; Chap. 4 investigates the development status and future of China's shale oil and gas industry. The second part is a micro-analysis of oil and gas companies, consisting of four chapters: Chaps. 5 and 6 discuss the impact of shale technology on corporate efficiency and the interactions among companies in the global oilfield (oil service) market; Chaps. 7 and 8 discuss the impact of ownership on oil and gas production behaviors and the competition among oil and gas companies based on data of global top petroleum enterprises.

In recent years, a large number of books on the Shale Revolution and petroleum industry have been published, which illustrate the importance of this revolution. Compared with other books on the same topic, this book has four main features. First, it is an academic book. The macro-analysis part is composed of four qualitative analyses of the oil and gas market, and the micro-analysis part is composed of four quantitative analyses of the oil and gas companies published in SSCI Q1 journals (Chaps. 5 and 8 are published in *Energy Economics*, while Chaps. 6 and 7 are published in *Energy Policy*). Second, it is a comprehensive book of the oil and gas market and the chapters are closely related. The first half of the book (the first four chapters) introduces the industry at macro-level: it first introduces the overall situation of the global oil and gas market, then studies the impact of Shale Revolution on the markets of natural gas and crude oil, respectively, and finally discusses the prospect and implications of shale oil and gas development in China based on the experience of the United States discussed above. The second half of the book (the next four chapters) is firm-level analysis that investigates the technical efficiency and productivity of both oil service companies and petroleum companies. Third, this book is based on many high-quality data. This book uses Rystad Energy's UCube database to build global oil and gas macro-data from 1990 to 2030, uses Spear's OMR database to build panel data from 114 major oil service companies worldwide from 1996 to 2014, and uses Energy Intelligence's Top 100 oil companies database to build panel data of 54 major oil and gas companies around the world from 2009 to 2016. These databases provide high quality data and most of the companies in the field use them quite often. Fourth, this book is suitable for different kinds of readers. Although this book includes many academic papers and theories, many are motivated to solve practical problems encountered by the author when working in the oil and gas industry. For example, this book gives the competitiveness rankings of global oil service companies and petroleum enterprises, and the list of major competitors of each company, thus answering questions in corporate management such as "who is on my list (who is my competitor)" and "am I on other's list (whose competitor am I)." In addition to scholars in the field of energy economics and industrial organization, practitioners, managers, and investors of the energy industry are also the target readers of this book.

I would never have been able to finish book without the guidance of my teachers, comments from other scholars, help from friends, and support from my family. I would like to express the deepest appreciation to Dr. Robin Sickles, Dr. Antonio Merlo, Dr. Tang Xun, Dr. Hulya Eraslan and Dr. Gustavo Grullon from Rice University, Karen David-Green, Suzanne Niemann and Bin Shao from Weatherford International, Dr. Peter Hartley and Dr. Kenneth Medlock from the Baker Institute for Public Policy, Dr. Jinhua Zhao and Dr. Songqing Jin from Michigan State University, Dr. Jianxing Yu (郁建兴), Dr. Zuhui Huang (黄祖辉), Dr. Wenrong Qian (钱文荣), Dr. Zhigang Chen (陈志钢), Dr. Sujian Guo (郭苏建) from Zhejiang University, Dr. Min Wang (王敏) from Peking University, Dr. Feng Song (宋枫) from Renmin University of China, Xianliang Zhao (赵先良), Yue Wang (王越) and Luxin Wang (王陆新) from the Ministry of Natural Resources of the People's Republic of China. My sincere thanks also go to Dr. Yuzhu Kang (康玉柱) from Chinese Academy of Engineering and Dr. Bi Fan (范必) from Research Office of the State Council for recommending this book. In addition, I am grateful to two distinguished scholars who gave me suggestions on future studies. Dr. Steven Chu encouraged me to cover the entire petroleum industry and apply the model to multinational firms. Dr. Roger Myerson suggested me to introduce the local agency idea into the model. I thank my students from Zhejiang University, Shurui Zhang (张书睿), Shuo Wang (王硕), Nan Zhang (章楠), Lingran Yuan (袁菱苒), Qizhen Zhang (张启正), Tingting Li (李婷婷), Kexuan Chen (陈可轩), Jiayi Li (李佳忆), Jinfeng Xu (许金凤), Yuqing Han (韩雨晴), Jiaxin Zhao (赵嘉欣), Huimin Xu (徐慧敏), and Zhenni He (贺桢妮) for their work. I acknowledge support by the National Natural Science Foundation of China (71903172), the Research Program for Humanities and Social Science Granted by Chinese Ministry of Education (18YJC790034), the Soft Science Research Program of Zhejiang Province (2020C25020), Qianjiang Talent Program (QJC1902008), Energy Center of Baker Institute for Public Policy, School of Public Affairs, China Academy of Rural Development (CARD), Environmental and Energy Policy Center, and Academy of Social Governance at Zhejiang University.

March 2020   Binlei Gong

Contents

Part I
Macro Analysis of Global Oil and Gas Market

Chapter 1
Analysis on the Structural Changes in the Global Oil and Gas Industry and Its Trend

Abstract The global oil and gas industry is facing opportunities and challenges. On the one hand, renewable energy squeezes the market share of conventional energy. On the other hand, the Shale Revolution adds momentum to the oilfield market. In this context, whether the structure of the industry will change is a key issue. This chapter uses Rystad Energy data to analyze the investments and productions of the global oil and gas industry from 1990 to 2030, focusing on the structural adjustment of the market and its trend. Overall, oil and gas will remain the dominant position in the global energy supply in the next 15 years. The internal structure of the oil and gas market faces the following changes: (1) the competitiveness of natural gas will increase significantly compared with crude oil; (2) offshore oil and gas exploration has a bright future; (3) Shale Revolution boosts unconventional oil and gas development. Geographically, the Middle East and North America will contribute half of the global supply; Asia, Africa and Latin America will maintain a relatively stable market share; and European countries will invest and produce less on the oilfield market.

Keywords Global oil and gas industry · Input and output analysis · Oil and gas competition · Onshore and offshore drilling · Shale Revolution and unconventional resources

1 Introduction

Oil and gas are the most important energy and strategic materials in the world. Since the drilling of the world's first oil well in Baku in the Caspian Sea in 1848, oil and gas resources have provided a solid material foundation for the evolution of human civilization. Fossil fuels (mainly three hydrocarbon resources of petroleum, coal and natural gas) account for about 80% of the world's total energy use. Major economies in the world, especially China and the United States, rely heavily on fossil fuels. China's fossil fuel consumption accounts for 92.6% of its total energy consumption, and the United States is 86.4% (Kolb 2013). Within fossil fuels, coal resources dominated in the first industrial revolution but its importance is declining for two reasons. On the one hand, the transportation cost of coal is higher than petroleum

© Zhejiang University Press 2020
B. Gong, *Shale Energy Revolution*,
https://doi.org/10.1007/978-981-15-4855-0_1

(Kolb 2013); on the other hand, coal has become an important control target for energy conservation and emission reduction in various countries due to its high emission of greenhouse gas. As a result, oil and natural gas have occupied a dominant position in the current global energy supply (Speight 2013), and the development and utilization of oil and gas resources are extremely important to the stability and development of the global economy. In the "Outline of the Thirteenth Five-Year Plan for National Economic and Social Development of the People's Republic of China" issued in March 2016 and the "Shale Gas Development Plan (2016–2020)" released in September 2016, China clearly stated that the exploration and production of unconventional oil and gas (especially shale gas) will be one of China's key projects and industries during the 13th Five-Year Plan (2016–2020).

The oil and gas industry is facing many pressures and challenges. First, many people are worried about resource depletion if we rely too much on oil and gas resources since they are disposable energy sources. Second, most of the high-quality and rich oil and gas fields in the world have been exhausted, leaving us with less productive oilfields, which leads to rapid improvement in resource extraction costs. Third, the world energy price fluctuates sharply, which has a significant impact on the economy and people's livelihood. Fourth, the Middle East and other regions with abundant oil and gas resources have poor political stability and cannot guarantee the supply of resources. Finally, with the increasing awareness of environmental protection, the rapid development of renewable energy sources has squeezed the market share of traditional energy sources. For these reasons, many countries are trying to get rid of their dependence on oil and gas resources.

At the same time, the technological revolution has brought opportunities to the oil and gas industry. First, oil and gas exploration technology has improved. As of 2019, the world has produced approximately 1.4 trillion barrels of crude oil. The US Geological Survey[1] estimates that global conventional (liquid) petroleum resources exceed 6.7 trillion barrels. The US Energy Information Administration[2] estimates that the total global geological reserves of crude oil are 9 trillion barrels, plus natural gas condensate, there are a total of 20.6 trillion barrels of oil resources. According to this calculation, the overall petroleum resources that humans have already extracted account for only 5–7% of the geological reserves. Data from the US Energy Information Administration also showed that in 1980, the proven oil reserves were 0.6 trillion barrels and the recoverable period was 28 years, which meant that the proven oil reserves at that time would be exhausted around 2007 without the discovery of new oilfields. However, up to date, not only is oil not exhausted, proven reserves and recoverable years are still increasing. According to 2019 *BP Statistical Review of World Energy*, the world's proven oil reserves reached 1.728 trillion barrels, and the oil reserve-production ratio increased to 50 years, thanks to the more advanced oil and gas exploration technologies. Secondly, the commercial

[1]The US Geological Survey's assessment is the most reliable and comprehensive assessment of the basic state of petroleum resources in the world.
[2]The Energy Information Administration is a statistical agency affiliated with the US Department of Energy, and its published energy data is highly authoritative.

exploitation technology of oil and gas resources is becoming increasingly mature. In 1950, the success rate of drilling and producing oil was only about 20%, which has been doubled to an average of 52–58% during the period of 2004 to 2006. The success of commercialization has also brought high returns to oil and gas companies. During the last 15 years in the 20th century, the return on investment (ROI) of major energy companies in the United States was about 2%. During the period of 2000 to 2008, however, the return on investment of these companies has risen to around 7%, which has exceeded the average rate of return for American manufacturing companies (Gorelick 2011).

The global oil and gas industry is faced with both environmental problems and the challenge of renewable energy, as well as development opportunities brought about by technological innovation and the Shale Revolution. What structural changes will take place in the petroleum industry in the next decade? This chapter uses data from Rystad Energy, a well-known Norwegian energy consulting company, to analyze the input and output of the global oil and gas market from 1990 to 2030, focusing on the structural adjustment of the oil and gas industry as well as the future development trend. Rystad Energy has close relationships with oil service companies, financial organizations, investors and governments around the world, and provides high-quality global macro and micro data of oil and gas industry. Its data and reports are often quoted and cited by analysts in well-known organizations such as the U.S. Energy Information Administration, oilfield companies, and petroleum enterprises. The research results in this chapter show that: (1) the global oil and gas market will continue to increase in terms of investment and output, but the growth rate of output is lower than the growth rate of investment, and the oil and gas output achieve its peak around 2030; (2) in the competition between crude oil and natural gas, the latter will witness significant improvement in production, market share, and competitiveness; (3) onshore high-quality oil and gas fields are during up and offshore oil and gas exploration has a bright future; (4) The Shale Revolution is boosting unconventional oil and gas production, and current low oil prices are difficult to prevent its continued development; (5) The Middle East and North America together occupy half of the global oil and gas supply and will continue to grow, the market share of Asia, Africa and Latin America will remain stable, whereas the share of Europe (and Russia) will continue to shrink.

2 Overview of Global Oil and Gas Industry

Table 1 shows the overall condition of the global oil and gas industry from 1990 to 2030, including investment amount, output and investment required per unit of production. The oil and gas market is significantly affected by the economic cycle. In order to eliminate the deviation caused by fluctuations, this table compares the changes in the average value decade by decade.[3]

---

[3]The data of the 1990s and 2000s are the average values of the actual output per decade (for example, the output of the 1990s is the average annual output of the 1990–1999 decade). The data of the

Table 1 Global overall oil and gas development

Variable name	1990s	2000s	2010s	2020s	2030
Annual investment (billion $)	207.0	561.9	1209.5	1818.7	2195.0
Average annual growth rate (%)	–	10.5%	8.0%	4.2%	4.3%
Annual production (billion barrels)	38.8	46.3	54.5	60.3	61.8
Average annual growth rate (%)	–	1.8%	1.6%	1.0%	0.0%
Investment per barrel of production ($)	5.33	11.89	22.25	30.11	35.51
Average annual growth rate/%	–	8.4%	6.5%	3.1%	4.3%

In terms of investment, the annual global oil and gas investment is expected to rise from an average of $207 billion in the 1990s to $2.2 trillion in 2030. In general, the growth trend of investment volume has gradually slowed down, from 10.5% per year in the first decade of the 21st century to 8% per year in the second decade of the 21st century, and it is expected further reduce to a growth rate of 4% after 2020.

In terms of production, global oil and gas production is still increasing, from an average annual output of 38.8 billion barrels of oil equivalent in the 1990s to approximately 61.8 billion barrels of oil equivalent in 2030. However, the growth rate of oil and gas production showed a gradual downward trend. Since 2000, the average growth rate every 10 years has dropped from 1.8 to 1.6% and then to 1.0%. By 2030, the growth rate of oil and gas production is expected to drop to zero, which means that the peak of global oil and gas production is around 2030. This is in line with the forecast of the U.S. Department of Energy's prediction that peak oil production will occur in 2030 (Gorelick 2011).

From the perspective of the investment required per unit of production, global unit output investment is increasing rapidly due to the fast growth rate in investment relative to the output growth. The average investment needed to produce a barrel of oil equivalent resources in the 1990s was only $5.33, which increased 8.4% annually to an average of $11.89 in the first decade of the 21st century. Then the growth rate slowed down to 6.5% per year, rising the investment required per unit of production to $22.25 in the second decade of the 21st century. In the next decade (2020–2029), the growth rate in per unit cost is expected to decline to 3.01%, resulting in an average investment of $30 to produce one barrel of oil equivalent resources. In 2030, this number will further improve to $35, which means it will be more and more expensive to produce oil and gas resources.

2010s is the average of the actual value of 2010–2015 and the predicted value of 2016–2019. The data of the 2020s is the average value of the estimated value of the decade 2020–2029, and 2030 is the year expected value.

3 Crude Oil Versus Natural Gas Production

According to the type of output, global oil and gas production can be divided into two categories, including crude oil and natural gas. After the 2007–2009 financial crisis, the world has entered an era of climate legislation. Climate legislation often covers most industries and sets demanding emission reduction targets (Chen 2012). Compared to coal and crude oil, natural gas is a clean energy source. When used as fuels of heating or industrial raw materials, natural gas with the same calorific value emits 25–30% less carbon dioxide than crude oil and 40–50% less carbon dioxide than coal; when used to generate electricity, natural gas emits 60% less carbon dioxide than coal (Geng et al. 2015). Therefore, when renewable energy cannot stably produce a large amount of supply in the short term, natural gas is regarded as an important transitional energy source, or even a major clean energy source for a long period of time, which draws increasing attention worldwide. Natural gas has an increasing market share in world energy consumption for two reasons. On the one hand, developed countries are using natural gas to replace coal for power generation. On the other hand, compressed natural gas (LNG) and liquefied natural gas (LNG) are more and more widely used in transportation sector.

Of course, there are also disadvantages of natural gas compared with crude oil. The natural gas market is not a global market as sophisticated as the oil market, and superior suppliers in different regions can monopolize the market to gain excess profit. Long-distance pipeline transportation is a solution for resource allocation across regions, but it requires a huge amount of long-term investment, which is very risky since many of the major natural gas suppliers are not in peace zone. As a result, the imbalance between supply and demand of natural gas is still difficult to improve in many areas. And a global market such as the oil market has not been established. The development of liquefied natural gas (LNG) market is a promising tool to break this regional monopoly in the medium or long term, because liquefied natural gas it easy to transport and becomes a real alternative to crude oil (El-Gamal and Jaffe 2009). However, how to reduce the high cost of liquefaction, transportation and gasification is the major task to fulfill the goal.

Table 2 divides the input and output of global oil and gas industry into two parts, including crude oil and natural gas, and then compares the trend in absolute value and market share for crude oil and natural gas.

From the perspective of investment, the ratio of oil and gas investment is expected to remain stable at 63:37 from 1990 to 2030. This shows that the growth rates of investment in these two energy sources are consistent, and crude oil will still receive more financial investment in the next decade.

However, the growth rate of crude oil production is much lower than the growth rate of natural gas production. Oil yield is stable at around 30 billion barrels per year and is approaching its peak in 2030, while natural gas production will continue to achieve significant growth in the next decade. This conclusion is mainly based on the following two reasons. On the supply side, new technologies brought by the Shale Revolution have a larger positive impact on natural gas production. On the demand

Table 2 Global oil and gas development

Category	Variable name	Type	1990s	2000s	2010s	2020s	2030
Input	Annual investment (billion $)	Oil	124.7	336.2	753.0	1148.6	1386.7
		Gas	72.5	200.1	429.5	670.1	808.3
	Market share (%)	Oil	63.2	62.7	63.7	63.2	63.2
		Gas	36.8	37.3	36.3	36.8	36.8
Output	Annual production (billion barrels)	Oil	23.1	26.4	29.2	31.1	31.2
		Gas	15.1	18.8	23.6	27.2	28.5
	Market share (%)	Oil	60.4	58.5	55.3	53.3	52.2
		Gas	39.6	41.5	44.7	46.7	47.8
Input-output efficiency	Investment per barrel of production ($)	Oil	5.39	12.53	25.86	36.91	44.49
		Gas	4.79	10.41	18.25	24.56	28.34
	Input-output index (Global average is 1)	Oil	1.01	1.05	1.16	1.23	1.25
		Gas	0.9	0.88	0.82	0.82	0.8

side, natural gas is clean energy that produces less emission, which makes it more popular in the context of climate change. Therefore, the proportion of gas production in the total oil and gas industry is expected to rise from 40% in the 1990s to 48% in 2030, which is close to half of the total oil and gas production.

In addition, Table 2 reports the investment required for per barrel of oil and gas as well as the input-output index using average investment required for the overall yield as the baseline. It is worth noting that an input-output index larger than one indicates that the per-unit cost is higher than the industry average and an input-output index smaller than one indicates that the per-unit cost is lower than the industry average. Table 2 shows that the input-output ratio of natural gas is lower than crude oil since the 1990s, and the gap between these two resources are increasing over time, which indicates that natural gas has a lower unit price and hence more competitive than crude oil. Moreover, this advantage in cost is increasing as time goes by. In 2030, per barrel of oil equivalent natural gas is expected to be one-third cheaper than one barrel of crude oil. The price advantage of natural gas is conducive to economic growth as well as emission reduction. The Financial Times believes that low energy costs will bring 1% GDP growth in the United States in the next ten years, and natural gas will drive the overall boom of the U.S. economy (Kolb 2013).

4 Onshore Versus Offshore Production

According to the distribution of drilling platforms, global oil and gas market can be divided into onshore activities and offshore activities. With the depletion of onshore oil and gas resources, many oil-producing countries are increasing their investment in deep water activities. Offshore drilling is a drilling project in the continental shelf area to explore and produce oil and gas. Compared with onshore drilling, offshore drilling has four major difficulties to deal with: (1) how to build a stable derrick that resists wind and waves; (2) how to isolate seawater from the wellbore; (3) how to drill and produce oil in the small platform and how to meet the high explosion-proof requirements; and (4) the need of underwater robots for underwater monitoring and underwater manipulation (Han et al. 2012). Because of these difficulties, the cost of offshore drilling for oil and gas is generally higher than onshore drilling activities. Table 3 describes the input-output condition of oil and gas resources extracted through onshore activities and offshore activities.

In terms of investment volume, the funds invested in onshore oil and gas fields accounted for 56.5% of the total investment in the 1990s, which improved to 61.4% in the first decade of the 21st century and further increased to 63.6% in the second decade of the 21st century. It can be seen that petroleum enterprises are still prefer to invest in oil and gas resources on land until now. Although share of investment in offshore activities has declined relative to onshore activities, the output share of

Table 3 Global onshore and offshore oil and gas development

Category	Variable name	Type	1990s	2000s	2010s	2020s	2030
Input	Annual investment (billion $)	Onshore	116.9	344.9	769.0	1115.4	1322.8
		Offshore	90.1	216.9	440.5	703.4	872.3
	Market share (%)	Onshore	56.5	61.4	63.6	61.3	60.3
		Offshore	43.5	38.6	36.4	38.7	39.7
Output	Annual production (billion barrels)	Onshore	28.0	32.1	38.6	41.7	41.1
		Offshore	10.8	14.2	15.9	18.6	20.7
	Market share (%)	Onshore	72.3	69.3	70.8	69.2	66.5
		Offshore	27.7	30.7	29.2	30.8	33.5
Input-output efficiency	Investment per barrel of production ($)	Onshore	4.17	10.52	19.99	26.74	32.1
		Offshore	8.39	14.98	27.77	37.64	42.16
	Input-output index (Global average is 1)	Onshore	0.78	0.89	0.9	0.89	0.91
		Offshore	1.57	1.26	1.25	1.25	1.19

offshore oil and gas production has increased year by year, from 27.7% in the 1990s to 33.5% in 2030. This is because high-quality onshore oilfields are gradually depleting, whereas the development of deep-sea oil and gas production becomes increasingly mature, which leads to a significant reduction in offshore exploration and production costs. From the perspective of input-output ratio, the input-output ratio of offshore oil and gas production is still higher than that onshore oil and gas production, but the gap between these types of activities is decreasing. Investment per unit of resource through offshore activities in the 1990s was 1.6 times of the baseline (global average) and twice as much as the same amount of output produced by onshore activities. By 2030, the unit cost of offshore production is expected to be only 20% higher than the baseline (global average) and 30% higher than the unit cost of onshore production (see Table 3).

5 Conventional and Unconventional Production

Conventional oil and gas resources are mostly stored in underground sandstone or carbonate rocks. Through vertical drilling, it is easier to extract and produce conventional oil and gas. The producing process is like inserting a straw into a bottle of orange juice, which is easy to receive large output at low cost. Unconventional oil and gas resources, such as those stored in shale, coal seam or tight sandstone, are difficult to exploit due to their low mobility. It is difficult and unproductive to use traditional vertical drilling techniques to produce unconventional oil and gas, just as it is difficult to suck juice out of an orange through a straw.

The first successful commercial exploitation of unconventional oil and gas resources was the George Michel project. The project used hydraulic fracturing to extract shale gas in 1998 (Kong 2014). Two technological innovations, hydraulic fracturing and horizontal drilling, unlocked the shale gas extraction and triggered a revival of American energy industry (Kolb 2013; Shu 2014; Zhang et al. 2015). The new well factory drilling technology and 3D imaging technology have further promoted the commercialization of shale gas extraction. Take the Marcellus shale in Pennsylvania as an example, the volume of a single horizontal well can be developed more than 4,000 times that of a vertical well (Speight 2013).

The shale gas revolution will enable the United States to achieve "energy independence" (Gao 2012; Qian 2014; Li et al. 2014; Zhang 2014). Some studies suggest that shale gas and newly discovered conventional natural gas can meet domestic consumption in the United States in the next 200 years or more (Yuan 2012). This revolution will push the United States to continue its strategic contraction in the Middle East, which will trigger a series of geopolitical chain reactions (Lang et al. 2008; Guan et al. 2013; Wang 2014). At the same time, the revolution will stimulate interest in the development of shale gas industry in energy importing economies such as Europe and China (Riley 2012). The large-scale development of shale gas will also push the world energy market into the era of cheap natural gas, which will squeeze the market share of renewable energy sources such as wind and solar energy

(Liu 2013; Qian 2014), and will also hinder the shift of global energy consumption to renewable energy (Jaffe 2010).

Petroleum enterprises, such as Continental Petroleum and Lyco Energy in the Bakken region, have proved that using shale technology, not only natural gas but also crude oil can be extracted from hard rocks (Xu 2013). Oil molecules move more easily in rocks than gas molecules (Zuckerman 2013). Horizontal drilling technology, large-scale fracturing technology and real-time microseismic monitoring technology are the three key technologies for shale oil production. Chaudhary (2011) found that multi-stage fracturing of horizontal wells can increase the ultimate production rate of shale oil by 6% (Sun et al. 2015).

With the large-scale commercialization of shale gas and shale oil, unconventional oil and gas resources have become a new force that cannot be ignored in global oil and gas market. Table 4 divides global oil and gas resources into conventional and unconventional categories, and analyzes the development trend of their input and output, respectively.

In terms of investment, unconventional oil and gas investment accounted for less than 10% of the total investment in the oil and gas industry in the 1990s, and has now soared to 25%. Although investment growth will slow down in the future, it is expected to increase to 28.7% by 2030. In terms of output, the proportion of unconventional oil and gas has increased from 5% in the 1990s to 16.2% today, and this high growth rate is expected to continue, and it is expected to increase by another 10% by 2030.

Table 4 Global conventional and unconventional oil and gas development

Category	Variable name	Type	1990s	2000s	2010s	2020s	2030
Input	Annual investment (billion $)	Conventional	180.6	462.5	884.2	1309.7	1565.6
		Unconventional	16.5	73.8	298.4	509.1	629.4
	Market share (%)	Conventional	91.6	86.2	74.8	72.0%	71.3%
		Unconventional	8.4	13.8	25.2	28.0%	28.7%
Output	Annual production (billion barrels)	Conventional	36.4	42.2	44.2	44.2	44.2
		Unconventional	1.9	3.0	8.6	14.1	15.5
	Market share (%)	Conventional	95.1	93.3	83.8	75.8	74.0
		Unconventional	4.9	6.7	16.2	24.2	26.0
Input-output efficiency	Investment per barrel of production ($)	Conventional	4.96	10.81	20.01	29.64	35.42
		Unconventional	8.84	22.67	36.32	35.94	40.63
	Input-output index (Global average is 1)	Conventional	0.93	0.91	0.9	0.98	1
		Unconventional	1.66	1.91	1.63	1.19	1.14

According to the change of input-output ratio, it can be found that the investment required to produce unconventional oil and gas is increasing rapidly over time, so does the investment required to produce conventional oil and gas. As a result, the unit cost of unconventional oil and gas is still relatively high compared to conventional oil and gas (the unit cost ratio of unconventional oil and gas to conventional oil and gas in the 21st century was 1.63: 0.9). A major change in the future is that the continuous increase in unconventional oil and gas production will rely more on technological advances rather than extensive growth, so the input-output ratio of unconventional oil and gas will decline in the next decade. For conventional oil and gas, however, the investment for per barrel of oil equivalent of resources will increase from $20 to $30 in the next decade. Accordingly, the difference in unit cost between unconventional and conventional oil and gas will decrease dramatically (the unit cost of unconventional oil and gas will be only 20% higher than conventional oil and gas in the 2020s), which means that the competitive advantage of conventional oil and gas will be significantly reduced. In 2030, the cost gap between these two resources is expected to further reduce to less than 15%.

6 Oil and Gas Production Across Regions

This section analyzes the oil and gas development in eight regions including the Middle East, North America, Asia, Africa, South America, Europe, Russia, and Oceania from three aspects: input, output, and input-output ratio. According to data source, Russia is listed separately from Europe in the analysis of the oil and gas industry for three reasons: geopolitically, Russia is an important oil and gas producer but not a member of the European Union; geographically, most of Russia's oil and gas producing regions are in Asia; in terms of resource endowment, Russia is very different from most parts of Europe, and the cost of resource production is relatively low.

Table 5 reports the oil and gas investment in various regions of the world. In terms of investment, the amount of oil and gas investment in all regions has increased over time, but the growth rate varies across regions, which implies that the market shares are changing in different regions. The investment in North America is the largest, and it has remained around 30% of the entire world. The amount of investment in the Middle East has steadily increased from 11.1% in the 1990s to 12.4% now, and will continue to increase. By 2030, it is expected to exceed 15% of the total investment in the global oil and gas industry. Asia's oil and gas investment has remained at a slightly higher level than the Middle East since the 1990s, and achieved its peak over 15% in the 2010s. However, the share of investment in Asia will decline in the next decade, and it is expected that by 2030 it will be as low as 11.5% of global investment. The investment volume of Africa and South America has maintained a steady growth trend. It is expected that both regions will increase to the same share as Asia by 2030, reaching about 11% of the global total investment. During the same period, European and Russian market shares have fallen sharply. European oil and

Table 5 Oil and gas input in various regions of the world

Variable name	Region	1990s	2000s	2010s	2020s	2030
Annual investment (billion $)	Middle East	23.0	65.2	149.8	257.1	333.5
	North America	55.7	164.0	371.1	556.4	661.2
	Asia	25.2	81.3	186.7	240.6	252.1
	Africa	17.5	59.1	115.5	195.2	250.5
	South America	16.1	53.2	124.0	194.8	239.6
	Europe	37.6	59.6	96.7	132.9	170.8
	Russia	27.9	67.9	119.4	176.7	196.3
	Oceania	4.0	11.5	46.2	65.0	91.0
Market share (%)	Middle East	11.1	11.6	12.4	14.1	15.2
	North America	26.9	29.2	30.7	30.6	30.1
	Asia	12.2	14.5	15.4	13.2	11.5
	Africa	8.5	10.5	9.6	10.7	11.4
	South America	7.8	9.5	10.3	10.7	10.9
	Europe	18.2	10.6	8.0	7.3	7.8
	Russia	13.5	12.1	9.9	9.7	8.9
	Oceania	1.8	2.0	3.7	3.7	4.2

gas investment has fallen by more than half, from 18.2% in the 1990s to 8% in the 2010s, and is expected to further reduce to 7.3% in the next decade. Investment share in Russia also suffered from significant reduction, from 13.5% in the 1990s to 10% in the 2010s. Moreover, another one percentage point decrease is expected, leading Russia's share of global oil and gas investment to 8.9% in 2030. Finally, Oceania's investment is the smallest among all regions, accounting for only 2% of the global investment in the 1990s, but its growth rate is the highest, and its market share is expected to exceed 4% by 2030.

Table 6 reports the oil and gas output in various regions of the world. North America has the world's largest investment, which is twice as much as the investment received by Middle East. Using this large amount of investment, North America was able to produce almost a quarter (24.6%) of the global total supply in the 1990s. This share has reduced to 21.8% in the first decade of the 21st century. Thanks to the Shale Revolution, the market share of North America inclined to 23.4% in the second decade of the 21st century. Although receiving less than half of the investment than North America, Middle East's oil production share has increased from 21% in the 1990s to 22.7% in the first decade of the 21st century, and hence surpassed that of North America due to rich oil and gas endowment. It is expected that the market share of both Middle East and North America will continue to grow, contributing to 27.1% and 26.5 of global output by 2030, respectively. The sum of oil and gas production in these two regions will exceed the total output of other regions in the world.

Table 6 Oil and gas output in various regions of the world

Variable name	Region	1990s	2000s	2010s	2020s	2030
Annual production (billion barrels)	Middle East	8.15	10.50	13.99	16.42	16.76
	North America	9.54	10.08	12.74	16.05	16.41
	Asia	4.51	6.11	7.56	7.21	7.17
	Africa	3.16	4.40	4.54	4.51	5.17
	South America	2.49	3.49	3.98	4.34	4.89
	Europe	4.15	4.36	3.28	3.05	2.89
	Russia	6.25	6.77	7.65	7.38	6.65
	Oceania	0.51	0.57	0.75	1.36	1.87
Market share (%)	Middle East	21.0	22.7	25.7	27.2	27.1
	North America	24.6	21.8	23.4	26.6	26.5
	Asia	11.6	13.2	13.9	12.0	11.6
	Africa	8.2	9.5	8.3	7.5	8.4
	South America	6.4	7.5	7.3	7.2	7.9
	Europe	10.7	9.4	6.0	5.1	4.7
	Russia	16.1	14.6	14.0	12.2	10.8
	Oceania	1.3	1.2	1.4	2.2	3.0

The proportion of Asian output in the world has increased from 11.6% in the 1990s to 13.2% in the first decade of the 21st century, and further improved to 13.9% in the second decade of the 21st century. However, this share is expected to decline in the future. By 2030, the market share of Asia will return to the level of 1990, accounting for 11.6% of the world total output. The market share of Africa and South America are relatively stable, each accounting for about 8% of the global total during the period of 1990–2030. The market share of Europe and Russia is declining rapidly as the share of investment declines. Europe produced 4.14 billion barrels of oil and gas per year in the 1990s, which accounted for 10.7% of global oil and gas production. Annual production of Europe slightly increased to 4.36 billion barrels of oil and gas, but its market share shrank to 9.4% in the first decade of the 21st century, mainly due to the high growth in other regions. In the second decade of the 21st century, however, the oil and gas production of Europe decreased to 3.28 billion barrels a year, which accounted for only 6% of global oil and gas production. Moreover, the production of Europe will continue to decrease, resulting in less than 5% market share in 2030, which is less than half of the market in the 1990s. In terms of Russia, its production level increased slightly from 1990s to 2010s and is expected to drop since then. Russia's market share of oil and gas output, on the other hand, kept decreasing, from 16% in 1990s to 11% in 2030. Oceania's share of output has been stable at about 1.3% during the period of 1990–2019, but is expected to rise rapidly to 3% of global output by 2030. It is worth noting that the oil production of the whole American continent will increase from 30.7% today to 34.4% in 2030, surpassing that of the Middle East both in total amount and in growth rate, which

Table 7 Oil and gas input-output efficiency in various regions of the world

Variable name	Region	1990s	2000s	2010s	2020s	2030
Investment per barrel of production ($)	Middle East	2.84	6.00	10.71	15.63	19.90
	North America	5.82	16.21	29.37	34.61	40.29
	Asia	5.57	12.78	24.67	33.41	35.15
	Africa	5.49	12.84	25.51	43	48.48
	South America	6.49	14.87	31.18	44.66	48.96
	Europe	9.14	14.11	29.51	43.53	59.1
	Russia	4.46	9.8	15.61	24.1	29.51
	Oceania	7.75	20.81	69.9	47.39	48.7
Input-output index (Global average is 1)	Middle East	0.53	0.5	0.48	0.52	0.56
	North America	1.09	1.36	1.32	1.15	1.13
	Asia	1.05	1.07	1.11	1.11	0.99
	Africa	1.03	1.08	1.15	1.43	1.37
	South America	1.22	1.25	1.4	1.48	1.38
	Europe	1.72	1.19	1.33	1.45	1.66
	Russia	0.84	0.82	0.7	0.8	0.83
	Oceania	1.46	1.75	3.14	1.57	1.37

support the prediction that the world oil and gas center will "shift westward" from the Middle East to the Americas (Lin 2012; Wu 2014).

Table 7 reports the input-output efficiency of oil and gas in different regions of the world. From the perspective of the input-output index, oil and gas costs in the Middle East have been relatively low, and the input required per unit of output is only about half of the global average during the period of 1990 to 2030. Russia's oil and gas resources also have a low input-output ratio, and the unit cost is stable at 80% of the global average during the period of 1990 to 2030. Asia's input-output ratio has remained at the global average. The input-output ratio in North America was about 10% higher than world average in the 1990s, which has increased to 30% higher than world average in the first two decades of the 21 century. Thanks to the development of share techniques and the lower of cost unconventional oil and gas as we discussed in Table 4, unit cost of oil and gas in North America will return to 1990s levels by 2030, which is about 10% higher than the world average. The unit cost of Africa is expected to gradually increase from the global average in 1990 to 37% above the global average in 2030. South America's input-output ratio has been stable at about 1.3 times of the global average during the period of 1990 to 2030. In terms of Europe, its oil and gas exploration and production costs were 72% higher than world average, which has reduced in the first two decades of the 21st century but is expected to incline again in the next decade. In 2030, the unit cost of oil and gas production in Europe will be two-thirds higher than global average, close to the high level in the 1990s. Finally, Oceania's oil and gas input-output ratio has grown rapidly, but it is expected to decrease in the future, reaching one-third higher than world average level in 2030.

7 Summary

In general, the global oil and gas market output will continue to grow steadily. It is expected to reach its peak by 2030, and oil and gas will maintain the dominant position in the global energy supply for a long time. However, with the depletion of high-quality, low-cost oil and gas fields, the investment required to maintain a high level of supply will increase significantly, which is good news for companies in the oilfield market.

Judging from the internal structure of the oil and gas industry, significant changes will be witnessed in the next ten years. First, in terms of the proportion of crude oil and natural gas, the proportion and competitiveness of natural gas have been significantly improved. Natural gas will become a major clean energy and its advantages compared with crude oil will be further enlarged in the future. Second, offshore oil and gas exploration and production will have a bright future due to technological progress and the depletion of high-quality onshore oilfields. Third, the Shale Revolution represented by horizontal drilling and hydraulic fracturing has promoted the commercial development of unconventional oil and gas. Today's low oil prices are difficult to prevent its continued growth, and the gap in unit cost between unconventional and conventional oil and gas will narrow in the future.

From the perspective of the regional distribution of oil and gas activities, the Middle East and North America have occupied half of the global market for a long time and will continue to dominate this market in the next decade. Asia, Africa and Latin America will maintain a relatively stable position and market share in the global oil and gas market. Therefore, the developing countries in these three regions should not overly rely on the energy industry and ignore other sustainable industries to prevent them from falling into the curse of resources. The oil and gas market in Europe (including Russia) is expected to continue to shrink, which is closely related to Europe's forefront in the development of renewable energy sources and the public's environmental awareness. Its path from fossil energy to renewable energy is worth learning from other regions.

References

Chaudhary A S. Shale oil production performance from a stimulated reservoir volume[Z]. Texas A&M University, 2011.

Chen B. Low-carbon big change: What shall we do in the next 30 years[Z]. Beijing: Petroleum Industry Press, 2012.

El-Gamal M A, Jaffe A M. Oil, dollars, debt, and crises: The global curse of black gold[M]. Cambridge University Press, 2009.

Gao H. The Shale gas revolution in the United States and its impact on our country[J]. Development Research. 2012, 12: 4.

Geng X, You S, Wu Y, etc. Study on the financial problems of shale gas industryand policies suggestion[J]. China Minging Magazine. 2015(10): 68–71.

Gorelick S M. Oil panic and the global crisis: predictions and myths[M]. John Wiley & Sons, 2011.

Guan Q, Li J. "Shale Gas Revolution" and Global Political and Economic Structure[J]. Westen Resources. 2013(3): 48–52.

Han M, Teng Y, Wang H, etc. Design of Offshore Platform Drilling System[J]. Ship Standardization Engineer. 2012, 45(2): 42–44.

Jaffe A M. Shale gas will rock the world[J]. Wall Street Journal. 2010, 10.

Kolb R W. The natural gas revolution: At the pivot of the world's energy future[M]. FT Press, 2013.

Kong X. An Analysis of America's "Shale Gas Revolution" and Its Impact: Some Thoughts on Exploration and Production of Shale Gas in China[J]. International Forum. 2014(1): 71–76.

Lang Y, Wang L. Evolution of Petroleum Geopolitical Patterns and China's Policy Response [J]. Resources Science. 2008(12): 1778–1783.

Li Q, Xu K, Wei W. Current Situation of Supply and Demand of International resources And Its Influence on China[J]. Social Sciences of Beijing. 2014(7): 121–128.

Lin L. "Westward Move" of the World Oil and Gas Center and Its Geopolitical Impact[J]. Contemporary International Relations. 2012(9).

Liu C. American shale gas revolution affects world energy pattern[N]. Chinese Social Sciences Today. 2013-04-10(A6).

Qian X. The Impact of American "Energy Independence" and Its Enlightenment to China[J]. Theoretical Horizon. 2014(12).

Riley A. The shale revolution's shifting geopolitics[J]. The New York Times. 2012.

Shu J. Impact of Shale Gas Revolution on American Energy Dominance[J]. International Review. 2014(5): 78–89.

Speight J G. Shale gas production processes[M]. Gulf Professional Publishing, 2013.

Sun Z, Tian Q, Wu X, etc. Advancements in global tight oil exploration and exploitation and the implications for China[J]. China Mining Magazine. 2015(9): 7–12.

Wang L. Shale Gas Revolution and Its Impact on Global Geopolitics[J]. Journal of China University of Geosciences (Social Sciences Edition). 2014, 14(2): 35–40.

Wu Z. Analysis of the Geopolitical Influences of America's "Energy Independence"[J]. International Forum. 2014(4): 7–12.

Xu X. The US Energy Development Trend and Its Global Impacts[J]. International Economic Review. 2013(2): 34–45.

Yuan J. The Challenge of Shale Gas Revolution to US Climate Policy[J]. International Studies. 2012(6): 39–49.

Zhang M. The Prospect of U.S. "Energy Independence"and Its Geoeconomics Impacts[J]. Contemporary International Relations. 2014(7).

Zhang D, Zhang J, Wang Y, etc. China's unconventional oil and gas exploration and development:progress and prospects[J]. Resources Science. 2015, 37(5): 1068–1075.

Zuckerman G. The frackers: The outrageous inside story of the new billionaire wildcatters[M]. Penguin, 2013.

Chapter 2
The Development and Implication of Nature Gas Market in the Context of the Shale Revolution

Abstract The United States is the global leader in the natural gas industry with high production and rich experience. Donald Trump's victory will lift the shale gas development to the next level. Since natural gas is the most important energy in China's 13th Five-Year Plan, studying the American experience in shale gas revolution is of great significance. This chapter first reviews the background and the development of the U.S. shale gas revolution and summarizes the reasons of its commercial success. The global trends of natural gas in the next 25 years are predicted and the influence of the revolution is analyzed. Research shows that: (1) the "energy independence" is the motivation of the development; (2) the support from the government, the cooperation and innovation across firms, the mature financial and capital markets, and the strong industrial potential are the keys to create the technological revolution. Shale gas revolution reshapes the U.S. natural gas market, with its influence spreads from the U.S. to the world and from gas to oil industry. Moreover, the development of shale industry also has tremendous impacts in all aspects of the society.

Keywords Shale gas revolution · U.S. natural gas industry · Industrial policy · Technical innovation

1 Introduction

Energy is the material basis of human activities. Civilization cannot develop without the upgrade of high-quality energy and the innovation of advanced energy technologies. In the first industrial revolution and the second industrial revolution, coal and oil played the leading role in energy consumption, respectively; in the third industrial revolution, renewable energy played an increasingly important role. However, unlike traditional hydrocarbon energies, renewable energy cannot be obtained through direct mining and simple processing, and it is difficult to achieve a stable and large amount of supply in the short term. In this context, natural gas will be the No. 1 choice among hydrocarbon fuels in the coming decades due to its relative cleanliness, and it will become a transition bridge from traditional energy sources to renewable energy sources (Hausfather 2015; Zhang et al. 2016). The 21st century may become the "century of natural gas" (Yergin and Ineson 2009). In the 1970s,

© Zhejiang University Press 2020   19
B. Gong, *Shale Energy Revolution*,
https://doi.org/10.1007/978-981-15-4855-0_2

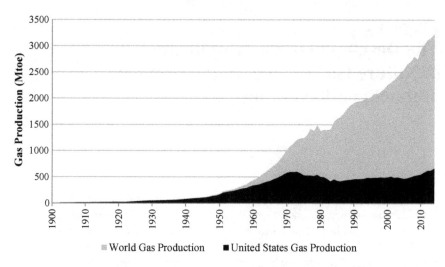

Fig. 1 US and global natural gas production from 1900 to 2014. *Data source* 1990–1980 from Etemad et al. (1998), 1981–2014 from the United States Energy Information Administration (EIA)

Kissinger once said, "who controls the energy can control whole continents." In the 21st century, the world may become that "who finds shale gas will not be controlled." The United States has always been a leader in the global natural gas industry. Figure 1 reports the changes in the U.S. and global natural gas production from 1900 to 2014. In the first half of the 20th century, most of the global natural gas was produced in the United States. The market share of U.S. natural gas production in the world remained over 60% until the year of 1969. From 1900 to 1970, the average market share of U.S. natural gas production in the world was 89%, and its cumulative production accounted for 75% of the world's total supply. However, U.S. natural gas reserves account for only 5.1%[1] of the world's total reserves. Overexploitation has led to rising costs. In addition, other countries have begun to pay attention to the natural gas industry, which has caused the market share of U.S. natural gas production to decrease over time. In the 1970s, with the victory of the Organization of Petroleum Exporting Countries (OPEC) in a series of negotiations, the market power began to shift. The outbreak of the first oil crisis in 1973 made the United States aware of the potential danger of over-reliance on imported energy. In the same year, President Nixon promulgated the Energy Independence Plan, and the United States has thus embarked on the search for "energy independence" (Wang 2014). However, due to the depletion of high-quality conventional oil and gas fields, large oil and gas companies have moved most of their exploration and production (E&P) spendings overseas, and therefore the United States is unable to significantly increase conventional oil and gas production. On the other hand, economic development increased the demand for energy. As a result, the rate of self-sufficiency in primary energy is decreasing

---

[1]Data sourced from the Energy Information Administration (EIA).

dramatically over time in the United States[2] (Zhang 2014). After the second oil crisis broke out in 1978, the United States quickly stipulated tax subsidy policies to encourage the commercial development of unconventional oil and gas. With the strong support of the U.S. government, the first shale gas well in Barnett, Texas, was finally launched in 1981 (Zhang and Yu 2013), and the Shale Gas Revolution officially began.

Since 1970s, when the United States sought energy independence and encouraged the development of unconventional energy sources, what achievements have been delivered in the shale gas revolution? What experience and implications have been concluded to help other countries? What impact and changes will the shale gas revolution bring to the oilfield market in the United States and the world in the next two decades? The Outline of the 13th Five-Year Plan for National Economic and Social Development of the People's Republic of China issued in March 2016 and the Shale Gas Development Plan (2016–2020) released in September 2016 clearly defined natural gas (especially shale gas) market as one of China's key projects and industries during the 13th Five-Year Plan period. At the end of the same year, the National Energy Administration, the Development Research Center of the State Council, and the Ministry of Land and Resources jointly made an official statement that "China will gradually treat natural gas as the main energy source." Therefore, summarizing the trajectory of shale gas development in the United States and concluding its development experience are of great significance for the completion of China's 13th Five-Year Plan.

This chapter introduces the development of the U.S. shale gas revolution. It uses Rystad Energy's data to analyze the trend of natural gas production both globally and in the United States from 1970 to 2040. The shale gas revolution in the United States began in the 1970s in the context of the energy crisis, developed with the investment from the U.S. government and private companies in the 1980s, and witnessed the technological innovation breakthrough such as hydraulic fracturing in the 1990s. At the beginning of the 21st century, shale gas development has achieved commercialization and economy of scales by joint utilization of different technologies (i.e. the combination of hydraulic fracturing and horizontal drilling technology). Since then, many giant international petroleum enterprises have returned to the United States, acquired core shale gas technologies from different innovation firms and continued investing in new technologies, which has led to a rapid growth in shale gas production and a decline in natural gas prices. In addition, oil and gas companies have also carried out two strategic shifts in recent years. One is to improve and use shale gas technologies on shale oil (tight oil) production in the United States, and the other is to apply shale gas technologies to unconventional oil and gas production overseas.

---

[2]Data from the United States Energy Information Administration show that from 1982 to 2005, the primary energy self-sufficiency rate in the United States continued to fall from 91.1% to a historical low of 69.2%.

In summary, the shale gas revolution is a joint product that expanded dramatically with the support from U.S. government and innovation from private enterprises. The impact of the shale gas revolution on the global oil and gas market can be concluded as "from the United States to the world, and from the natural gas market to the crude oil market."

2   Development Track of the Shale Gas Revolution

There are two types of natural gas resources: conventional and unconventional. On the one hand, conventional natural gas refers to the resources that can be obtained from reservoirs using traditional drilling, pumping and compression techniques. On the other hand, unconventional natural gas refers to the resources that can be produced from sources of production that are, in a given era and location, considered to be new and different from conventional natural gas. There are three major types of unconventional natural gas resources, including shale gas, tight gas, and coalbed methane. The International Energy Agency (IEA) states that the boundary between conventional and unconventional oil and gas resources will change as technology changes. The "shale gas revolution" in the narrow sense refers to the sharp increase of natural gas production and the change of structure of energy consumption caused by breakthroughs and innovations in related mining technologies. The broad sense of the "shale gas revolution" includes not only the global unconventional gas production but also unconventional oil production due to this technological breakthrough, which will completely change the supply and demand structure of the energy sector (Dong 2014).

The United States was the first country to conduct research and exploitation of shale gas. The earliest shale gas well in North America was drilled in the eastern United States in 1821 (Zhang et al. 2015). In 1926, the commercial development of shale gas was successful in the Appalachian Basin. In the mid-1970s, American shale gas entered a large-scale development stage (Zeng et al. 2013). Mitchell Energy Corporation in the United States began liquid fracturing in the Barnett Shale in 1981, and it cooperated with the U.S. government to develop and apply new fracking technologies since 1991. In 1997, Nick Steinsberger, an engineer of Mitchell Energy, applied the slickwater fracturing technique, using more water and higher pump pressure than previous fracturing techniques. This new hydraulic fracturing technique turned out to be very successful in 1998. With the maturity of horizontal drilling technology and 3D geological imaging technology in the early 21st century, the efficiency of shale gas extraction has been further improved (Zuckerman 2013). This series of technological innovations originated from over 8,000 companies in the US oil and gas industry. As giant international oil and gas companies have paid more attention to oil and gas production outside of the United States, 85% of U.S. natural gas production is produced by Small and Medium-sized Enterprises (SMEs). The market-oriented business environment and severe competition have prompted many SMEs to continue technological innovation, which has become the main driving force for the rapid development of shale gas extraction technology in the United States. When shale gas technology became sophisticated, oil and gas giants returned and reinvested in the United States (Qian 2014). The small and medium-sized independent oil and gas developers are more flexible and good at technological innovation, whereas large companies are more stable and have more fundings. Large companies were witnessed to make acquisitions and capital injections after small and medium-sized companies achieved technological innovations.[3] This has greatly optimized resource allocation,[4] enriched and improved the industrial chain, and promoted the rapid development of the U.S. shale gas industry (Zeng et al. 2013). In 2009, the United States replaced Russia as the world's largest natural gas producer (Zhang and Qin 2014; Zhang et al. 2015). In 2012, President Obama stated in his State of the Union address that the U.S. government will take all possible measures to develop shale gas safely (Obama 2012). Two years later, President Obama in the State of the Union address proposed a strategy that maintains increased natural gas supply and develops a low-carbon economy (Obama 2014). President Trump has stated on several occasions that the United States will work hard to increase the exploitation of its own oil and gas resources and remove restrictions on the exploitation and use of shale gas. As the energy self-sufficiency rate continues to grow, the United States is expected to achieve "energy independence" by 2030 (Wu 2014). The center of the world oil and gas industry is "moving west" from the Middle East to America (Lin 2012).

3 Reasons for the Success of the Shale Gas Revolution

There are three main reasons for the success of the U.S. shale gas revolution. The first reason is the support of the U.S. government. Since the 1980s, the US government has invested more than \$ 6 billion in the shale gas industry (Zhai et al. 2013; Qu 2016). Government support is mainly given through three aspects: preferential policies, research investment as well as supervision and management (Wang 2014). (1) Preferential policies. U.S. subsidies for shale gas began since the Eastern Shale Gas Project in 1976. In 1978, shale gas and tight gas were subject to tax deductions and ad valorem cash subsidies. The Windfall Profit Tax Act was introduced in 1980, of which Chapter 29 provided preferential policies for unconventional natural

---

[3]For example, from 2001 to 2002, Devon Energy Co., Ltd. spent \$3 billion to acquire Mitchell Energy (Li et al. 2010). In 2009, Exxon acquired XTO energy company with a massive potential of unconventional resources at the expense of \$41 billion (Xu 2013; Kong 2014). ConocoPhillips spent \$15 billion in 2011 to acquire more deep-water and shale resources (Liu et al. 2012).

[4]For example, after Mitchell Energy invented the hydraulic fracturing techniques, it encountered financial obstacles in the process of large-scale application. At this time, Devon Energy Co., Ltd. with more financial resources acquired Mitchell Energy. One year after the acquisition, Mitchell Energy's daily output increased from 350 million cubic feet to 500 million cubic feet. At the same time, Devon has combined its own horizontal drilling and Mitchell's fracturing techniques, which has dramatically increased natural gas production (Yin and Zhang 2013).

gas production tax. In 1990, Texas waived production tax for shale gas exploration and production, and provided subsidies for related investments. The government extended the subsidy period and adjusted the intensity of subsidies for shale gas in 1997 and 2006. Moreover, the federal government proposed a ten-year shale gas subsidy policy in 2004 (Gao et al. 2015). It is estimated that about 30% of the initial US shale gas profits came from preferential policies (Yang, 2014). To summarize, the shale gas business in the United States enjoyed not only various preferential tax policies that applies to oil and gas, but also particular policies and funds to support this unconventional resource. (2) Research investment. In the 1970s, the Eastern Shale Gas Project co-sponsored by the U.S. Bureau of Mines and the U.S. Energy Technology Laboratory laid the basic prototype of directional drilling technology. The short diamond bit developed by the United States Department of Energy and General Electric improved the drilling efficiency of shale formations. In addition, U.S. shale gas producer Mitchell Energy Corporation has also received strong government support (Li 2011). This company adopted various technology platforms developed early by government agencies and received direct funding from the American Gas Institute to build the first horizontal well. (3) Supervision and management. The United States regulates the natural gas market at three levels: the federal, state, and local governments. At the federal government level, the Environmental Protection Agency is mainly responsible for implementing relevant laws and regulations. Under the supervision of the federal government, state governments regulate shale gas extraction. At the same time, local governments also set additional requirements for shale gas extraction (Li and Mou 2013). This strict supervision mechanism is conducive to the stable and orderly development of the market.

The second reason for the success of the U.S. shale gas revolution is the fully open capital market. Because of the "three lows" shale gas reservoir development has, which are low gas pressure, low daily production per well, and low recovery rate (Peng et al. 2016), the exploitation risk of a single well is far greater than that of conventional oil and gas fields, so is the production cost[5] (Liu et al. 2016). However, the production cycle of a single shale gas well is relatively long, generally 30 to 50 years (Dong et al. 2011). Therefore, unlike conventional natural gas that is focused on "finding gas", the key to shale gas development is "exploiting gas." To increase shale gas production as much as possible, it is necessary to drill far more production wells than conventional gas fields (Speight 2013). Once there is large-scale funding support, a massive amount of production can be achieved in a short period (Lv and Qu 2012). For example, there are about 14,000 shale gas wells (30% in vertical wells and 70% in horizontal wells) in the Barnett area of Texas (Jia et al. 2012; Li and Mou 2013), and the cost of a single well is above two million dollars (Zhang et al. 2015). In summary, shale gas is a technology-intensive and capital-intensive industry and requires a large amount of financial support. The support of government and the innovation of private companies have made the successful commercialization of shale

---

[5]For example, 100,000 to 220,000 wells need to be drilled to develop muddy rock formations in the largest Marcellus shale gas field in the United States. The investment for drilling alone is at least $ 300 billion (Sun 2011; Zhao 2011).

gas technology, which has greatly attracted domestic and international capital in the United States. The combination of these two types of capital has promoted the scale of shale gas production. Since 2008, the U.S. shale gas projects have attracted a total investment of $133.7 billion, of which $26 billion are foreign investments that participated in 21 U.S. shale gas projects. The shale gas industry is an example in the United States that successfully attracts backflow of foreign capital in recent years (Wang 2015). The International Energy Agency predicts that this investment trend will be maintained in the next decade (IEA 2013).

The third reason for the success of the shale gas revolution is the growing demand for natural gas. On the one hand, natural gas is a clean energy. With the same energy, the carbon dioxide emissions of natural gas are only 56% and 71% of the emissions produced by coal and oil, respectively, the nitrogen oxide emissions are 20% of the emissions produced by coal and oil, and the emissions of sulfur dioxide and dust particles are almost negligible. With the increasing awareness of environmental protection nowadays, governments have imposed restrictions on carbon emissions, which has led to a surge in demand for natural gas worldwide. On the other hand, the efficiency of natural gas in various application fields has remained high. The combined energy utilization efficiency of DES/CCHP (Distributed Energy System/Combined Cooling, Heating and Power) can exceed 80%, which is much higher than the 35% average energy utilization efficiency of thermal power generation (Qu 2016). Considering the cleanliness and efficiency of natural gas, the United States has replaced oil and coal with natural gas in power generation. In the transportation department, in addition to powering electric vehicles by generating electricity, natural gas can also directly used in compressed natural gas (CNG) and liquefied natural gas (LNG) vehicles (El-Gamal and Jaffe 2009). Moreover, the United States is the earliest country to develop the natural gas chemical industry, and its product variety and output rank No. 1 in the world. More than half of the total amount of raw materials and fuel consumed by the U.S. chemical industry comes from natural gas. It is mainly used to produce methanol, acetylene, and synthetic ammonia, and to further manufacture industrial products such as fertilizers, pesticides, plastics, fibers, dyes, coatings, spices, medicine, and feed. Large chemical companies such as Dow Chemical have expanded their production capacity in the United States in recent years, which has also significantly increased the demand for natural gas.

The success of the U.S. shale gas revolution has vividly illustrated that science and technology are the main driving forces of productivity improvement. Mitchell's engineers successfully reduced shale splitting costs from $250,000–300,000 to less than $100,000 using hydraulic fracturing technology. This technological breakthrough is considered as a milestone in strengthening the commercial competitiveness of shale gas (Li et al. 2013). Another key technology, horizontal drilling or directional drilling, can reduce the impact of drilling on the environment and increase recovery ratio. Advances in shale gas horizontal well production technology and fracturing technology have increased the production per well in the United States, while reducing the input required for a single well to 62.5% of the input required by a traditional natural gas well (Zhang and Yu 2013). In Texas, where shale gas is mainly produced, the unit production of horizontal wells is as low as 30–50% of that of traditional vertical wells (Zhang 2015). Due to the reduction in costs and the increase in production, the U.S. shale gas production cost per cubic meter has decreased from $0.073 in 2007 to $0.031 in 2010, which is 40% lower than the cost of conventional natural gas. With the further development of the new technology, the cost of shale gas production is expected to drop to less than half of the cost of conventional natural gas (Zhang and Qin 2014). New technologies have made shale gas and newly proven conventional natural gas enough to satisfy the demand of the United States for at least 100 years (Wright 2012; Yuan 2012).

The development and utilization of shale gas can significantly reduce energy costs. After the large-scale application of U.S. shale gas, natural gas future prices have decreased by 86% from their peak in July 2008, which has also led to a rapid 77% decline in the price of natural gas power plants (Li et al. 2013). However, weak natural gas prices have not hindered the continued development of shale gas. Compared with conventional natural gas, shale gas has a higher content of natural gas condensates (NGLs). In shale zones with high natural gas content, the natural gas condensates alone can fully compensate the production cost. Therefore, the extracted natural gas becomes almost cost-free by-products (Speight 2013). The production of U.S. natural gas condensates also benefited from the shale gas revolution, increased from 110 million tons in 2005 to 140 million tons in 2010. It is worth noting that U.S. total crude oil production improved from 310 million tons to 350 million tons during the same period (Liu et al. 2012), which means that natural gas condensates contributed 75% of the growth in crude oil within that period. By 2010, the proportion of NGLs in overall crude oil production has reached 40% in North American (Yang, 2014). It can be seen that the shale gas revolution not only increased natural gas supply, but also improved the supply of crude oil.

4 Impact of the Shale Gas Revolution on the Natural Gas Market

This chapter divides U.S. natural gas into four types, including "onshore conventional", "offshore conventional", "onshore unconventional" and "offshore unconventional". Table 1 reports the changes and trends of output for each of the four types from 1970 to 2039. The energy market is significantly affected by the economic cycle. In order to eliminate the deviation caused by fluctuations, this chapter compares the changes in the average value for each decade.[6] In general, unconventional natural

---

[6]The data from the 1970s, 1980s, 1990s, and 2000s are the average values of the actual output per decade (e.g., the 1970s output was the average annual output of the decade from 1970 to 1979). The data of the 2010s is the actual values of 2010–2015 and the predicted values of 2016–2019. The data of the 2020s and 2030s are the average values corresponding to the predicted output for those two decades.

Table 1 Changes in U.S. natural gas structure from 1970 to 2039

Classification	Time	Onshore		Offshore	
		Production (million barrels)	Market share (%)	Production (million barrels)	Market share (%)
Conventional gas	1970s	2771	79	590	17
	1980s	1910	66	753	26
	1990s	1779	58	824	27
	2000s	1517	48	598	19
	2010s	955	23	230	5
	2020s	687	13	126	2
	2030s	634	13	109	2
Unconventional gas	1970s	143	4	0	0
	1980s	216	8	0	0
	1990s	480	16	1	0
	2000s	1054	33	1	0
	2010s	3001	72	1	0
	2020s	4322	84	1	0
	2030s	4026	84	0	0

Data source Rystad Energy

gas is mainly produced onshore and has grown rapidly, while conventional natural gas production has shrunk in both onshore and offshore sectors.

According to the data in Table 1, the onshore output of conventional natural gas reached 2.8 billion barrels of oil equivalent in the 1970s, accounting for 79% of the total natural gas production in the United States at that time. But the production and proportion subsequently declined all the way. In recent years, annual onshore conventional natural gas production is around 1 billion barrels of oil equivalent, and its market share has fallen to 23%. It is estimated that by the 2020s, the production of onshore conventional natural gas will fall below 700 million barrels of oil equivalent, accounting for 13% of the national natural gas production, and the onshore conventional natural gas production and proportion is expected to continue to decline in the 2030s.

Offshore conventional natural gas production was 600 million barrels of oil equivalent in the 1970s, accounting for 17% of U.S. natural gas production at that time. By the 1980s, annual conventional natural gas extracted at sea increased to 800 million barrels of oil equivalent, and its proportion in total natural gas increased to 26%, and this proportion is maintained until the 1990s. Since the beginning of the 21st century, the output of offshore conventional natural gas started to decline, from nearly 600 million barrels in the first decade declined to 200 million barrels in recent years, and its market share has fallen to 19% in the first decade of the 21st century and further reduced to 5% in the second decade of the 21st century. By the 2020s, the annual output of offshore conventional natural gas for offshore is expected to shrink to 100 million barrels, accounting for only 2% of the total natural gas production in the United States.

The production of onshore unconventional natural gas was only 150 million barrels of oil equivalent in the 1970s, accounting for 4% of the total natural gas production in the United States. With the advent of the shale gas revolution, its output and proportion have almost doubled decade by decade: output of onshore unconventional natural gas exceeded 200 million barrels in the 1980s (8% of total production), then reached 500 million barrels in the 1990s (16% of the total output), and achieved nearly 1.1 billion barrels a year (33% of the total output) in the first decade of the 21st century, which exceeded the offshore conventional natural gas production (19% of the total output). In recent years, the annual output of onshore shale gas is about 3 billion barrels of oil equivalent, which accounts for 72% of the total natural gas production in the United States. It is expected that by the 2020s, onshore unconventional natural gas will maintain a strong growth trend, reaching a peak of 4.3 billion barrels of oil equivalent per year, accounting for 84% of US natural gas production. By the 2030s, the expected production of unconventional natural gas will decline, but still account for more than 80% of the U.S. natural gas production. At that time, shale gas is expected to account for 85% of unconventional natural gas and 69% of total natural gas production (EIA 2016).

Offshore unconventional natural gas is negligible and is expected to achieve no significant growth by 2040. This is mainly due to the high cost of offshore development projects. After a large amount of cheap onshore shale gas enters the market, the price of natural gas in the United States will be low, so the offshore shale gas development project is temporarily uncompetitive. But when the terrestrial high-quality shale resources are exhausted, if renewable energy development fails to achieve breakthroughs, the next hot spot may be the development of unconventional natural gas at sea.

In summary, the onshore unconventional natural gas has accounted for more than 70% of the natural gas in the United States and will continue to increase significantly in the next decade. The production of conventional natural gas will continue to shrink. The main reason is that unconventional natural gas, mainly shale gas, has reduced unit costs through technological innovation, making conventional natural gas less competitive. As mentioned above, the cost of shale gas production in 2010 was 60% of conventional natural gas and will continue to decline. In general, onshore production dominates the natural gas market. With the successful substitution of conventional natural gas by shale gas, onshore business will account for more than 90% of the total natural gas activities. Natural gas recovered at sea once accounted for more than a quarter of the total output in the 1980s and 1990s, but with the advent of the shale gas revolution, its market share has shrunk over time, and it is expected to only account for 2% of U.S. natural gas production in the next two decades.

Table 2 compares the changes in natural gas production between the United States and the rest of the world from 1970 to 2039 and the market share of unconventional natural gas to analyze the impact and development trend of the shale gas revolution in the United States and all over the world.

Table 2 Changes in US and world natural gas production from 1970 to 2039

Area	Time	1970s	1980s	1990s	2000s	2010s	2020s	2030s
The United States	Production (million barrels)	3505	2880	3083	3171	4188	5136	4770
	Market share of unconventional gas (%)	4	7	16	33	72	84	84
Rest of the world	Production (million barrels)	4187	7405	10147	13197	14690	18614	21262
	Market share of unconventional gas (%)	2	2	2	2	7	12	19

Data source Rystad Energy

The development of natural gas in the United States has always been at the forefront of the world, but large-scale production in early years has exhausted high-quality conventional gas resources. After the U.S. oil and gas production peaked in the 1970s, oil and gas giants such as Exxon, Shell, and Chevron successively shut down drilling projects in various parts of the United States, and went to Africa, Asia and South America to develop higher quality natural gas resources with lower cost (Zuckerman 2013). As shown in Table 2, from the 1980s to the beginning of the 21st century, natural gas production in the United States has not been able to recover to the level of the 1970s, while natural gas production in other regions of the world has soared from 4.2 billion barrels to 13.2 billion barrels of oil equivalent during the same period, which is more than tripled. As analyzed above, although shale gas technology was supported by scientific research funding in the 1980s and successfully commercialized in the late 1990s, the applicants of these new technologies were mainly small and medium-sized oil companies in the United States, and they do not have enough money to produce large amount of unconventional gas by themselves. Therefore, in the three decades after 1980, total natural gas production in the United States increased by only 300 million barrels of oil equivalent, while natural gas in the rest of the world increased by 5.8 billion barrels of oil equivalent. However, it is worth noting that the proportion of unconventional natural gas in the United States increased from 7% to 33% during this period, while the rest of the world remained at only 2%. Therefore, shale gas achieved tremendous growth during those 30 years, but the overall natural gas production in the United States did not improve a lot due to significant decrease in conventional natural gas production.

At the beginning of the 21st century, the success of domestic shale gas development in the United States attracted large international oil and gas companies to return to the U.S. market. They acquired small and medium-sized enterprises with shale technologies and purchased/rent a large number of lands to develop shale gas business. The shale gas projects of these large companies have been prepared for a period of time, and they have started production in recent years. Compared with the first decade of the 21st century, the average annual output of natural gas in the 2010s increased by 1 billion barrels of oil equivalent, surpassing the peak level in the 1970s, and the proportion of unconventional natural gas increased to 72%. During the same period, the natural gas production in other parts of the world increased by 1.5 billion barrels of oil equivalent a year, of which the proportion of unconventional natural gas increased to 7%, which shows that the rest of the world is still mainly focused on the production of conventional natural gas. With the mastery and improvement of shale technology by giant international petroleum enterprises, the future of U.S. shale gas market will be brighter. It is expected that the U.S. natural gas production will increase by another 1 billion barrels of oil equivalent per year in the 2020s, reaching a staggering 5.1 billion barrels of equivalent per year, more than 80% of which are unconventional natural gas. The proportion of unconventional natural gas in natural gas production in other parts of the world will increase from 7% to 12%, and will contribute more than 30% of the 4 billion barrels increase in annual production in the next decade. This indicates that the next decade will be a decade for the shale gas revolution to go from the United States to the world. The main reason for this change is the spillover effects brought by the international oil and gas companies who will apply new shale gas technologies to their business abroad. It is estimated that by the 2030s, although the total output of natural gas in the United States will decline, the proportion of unconventional natural gas is still expected to remain above 80%. During the same period, the proportion of unconventional natural gas in other parts of the world will increase dramatically from 12% in the 2020s to 19% in the 2030s, which directly accelerated the growth of total overseas natural gas production.

In general, the shale gas revolution began in the 1970s in the context of the energy crisis, developed fast in the 1980s under the support of the U.S. government and the R&D investment of oil and gas companies, and became more sophisticated in the 1990s in the United States due to the technological innovation and application of many small and medium-sized oil and gas companies. By the early 21st century, shale gas extraction has been successfully commercialized. Since then, large international oil and gas companies have returned to the United States, acquired core technologies of shale gas and extensively exploited shale resources, which has led to a sharp increase in shale gas production. Unconventional natural gas, mainly shale gas, has become the protagonist of the U.S. natural gas market. In the current market with low natural gas prices in the United States, many oil and gas companies have begun to apply shale technology to produce shale gas overseas, while others have applied shale technologies to produce shale oil, in addition to make profits by producing natural gas condensates (Xu 2013). Therefore, the impact of the shale gas revolution on the global oil and gas market can be described as "from the United States to the world, and from the natural gas market to the crude oil market."

5 Other Effects of the Shale Gas Revolution on the United States

The shale gas revolution has brought many impacts on the United States in terms of economics, politics, nature and social environment.

Economic and social aspects: Abundant supply of cheap shale gas has lowered the cost of many relevant industries in the United States that use natural gas as inputs and enhanced their international competitiveness (Zhang and Yu 2013). The advantages of low energy costs in the United States not only offset the advantages of low labor costs in developing countries such as China and India, but also offset the advantages of high quality producers in developed countries such as Germany and Japan, which accelerated the return of U.S. manufacturing. At the same time, lower energy prices and less energy imports have reduced the US trade and energy deficits,[7] cut U.S. household expenditures on energy (on average reduced expenditure by $1,000 per household per year[8]) (Altman 2012), and thereby increased the purchasing power of U.S. households, promoted the recovery of the U.S. economy and strengthened the economic security of the United States (Yu and Wu 2015). The development of shale gas is expected to increase U.S. total GDP by an additional 0.5–3 percentage points (Levi 2012; Wang 2014), and significantly increase government taxes[9] (Zhang 2014). In terms of social benefits, the prosperity of shale gas and related industries have dramatically boosted the U.S. job market. It is estimated that more than 1.7 million new jobs will be created in the United States, and the salaries of these jobs will be higher than the US average (Zhang and Yu 2013).

In terms of energy security and geopolitics: First, with the increase in energy production and the decline in the dependence of energy on foreign countries, the United States has gradually fulfilled the commitment to "guarantee that US foreign policy will never be coerced by external energy suppliers" put forward by George W. Bush in the 2001 National Energy Policy Report. Second, by producing more energy, the United States is able to reduce the energy price to suppress the influence of its political opponents such as Russia, Venezuela and Iran (Qian Xuming 2014), thereby weakening the geopolitical advantages of OPEC countries and the EU (Nye 2012; Troner 2013) and consolidating its global strategic dominance (Shu 2014). At the same time, the United States has implemented the necessary strategic contraction in the Middle East, paid less attention in Middle East affairs, and fully implemented the "Return-to-Asia" strategy. On the one hand, this can directly accumulate strength to restrict China's rise in the Asia-Pacific region (Wang 2014). On the other hand, it will create a vacuum of power in the Middle East, leading to further deterioration

---

[7] According to data from the US Energy Information Administration, from 2008 to 2013, the U.S. energy trade deficit fell from $415.8 billion to $232.5 billion.

[8] This number will exceed $2,000 by 2035 (Insight 2011).

[9] The tax revenue of the U.S. governments at all levels brought by shale gas production is expected to increase from $18.4 billion in 2010 to $36.8 billion in 2020, and then further increased to 56.7 billion in 2035. The cumulative tax revenue of the U.S. governments at all levels from shale gas production is expected to reach $924.5 billion during the same period (Insight 2011).

of the situation and the breeding of terrorist organizations such as ISIS (Li et al. 2015). This will indirectly affect China's energy security and stability, since China imports a large amount of crude oil from the Middle East. In addition, countries eager to acquire shale technologies must cooperate with the United States (Zhang and Yu 2013), increasing the number of American allies. Finally, the shale gas revolution has optimized the U.S. energy structure and reduced greenhouse gas emissions, which has strengthened the United States' discourse power on global climate issues, and reflects the confidence and responsibility of American society to cope with global climate change. In the international climate negotiations, more production and consumption of clean natural gas benefits the United States to put more pressure on China, India and other developing countries who cannot produce enough natural gas or renewable energies, and therefore achieving the purpose of curbing their rise (Zhang and Yu 2013).

In terms of environmental protection: The proportion of natural gas in the United States' energy consumption has begun to increase, while the proportion of crude oil and coal has decreased accordingly. This change has optimized the United States' energy structure and reduced carbon dioxide emissions (Zhang and Yu 2013). However, shale gas also poses risks to the environment. First of all, the development of shale gas resources may bring pollution to the water in the same area. For example, fracturing fluids containing a large number of chemicals may infiltrate the underground aquifers and cause groundwater pollution, and groundwater methane pollution that may be caused during production (Peng et al. 2016). Secondly, shale gas will cause atmospheric pollution during the producing process, such as methane emissions, exhaust emissions from machinery equipment, shale gas combustion, volatilization, leakage and blowout, and evaporation of toxic substances. Statistics on shale gas production in the United States show that methane emissions and leaks are significantly higher than the average values of conventional natural gas production during the drilling, fracturing and completion of the shale gas wells (Howarth et al. 2011; Ke et al. 2012).

6 Implications from the Shale Gas Revolution

The success of the U.S. shale gas revolution has brought us the following four points:

First, marketization and commercialization are the keys to a significant breakthrough in shale gas boom in the United States. In the United States, there is no mutual restraint among natural gas production, transportation, and sales activities. Third parties also have the right to bid for the transportation business that transports natural gas to downstream markets. This guarantees that natural gas producers and users have non-discriminatory access conditions for pipelines (Zeng et al. 2013). As a result, thousands of companies are active in the shale gas industry, thereby ensuring the diversification of shale gas exploration and production entities (Li et al. 2015). In many developing countries, however, state-owned oil companies or municipal engineering companies have monopoly power over natural gas supply infrastructure and have no motivation to innovate new technologies (Qu 2016).

Second, the government provided detailed and accurate geological survey data and established a great infrastructure of natural gas pipeline network facilities in terms of shale gas extraction and transportation. The United States has detailed geological structure records and oil and gas well production records. Natural gas extraction companies also need to disclose the production data of their rigs. These data, which are essential for the extraction of oil and gas, are available in libraries across the United States (Zuckerman 2013). The positive externalities generated by basic data sharing will help companies, especially small and medium-sized enterprises, to discover high-quality natural gas wells. In addition, the United States has more than 400,000 km of natural gas pipelines (China had 60,000 km of natural gas pipelines in 2014, with an average annual increase of about 5,000 km (He 2016), and a total mileage of 77,200 km in 2017). Well-developed pipeline facilities can compensate for the disadvantage of natural gas in transportation compared with crude oil.

Third, a healthy financial market provides sufficient funding support for shale gas development and is an important guarantee for the success of the US shale gas revolution. Due to the characteristics of low-abundance and low-quality unconventional oil and gas have, it is necessary to drill a large number of wells to obtain stable production and benefits. The initial return rate may not be ideal, so a large amount of capital investment is necessary (Qu 2016). It took the United States 30 years from the start-up phase of exploration to the early producing phase to the commercial producing phase. Technological breakthroughs and cost control are keys to achieve large-scale commercial development of shale gas resources in the United States. According to U.S. experience, the economic feasibility of shale gas development depends largely on the costs of drilling and completion. Interview information collected from experts also shows that the cost of drilling and completion of shale gas accounts for about 60–80% of the total operating cost (Liu et al. 2016). Therefore, the success of the U.S. shale gas revolution cannot be separated from the long-term support of mature, patient and visionary investors.

Fourth, the cooperation between large companies and SMEs have promoted the rapid growth of the U.S. shale gas industry. Since 1999, two-thirds of the world's oil and gas discoveries have come from only five private oil companies, including BP, ExxonMobil, Shell, Chevron and Total, all of which are active in the U.S. shale gas market. 50%-70% investments of these large companies are spent on unconventional resources. In the medium and long term major projects, 91% of ExxonMobil's funding and 88% of Shell's funding are used in unconventional resources (Qu 2016). The exploration and production business of large companies is outsourced to small companies and service companies. Given these stable supports, thousands of small and medium-sized independent oil and gas developers have the motivation and funding to innovate in different technical fields, which not only enriches and improves the industrial chain, but also promotes the rapid development of shale gas industry in the United States. This kind of cooperation mode is worthy of reference and attention of state-owned oil companies such as CNPC, Sinopec and CNOOC (Qu 2016).

References

Altman R. The US economy may surprise us all [J]. Financial Times on line. 2012.

Dong C. Rethinking the Shift of the Center of Gravity in Oil and Gas World: Based on an Assessment of the Shale Gas Revolution's Limitations [J]. Modern International Relations. 2014 (2).

Dong D, Zou C, Li J, et al. Resource potential, exploration and development prospect of shale gas in the whole world [J]. Geological Bulletin. 2011, 30 (2): 324–336.

EIA. Annual Energy Outlook 2016[R]., 2016.

EI-Gamal M A, Jaffe A M. Oil, dollars, debt, and crises: The global curse of black gold [M]. Cambridge University Press, 2009.

Etemad B, Luciani J, Bairoch P, et al. World Energy Production, 1800–1985[M]. DIANE Publishing Company, 1998.

Gao M, Wang Z, Fan T. A System Simulation Study of China's Shale Gas Subsidy Policy [J]. China Energy. 2015, 37 (4): 19–23.

Hausfather Z. Bounding the climate viability of natural gas as a bridge fuel to displace coal [J]. Energy Policy. 2015, 86: 286–294.

He M. Maintenance of ball valve in natural gas pipeline operation [J]. China Equipment Engineering. 2016 (8).

Howarth R W, Santoro R, Ingraffea A. Methane and the greenhouse-gas footprint of natural gas from shale formations [J]. Climatic Change. 2011, 106(4): 679–690.

Iea. Redrawing the energy-climate map: world energy outlook special report [R]., 2013.

Insight I G. The economic and employment contributions of shale gas in the United States [J]. Prepared for America's Natural Gas Alliance by IHS Global Insight (USA), Washington, DC: America's Natural Gas Alliance. 2011.

Jia C, Zheng M, Zhang Y. Unconventional hydrocarbon resources in China and the prospect of exploration and development [J]. Petroleum Exploration and Development. 2012, 39 (2): 129–136.

Ke Y, Wang Y, Zhou X, et al. Environmental Effects and Suggestions in Shale Gas Development [J]. Natural Gas and Petroleum. 2012, 30 (3): 87–89.

Kong X. An Analysis of America's "Shale Gas Revolution" and Its Impact: Some Thoughts on Exploration and Production of Shale Gas in China [J]. International Forum. 2014 (1): 71–76.

Levi M. Think again: the American energy boom [J]. Foreign Policy. 2012(194): 55.

Li K. Reform of the acquisition method of mining land use right [J]. Hunan Social Science. 2011 (3): 93–96.

Li F, Bai Y, Wang J, et al. Shale Oil and Gas Development Trend of America and Its Effect on the World Energy Structure [J]. China Land Resources and Economy. 2015 (10): 34–36.

Li Y, Mou B. Lessons of foreign development practices of shale gas for China [J]. China Mining Industry. 2013, 22 (3): 4–7.

Li S, Qiao D, Feng Z, et al. The status of worldwide shale gas exploration and its suggestion for China [J]. Geological Bulletin. 2010, 29 (6): 918–924.

Lin L. "Westward Move" of the World Oil and Gas Center and Its Geopolitical Impact [J]. Modern International Relations. 2012 (9).

Liu H, An H, Mei J. Development and Effect of Shale Gas in The United States [J]. Resources and Industry. 2012, 14 (6).

Liu Z, Guo J, Wang S. The Research on the Learning Curve of Technology Engineering Implementation for Shale Gas Development in China [J]. Science and Technology Management Research. 2016, 36 (3): 118–122.

Lv X, Qu Y. Problems and countermeasures in the development of China's unconventional natural gas resources industry [J]. Economic and Social Perspectives. 2012 (8): 79–82.

Nye Jr J S. The Geopolitics of US Energy Independence [J]. The International Economy. 2012: 23.

Obama B. The White House, Office of the Press Secretary. Remarks by the president in the state of union address. Washington, DC [Z]. 2012.Yergin D, Ineson R. America's natural gas revolution [J]. The Wall Street Journal. 2009, 2.

Obama B. The White House, Office of the Press Secretary. Remarks by the president in the state of union address [Z]. Washington, DC. Retrieved, from www. whitehouse. gov/thepress-office/2014/01/28/remarks-president-state-union-address, 2014.

Peng M, Lei M, Yang H, et al. Environmental Regulation Policy Choices of the Shale Gas Resource Development: Based on Environment Space Differences [J]. Ecological Economy. 2016, 32 (4): 208–213.

Qian X. The Impact of American "Energy Independence" and Its Enlightenment to China [J]. Theoretical Perspectives. 2014 (12).

Qu G. Technical and economic development of shale gas industry [M]. China Petrochemical Press, 2016.

Shu J. Impact of Shale Gas Revolution on American Energy Dominance [J]. International Watch. 2014 (5): 78–89.

Speight J G. Shale gas production processes [M]. Gulf Professional Publishing, 2013.

Sun Y. The shale gas problem [J]. China Energy. 2011 (3): 54.

Troner A. Natural gas liquids in the shale revolution [R]. Baker Institute for Public Policy, Rice University, 2013.

Wang Z. From "Shale Gas Revolution" to "Energy Independence": Prospects, Impacts and Challenges [J]. Theory Monthly. 2014 (3): 143–148.

Wang L, Wang Z. Impact of the Shale Gas Revolution on the US Economy and China's Countermeasures [J]. China Energy. 2015, 37 (5): 22–25.

Wright S. An Unconventional Bonanza: Special Report Natural Gas [M]. Economist Newspaper, 2012.

Wu Z. Analysis of the Geopolitical Influences of America's "Energy Independence" [J]. International Forum. 2014 (4): 7–12.

Xu X. The Global Impact of US Energy Independence Trend [J]. International Economic Review. 2013 (2): 34–45.

Yang L. The Impacts of Shale Gas on International Demand of Energy and China's Development Strategy [J]. China Circulation Economy. 2014, 28 (4): 117–121.

Yergin D, Ineson R. America's natural gas revolution [J]. The Wall Street Journal. 2009, 2.

Yin S, Zhang Y. Analysis on the International Experience and China's Countermeasures of the Shale Gas Industry Development [J]. Reform. 2013 (2): 28–36.

Yuan J. The Challenge of the Shale Gas Revolution to US Climate Policy [J]. International Studies. 2012 (6): 39–49.

Yu G, Wu Q. The strategic revelation in view of the new energy security according to the America experience of shale gas development [J]. China Mining Industry. 2015 (11): 1–4.

Zeng S, Yang L, Zeng K. Status, Problems and Solutions to China's Shale Gas Development [J]. China Population: Resources and Environment. 2013, 23 (3): 33–38.

Zhai D, Cai W, Zhang J, et al. International Research Trend of Shale Gas Technologies Based on Patents [J]. Information Magazine. 2013 (11): 11–15.

Zhang L. Exploring shale gas exploration and development technology and its enlightenment in Texas, USA [J]. Low Carbon World. 2015 (23): 121–123.

Zhang M. The Prospect of U. S. "Energy Independence" and Its Geoeconomics Impacts [J]. Modern International Relations. 2014 (7).

Zhang H, Qin P. Remodeling Effect of "Shale Gas Revolution" on International Political and Economic Relations [J]. Journal of Anhui Normal University (Humanities and Social Sciences), 2014, 42 (2): 185–191.

Zhang H, Yu G. Benefits and Risk Analysis of the "Shale Gas Revolution" in the United States [J]. Theory Monthly. 2013 (11): 140–142.

Zhang X, Myhrvold N P, Hausfather Z, et al. Climate benefits of natural gas as a bridge fuel and potential delay of near-zero energy systems [J]. Applied Energy. 2016, 167: 317–322.

Zhang D, Zhang J, Wang Y, et al. China's unconventional oil and gas exploration and development: progress and prospects [J]. Resources Science. 2015, 37 (5): 1068–1075.

Zhao H. The current status of shale gas development in the world and its impact [J]. Modern International Relations. 2011 (12): 44–49.
Zuckerman G. The frackers: The outrageous inside story of the new billionaire wildcatters [M]. Penguin, 2013.

Chapter 3
The Development and Implication of Crude Oil Market in the Context of the Shale Revolution

Abstract The development of unconventional oil helps the United States to achieve energy independence and to consolidate its leading position in the global energy market. With Trump winning the election, the United States will further enhance the role of crude oil in its energy policy. Therefore, it is of great significance to study the Shale Revolution that improves the oil production in the United States. This chapter first reviews the history of the oil industry in the United States and the world. Then we introduce the technical innovation in unconventional oil production and predict the future development of the industry. Finally, the impacts of the Shale Revolution as well as its enlightenment are presented. The research shows that the development of unconventional oil has been successfully commercialized in the U.S., which will affect the energy security, geopolitics, economy and many other aspects in the United States.

Keywords Unconventional oil · Crude oil production · Energy independence · Shale Revolution

1 Introduction

Known as "black gold" and "industrial blood", crude oil is not only one of the world's main energy sources, but also a strategic resource that has an important influence on the politics, economy, and military of all countries in the world (Kolb 2013; Speight 2013). As the birthplace of the modern petroleum industry, the United States has occupied the dominant position of the world's petroleum resources for a long period. Since the middle of the 20th century, with the depletion of conventional oil resources in the United States, as well as the exploration of oil reserves in Saudi Arabia, Iraq, Iran, Russia and other countries, the United States has deepened its dependence on imported oil and its position as the world's energy leader has been threatened. In this context, the United States has proposed the strategic goal of "energy independence" which asked for the development of exploration and production technologies of unconventional oil and gas. After entering the 21st century, the commercialized and large-scale development of the Shale Revolution made the United States once

© Zhejiang University Press 2020
B. Gong, *Shale Energy Revolution*,
https://doi.org/10.1007/978-981-15-4855-0_3

again become the "leader" in the world energy order. After winning the U.S. election, President Trump said that oil should be the core of the U.S. energy policy, and it is important to further deregulate the petroleum industry and increase its production level. Besides, the new authorities will abolish the Obama administration's policy of restricting the use of hydraulic fracturing technology. Therefore, the United States is likely to be the engine and locomotive for increasing world oil production continuously.

Prior to 2008, the U.S. oil production had experienced decades of stagnation and decline. The average annual growth rate of oil dropped from 7.6% during the period of 1900–1945 to 3.0% during the period of 1946–1970 and −0.2% during the period of 1971–2008. At the same time, the growth rates in the rest of the world were 5.3% (1900–1945), 11.2% (1946–1970), and 1.9% (1971–2008), respectively. As a result, the average share of the United States in global oil production fell from 64% during the period of 1900–1945 to 21% during the period of 1946–1970 to 10% during the period of 1971–2008. After the 2007–2009 financial crisis, the growth rate of oil outside the United States further declined to 1%, while the growth rate of the United States during the same period reached an astonishing 8.9%, exceeding any period in history. Its oil production not only stood at a record high of 600 million tons in 2013 but also exceeded the 700 million tons mark in 2014. At this stage, the United States contributed 56% of the world's oil increase, and its proportion of oil production also increased from 10% in 2008 to 15% in 2014. In 2017, the United States surpassed Saudi Arabia to become the world's largest oil producer.

After a long recession, why did the U.S. oil production win 8.9% strong growth after the 2007–2009 financial crisis? How long can this growth last? Can the growth of the United States lead the growth of oil production in the rest of the world? This chapter reveals the reasons for the increase in the U.S. oil production, predicts the structural changes and production trends of the U.S. and global oil production in the next two decades, and analyzes the impact of changes in the petroleum industry on American society and the world's political economy as well. The result shows that: (1) the U.S. Shale Revolution has directly contributed to the commercialization and large-scale development of unconventional petroleum resources, and increased the U.S. crude oil production; (2) the U.S. crude oil supply will continue to grow rapidly in the next ten years and maintain a high level in the 2030s; (3) The technology of the Shale Revolution will spread to other countries, ensuring a stable supply of global crude oil before the 2040s; (4) The Shale Revolution will change the world's energy pattern, and the United States will seize the initiative in political, economic, social and other aspects.

2   Development History of the Petroleum Industry

Figure 1 shows the changes of oil production in the United States and in the world from 1900 to 2014.

As shown in the figure, this chapter divides the world petroleum history into four stages.

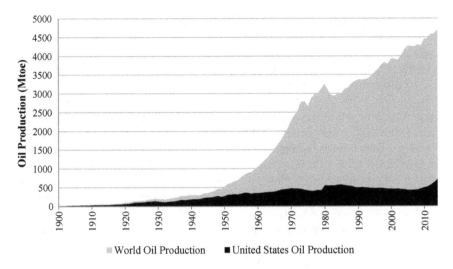

Fig. 1 Changes of oil production in the U.S. and global from 1900 to 2014 *Data source* 1990–1980 from Etemad et al. (1998), 1981–2014 from EIA

The first stage (before 1946): the oil production of the United States increased from 8.48 million tons in 1900 to 230 million tons in 1945, 26 times higher, with an average annual growth rate of 7.6%. Over the same period, global oil production increased 16 times from 20.20 million tons to 350 million tons, with an average annual growth rate of 6.6% (5.3% for regions other than the United States). During this time, the cumulative oil production of the United States accounted for 64% of the world's total. Although the growth rate of oil in the United States and the world remains high, the growth rate in the United States (7.6%) is far higher than that in the rest of the world (5.3%) during this period.

From the end of the 19th century to the beginning of the 20th century, the rise of the Second Industrial Revolution made crude oil gradually replace coal as the primary energy. Due to the need of advanced technology, financial support and consumer market, the exploration and production of crude oil was first carried out in the western developed countries. At that time, the U.S. oil production accounted for more than half of the world's total for a long time, mainly due to three reasons: (1) the United States has the most abundant oil resources among western developed countries; (2) the geographical advantages of the United States made the war far away from its mainland for a long time, ensuring the smooth progress of the exploration and production of the petroleum industry; (3) the large-scale production of fuel vehicles by the U.S. automobile companies such as Ford greatly increased the demand for crude oil in the United States. In the two world wars, crude oil is a very important strategic material. In the third year after the beginning of the World War I (1916), the oil crisis broke out due to the increasing demand for crude oil by the armies of all countries, especially the popularity of fuel warships. The Central Powers, led by Germany, suffered from a shortage of crude oil resources. However, the huge industrial capacity of the United

States in the Entente Powers could not only increase the aircraft production from 400 in 1916 to 11000 in 1918, but also transport 5.5 million motor vehicles overseas. More importantly, the United States could provide abundant crude oil, which guaranteed the normal use of aircraft, warships, tanks and other equipment. The share of the U.S. oil production in the world increased from 63% in the year right before the war (1913) to 70% in the year of victory (1918), and then fell to 60% three years after the war (1921). World War II is very similar to World War I in terms of how oil market share of the United States changed during the war. In 1938, the year before World War II, the United States accounted for 60% of the world's oil production. In 1945, the last year of the war, the proportion increased to 66%. However, the proportion of the U.S. oil production fell back to 58% in three years after the war. The fact of the two world wars demonstrates that the U.S. oil industry can not only maintain more than half of the world's capacity at this stage, but also have the potential to increase production significantly in a special period and change the pattern of world wars. In short, the United States had an absolute advantage in both the stock and potential in crude oil production during this period.

The second stage (1946–1970): the oil production of the United States increased from 230 million tons in 1946 to 480 million tons in 1970. The output was more than doubled, with an average annual growth rate of 3.0%. Over the same period, global oil production increased from 370 million tons to 2.28 billion tons, a five-fold increase in production, with an average annual growth rate of 7.8% (11.2% for regions other than the United States). Since the end of World War II, the United States has slowed down the pace of exploitation and reduced the growth rate of production. At the same time, other countries began to build and develop the petroleum industry in peacetime. The growth rate of global oil was significantly higher than that in the first stage. Therefore, the share of the U.S. oil production in the world decreased from 63% in 1946 to 21% in 1970.

After World War II, the world entered a relatively stable post-war reconstruction period, which provided a historic opportunity for countries to develop the petroleum industry. In the 1950s, large international oil and gas companies were still the main force of oil development in the Middle East and other places. The United States still played the role as the global energy leader through its high proportion of oil production and its high development capacity overseas. However, the oil production of Middle East countries has increased significantly, and the Organization of Petroleum Exporting Countries (OPEC) was established in 1960, which is considered as the time point when the world oil and gas center began to move to the Middle East (Jaffe 2011). In 1966, the crude oil production in the Middle East accounted for 28.4% of the world's total output, surpassing the 27.9% in North America for the first time, which shifted the energy market from the "Mexico Gulf era" to the "Persian Gulf era" (Lang and Wang 2008). To sum up, the second phase of the rapid growth of the global oil industry is mainly due to the relative stability of the international environment and the development of large oil fields in the Middle East and other places. In the United States, the growth rate of oil production slowed down, on the one hand, because the production of the high yield oilfields began to exhaust, on the other hand, more attentions of the large oil companies in the United States were paid on more profitable oilfields overseas. In conclusion, in the second stage, the control power of the United States on global petroleum industry began to weaken, OPEC member countries began to become the engine and locomotive of the world petroleum industry, and the "oil depot" in the Middle East began to replace Houston in the U.S. to become the world oil and gas capital.

The third stage (1971–2008): the U.S. annual oil production decreased from 470 million tons in 1971 to 430 million tons in 2008. The production decreased by 7%, with an average annual growth rate of −0.2%. During the same period, the global oil production increased from 2.41 billion tons to 4.30 billion tons, with an increase of 78% in production and an average annual growth rate of 1.6% (the annual growth rate in regions other than the United States is 1.9%). The oil production of the United States has declined since the peak in 1970. Although the annual production rebounded to more than 500 million tons in the 1980s, it has been hovering around 450 million tons since then. During the third stage, the growth of the global oil market slowed down significantly compared with the second stage. In 2008, the market share of the U.S. oil production in the world fell to 10%.

In the 1970s, oil companies in OPEC countries were nationalized one after another, including Iraq in 1972 and Kuwait in 1975. Saudi Aramco also completed nationalization in 1976. Moreover, domestic market in the United States was greatly impacted. On the one hand, the high-quality oilfields dried up. Large oil and gas companies (Exxon, Shell, Chevron, etc.) closed the drilling projects in many places of the United States, and spent more investment in Africa, Asia, South America and other places (Zuckerman 2013). On the other hand, the development of supertanker and VLCC technology made it possible to import large amount of cheap crude oil from the Middle East. At the same time, with OPEC winning a series of negotiations, the pricing power of energy price began to shift. The first oil crisis in 1973 and the second oil crisis in 1978 both showed the strong influence of the Middle East on the world oil market and this crisis severely damaged the industrial productivity of the United States. Of course, the United States also took countermeasures: first, the United States began to pay attention to the institutional construction of the international energy order, reviving its leading position in energy by building the International Energy Agency (IEA) and establishing the Petrodollar System. Second, the United States' strong navy and military bases all over the world ensured that the United States can control the oil transportation channels and guarantee the international oil security (Shu 2014). Finally, after realizing the potential danger of over dependence on imported energy, President Nixon announced an initiative called Project Independence, which declared that American science, technology and industry could free America from its dependence on imported oil and establish its energy independence (Wang 2014). Since 1976, the United States has adopted a series of preferential policies to encourage the research and development of domestic oil and gas resources, especially unconventional oil and gas resources, which eventually led to the Shale Revolution. In the 1980s, the U.S. government and oil and gas enterprises increased their investment in scientific research on shale resource production. In the 1990s, small and medium-sized oil and gas companies in the United States started the commercial development of shale gas through technological innovations represented by hydraulic fracturing. At the beginning of the 21st century, the emergence of technologies such as horizontal drilling and 3D imaging made the large-scale development of shale gas possible. However, the Shale Revolution at this stage was mainly limited to the shale gas industry. Although it provided technical reserves for the U.S. oil industry, it made little contribution to oil production directly. At the same time, the growth rate of oil production in the rest of the world also dropped to a low level at 1.9%, due to the depletion of high-quality oilfields and the insufficient investment of state-owned oil companies from OPEC member countries in the exploration of new oilfields. During the whole third stage, the U.S. dependence of crude oil on foreign countries increased from 11% in 1970 to 61% in 2008. However, when the world's petroleum industry entered a low-speed growth stage, the U.S. oil industry has taken the lead in preparing for a renaissance.

The fourth stage (2009 to present): the oil production of the United States has soared from 460 million tons in 2009 to 710 million tons in 2014, with an increase of 53% and an average annual growth rate of 8.9%. In the same period, global oil production increased from 4.26 billion tons to 4.70 billion tons, with an increase of 10% and an average annual growth rate of 2.0% (1.0% for regions other than the United States). After the 2007–2009 financial crisis, the growth rate of oil production outside the United States fell to 1%, whereas the growth rate of the United States in the same period reached an astonishing 8.9%, which exceeded any period in history. Its oil production not only reached a record high of 600 million tons in 2013, but also exceeded the 700 million tons in 2014. During this period, the United States contributed 56% of the global oil increment, and its production proportion increased from 10% in 2008 to 15% in 2014.

With the large supply of shale gas, the price of natural gas in the United States has fallen sharply. Many oil and gas companies have begun to study how to apply shale gas technology to unconventional oil resources, including the exploitation of Tight Oil and Natural gas liquids (NGLs). On the one hand, NGLs is a liquid component condensed from condensate gas fields or oil field-associated natural gas. NGLs become liquid when produced to the surface. It is worth noting that both conventional and unconventional gas production are accompanied with NGLs, only the latter is defined as unconventional oil resources. With the substantial increase of shale gas production, a large number of NGLs has been produced at the same time, which is the contribution of Shale Revolution to the increase of unconventional oil resources in the United States. On the other hand, tight oil is directly extracted from shale. The U.S. Energy Information Agency (EIA) defines tight oil as "oil produced from petroleum-bearing formations with low permeability such as the Eagle Ford, the Bakken, and other formations that must be hydraulically fractured to produce oil at commercial rates. Shale oil is a subset of tight oil" (EIA 2012).[1] The development of tight oil started late, but in recent years, its production has greatly increased,

---

[1] There are different definitions of Tight Oil in the world. For example, according to the National Energy Commission of Canada, Tight Oil contains more types, including tight sandstone, siltstone, limestone, dolomite and other tight reservoirs in addition to shale oil (Shu 2014). Due to the comprehensive and authoritative data provided by EIA, the definition of Tight Oil by EIA is adopted in this chapter.

exceeding the total amount of NGLs and becoming the main role of unconventional oil resources, which also marked that the achievements of Shale Revolution such as horizontal drilling and multi-stage hydraulic fracturing technology have been successfully applied to the development of unconventional oil resources. The increase of NGLs and tight oil production has brought the highest oil growth rate of 8.9% per year since the financial crisis in the United States. In contrast, the rest of the world saw oil growth of only 1% over the same period. The contribution of the U.S. Shale Revolution is obvious.

3 Structural Change and Development Trend of the U.S. Oil Production

It can be seen from the analysis above that the U.S. oil production has achieved rapid growth after the financial crisis in 2008. However, to analyze the contribution of unconventional oil, we must observe the internal structural change of total oil production in the United States. Table 1 divides American oil into "land-conventional", "offshore-conventional", "land-unconventional" and "offshore-unconventional" by two dimensions of drilling platform distribution and oil types. It also describes the change and trend of production in 1970–2039. The energy market is obviously

Table 1 Changes of oil structure in the united states in 1970–2039

Classification	Time	Onshore		Offshore	
		Production (million barrels)	Market share (%)	Production (million barrels)	Market share (%)
Conventional oil	1970s	3300	86	448	12
	1980s	3118	84	409	11
	1990s	2383	76	534	17
	2000s	1748	65	653	24
	2010s	1258	31	616	15
	2020s	786	13	707	12
	2030s	598	11	687	13
Unconventional oil	1970s	108	3	3	0
	1980s	157	4	8	0
	1990s	191	6	20	1
	2000s	287	11	18	1
	2010s	2181	53	26	1
	2020s	4624	75	24	0
	2030s	3993	75	16	0

Data source Rystad Energy

affected by the economic cycle. In order to eliminate the deviation caused by the fluctuation, this chapter compares the change of the average value every ten years.[2] Generally speaking, conventional oil from land exploitation started early but its output continued to shrink. Conventional oil from offshore exploitation is stable but its potential is limited. Unconventional oil is mainly from land exploitation, which is growing rapidly. In the next two decades, unconventional oil will maintain its dominant position in oil supply, so as to ensure the overall supply of American oil.

In the 1970s and 1980s, the onshore conventional oil production in the United States remained at over 3 billion barrels per year, accounting for more than 80% of the total oil production in the United States. Since 1990, it has declined at 1% per year for two decades. In recent years, the conventional oil production of land mining is around 1.2 billion barrels per year, accounting for 31% of the national production, which is a significant decline. After 2020, the amount of onshore conventional oil will keep on decreasing rapidly, accounting for around 13% of the national oil production in the 2020s and 11% in the 2030s.

The production of offshore conventional oil in the United States is relatively stable, increasing steadily from 400 million barrels a year in the 1970s and 1980s to about 700 million barrels a year in the 2020s and 2030s. The market share of offshore conventional oil in the United States has increased from 10% in the 1970s and 1980s to 24% in the first decade of the 21st century, becoming an important growth point at that time. In the 2020s and 2030s, its market share will fall back to level in the 1970s because of the substantial increase of total oil production. By the 2030s, offshore conventional oil production will exceed onshore conventional oil production in the United States.

The production of onshore unconventional oil grew slowly in the 20th century, mainly relying on the NGLs from small-scale shale gas production, which steadily increased from 3% of the total oil production in the 1970s to 11% in the first decade of the 21st century. Nowadays, the onshore unconventional oil resources account for more than half of the total oil resources in the United States, due to the large amount of NGLs and tight oil production. However, the potential of the Shale Revolution in the petroleum industry has not been fully developed. It is predicted that the proportion will further rise to 75% in the 2020s and 2030s.

Analogous to conventional natural gas, offshore production of unconventional oil is not expected to have a breakthrough growth until 2040. This is because the large amount of onshore conventional oil production will weaken world oil price, and the offshore exploitation projects with huge investment are not competitive.

In summary, the commercial production of unconventional oil in the United States has entered a fast track, which will greatly reduce the price of crude oil. Due to the depletion of high-quality conventional oilfield resources and the increasing cost of onshore conventional oil, in addition to the weak crude oil price, the market

---

[2]The data of 1970s, 1980s, 1990s and 2000s are all the average values corresponding to the actual output of each decade (for example, the output of 1970s is the average annual output of 1970–1979). The data of the 2010s are the average of the actual output in 2010–2015 and the predicted output in 2016–2019. The data of the 2020s and 2030s are the average of the predicted production per decade.

share of onshore conventional oil production has been decreased dramatically in the past decades and will continue to decline in the future. Although the cost of offshore exploitation is relatively high, there are still many high-quality offshore conventional oilfields worth producing, and the output of offshore conventional oil will still increase, but the lower crude oil price will restrict the speed of its growth. By the 2020s, the share of unconventional oil production in the U.S. oil production will increase from half to three quarters and remain in the same level in the 2030s.

4 Technological Development of the U.S. Petroleum Industry

Table 1 shows that the Shale Revolution had generated a significant increase in unconventional oil production, which in turn increased the overall oil supply in the United States. Horizontal drilling technology, large-scale fracturing technology and microseismic based fracturing monitoring in Shale Revolution are three key technologies of tight oil production (Sun et al. 2015), which play roles in the process of oil production growth in the United States. At present, the horizontal drilling technology develops from single well to multi-branch well. The technology creates a secondary well at the bottom of the main well, and then continuously drills the next level of sub-wells, and therefore realizes the multi-development of oil and gas reservoirs in different depths of a single reservoir, reduces the drilling cost and improves production from a single well (Li et al. 2016).

Fracturing technology is one of the most important technologies in tight oil production. In petroleum geology, shale gas reservoirs are usually characterized by extremely low permeability and porosity. Therefore, the key of tight oil production is to fracture the rock effectively and then hold the fractures open with low cost. Mitchell Energy made a breakthrough in hydraulic fracturing technology on Barnett shale by changing the composition of fracturing fluid, which directly leads to the commercial exploitation in the US shale area. At present, in the development of low permeability and ultra-low permeability reservoirs, horizontal well multi-stage fracturing technology becomes one of the most widely used technologies. The combination of horizontal multi-stage fracturing technology and multi-branch horizontal well technology can increase the production area of crude oil and control the number of fractures, which has significantly improved the recovery rate of unconventional oil and gas reservoir. Chaudhary (2011) shows that the production of tight oil can increase by 6%, which proves the effectiveness of this technology.

In recent years, a variety of new fracturing technologies has been introduced and tested. The HiWAY flow-channel fracturing technology creates open pathways inside the fracture, enabling hydrocarbons to flow through the stable channels rather than the proppant, which optimizes connectivity between the reservoir and the wellbore and results in infinite fracture conductivity. (Pena et al. 2010). In the development of the Eagle Ford shale in the United States, the application of HiWAY flow-channel fracturing technology increased the condensate oil production by 46%, and the saving of proppant greatly reduced the cost and environmental pollution. Nowadays, this technology on average can increase production by 20%, reduce proppant by 40%, and save water by 25%, and has been applied in more than 20 countries around the world, which has become one of the most promising technologies in the exploitation of unconventional oil and gas resources (Sun et al. 2015). Perforating gun technology is derived from the U.S. military's proprietary ballistic missile. This technology can stably and continuously release higher pressure energy and generate multiple radial cracks, while avoiding a large amount of water outflow caused by crack channeling (Li et al. 2016). Perforating gun technology has been used in fracturing in the Appalachian and Illinois basins for more than 5,000 times. This technology has gradually been acknowledged in the North American market (Li et al. 2016). In addition, fracturing technologies using liquid carbon dioxide and liquid natural gas as media are constantly tested. Multistage cemented sliding sleeves, deflagration fracturing, and other technologies will also increase the controllability and accuracy of rock formation reform. These new technologies emerging in the Shale Revolution will continue to promote and lead the development of unconventional petroleum resources (Li et al. 2016).

Real-time micro-seismic monitoring technology is also an important technology in the reconstruction of unconventional oil reservoir in recent years. The technology uses the principles of acoustic emission and micro-seismic to realize the synchronous operation with fracturing technology. Through 3D space imaging, real-time observation and analysis of the fracture condition in the production process can provide information such as fracture orientation, length, width, height, dip angle and coverage range for further completion (Sun et al. 2015). The application of this technology can optimize the fracturing design, effectively improve the performance of the reservoir, maintain high production of oil and gas, and achieve a breakthrough in areas of low or no oil and gas production in the past, so as to control and manage the fractured rock more economically and effectively.

5   The Impact of Shale Revolution on the U.S. and Global Petroleum Industry

It is the technological innovations and breakthroughs mentioned above that enabled the U.S. oil production once again to become the focus of the world's energy market, and there is a trend of radiating and diffusing new technologies to the world. Table 2 compares the changes in crude oil production between the United States and the rest of the world from 1970 to 2039 and the market share of unconventional oil to analyze the impact and development trend of the Shale Revolution in the United States and all over the world. Moreover, this table also compares "Maker Share of Unconventional Oil" and "Maker Share of Unconventional Gas" to show the different starting point

Table 2 Changes in US and world crude oil production from 1970 to 2039

Area	Time	1970s	1980s	1990s	2000s	2010s	2020s	2030s
The United States	Production (million barrels)	3859	3693	3127	2706	4081	6140	5294
	Market share of unconventional oil (%)	3	4	7	11	54	76	76
	Market share of unconventional gas (%)	4	7	16	33	72	84	84
Rest of the world	Production (million barrels)	17105	18425	21889	26108	26581	28852	29341
	Market share of unconventional oil (%)	3	4	4	5	9	12	19
	Market share of unconventional gas (%)	2	2	2	2	7	12	19

Data source Rystad Energy

and development trend of shale technologies introduced in the oil market and gas market.

The average annual output of the U.S. oil dropped from a peak of 3.9 billion barrels per year in the 1970s to 2.7 billion barrels per year in the first decade of the 21st century, while the oil production for the rest of the world increased from 17 billion barrels per year to 26 billion barrels per year during the same period. Moreover, during the same period, the market share of unconventional oil gradually increased from 3 to 11% of the U.S. total oil production. In the first decade of the 21st century, although unconventional oil accounted for only 11% of total oil production, the shale gas revolution had already brought a large amount of shale gas into the U.S. market and accounted for 33% of the U.S. total natural gas production, which made the price of natural gas relatively low around 2010. Meanwhile, crude oil prices were still high. Therefore, some shale gas companies such as Continental Resources, Headington Energy Partners, EOG Resources and SandRidge Energy (Zuckerman 2013) shifted their focus to the production of unconventional oil since 2010. Moreover, large oil and gas companies also began to develop unconventional oil rapidly by mergers and acquisitions of SMEs with shale technology. A large number of shale gas technologies have been improved and applied to the production of unconventional oil, which contributed to annual oil production around 2010 in the

U.S. increased by 1.3 billion barrels (50% increase) for the first time in 40 years, reaching a historical peak of 4 billion barrels per year, of which the proportion of unconventional oil has increased from 11 to 54%. During the same period, the rest of the world was facing the dilemma of high-quality conventional resources depletion and the Shale Revolution still not spreading, with an increased output by only 0.4 billion barrels per year (up by 2%). Rystad energy's data shows the revival of the U.S. oil industry and the plight of the oil market in other regions in the 2010s, which is in line with the EIA data given in Sect. 2 (in the fourth stage after 2008, the growth rate of the U.S. oil production is 8.9%, whereas the growth rate is only 1.0% for the rest of the world). By the 2020s, as the shale technology mastered by transnational oil giants becoming more and more sophisticated, the U.S. oil production is expected to increase by an additional 2 billion barrels per year, significantly increasing to a total of 6 billion barrels per year, of which the share of unconventional oil will further increase to 76%, and the market share is expected to remain until the end of the 2030s. At the same time, it is also hopeful that oil production in other parts of the world will increase rapidly, mainly because multinational oil and gas enterprises gradually apply shale technology to overseas oilfields. It is predicted that by the 2030s, the share of unconventional oil in the total oil production for the rest of the world will increase from 9 to 19%.

Comparing the changes in the market share of unconventional oil and unconventional gas in the United States in Table 2, it can be found that the application of shale technology in the U.S. natural gas market is earlier than in crude oil market. However, in other parts of the world, the market share of unconventional oil and unconventional gas stay at the same level, which indicates that shale technologies are almost synchronized in the global oil and gas market. Large oil and gas companies have applied related shale technologies to overseas oil and gas development synchronously after mastering them. Although multinational companies can graft shale technology overseas, the speed of overseas development of unconventional oil and gas is restricted, due to the lack of census data, different geological structures and differences in industrial policies. Therefore, it is unlikely that unconventional oil and gas will explode globally in the short term.[3]

To sum up, from the 1970s to the first decade of the 21st century, oil and gas companies of small and medium size in the United States persisted in the innovation of shale technology and gradually increased the production of unconventional oil. This has, to some extent, curbed the trend of rapid decline in the U.S. total oil production, and provided a technical basis and experiences for the explosive growth of unconventional oil in recent years. After the 2007–2009 financial crisis, multinational oil giants have applied the shale technology which was previously more used for natural gas exploration to the development of unconventional oil resources as well. The successful utilization of shale technologies in unconventional oil production has significantly increased the U.S. oil production. At the same time, these large multinational oil and gas companies would gradually apply the unconventional oil extraction technology to the development of overseas unconventional oil resources,

---

[3]China may be the only exception because of its strong government and abundant shale resources.

which is conducive to increase production in the global oil market. In conclusion, the diffusion of shale technology mainly follows the pattern of "from the United States to the world, and from the natural gas market to the crude oil market."

6   Other Effects of the Shale Revolution on the United States

Not only does the Shale Revolution in the U.S. has a direct impact on the energy industry, but also have various influence on the U.S. in economic, political and social aspects.

First, Shale Revolution has important effects on energy security and geopolitics. On the one hand, with the advent of the Shale Revolution, US crude oil production has achieved a growth rate of 8.9% in recent years, and oil prices depends more on the production of unconventional oil, so the United States will have greater control over world oil markets, especially in terms of pricing power. On the other hand, crude oil, as a key strategic material, has typical political attributes (Xu 2013), which directly affects US diplomatic strategies. The development of the international situation also shows that the United States' "allies" and "opponents" in the Middle East both have used oil as a bargaining chip (Wu 2014). Once the United States achieves "energy independence", it will be more flexible to adjust its strategic layout in the Middle East to achieve its long-term national interests (Wu 2014). If taking the lead in oil development is the beginning of the U.S. energy dominance, and the establishments of International Energy Agency and the petrodollar system have reinvigorated the US energy dominance from the institutional level, then the Shale Revolution has strengthened America's dominant position in the international energy market from resource control, resource pricing, technology, market and other aspects (Shu 2014).

Second, Shale Revolution has significant impacts on in the economic and social aspects. The Shale Revolution has not only increased employment opportunities in the U.S. and raised wages of industrial workers, but also reduced manufacturing costs, attracted manufacturing backflow and foreign investment, as well as brought more benefits to American consumers (Peng et al. 2016). For example, in 2012, the per capita income of the oil and gas industry in Pennsylvania was $83,000, which is 1.7 times the average income of the United States, and is over 10% higher than that of the coal industry (Wang et al. 2015); The oil and gas industry added more than 130,000 jobs to the United States, ranking among the top industries in the U.S. in the same period (Wang et al. 2015). The increase of crude oil supply has pulled down the domestic oil price in the United States. The lower cost for refiners has stimulated oil export and improved refiner's economic profit (Dong 2014). In addition, due to its convenient storage, crude oil is still the most important fuel source in the transportation field (Dong 2014). On November 2, 2015, the technical outlook report issued by BP emphasized that liquid fuel, in the next two decades, will continue to be the dominant fuel in transportation sector, and the exploitation of shale oil will further promote the increase in US automobile sales, thus driving the growth of diesel and gasoline consumption. However, on the other hand, the market reaction of oversupply of crude oil will have a negative impact on the research and development process of alternative new fuel energy such as bioethanol. At the same time, low oil price exerts a severe challenge to the further exploration and development of unconventional oil, and also puts forward an urgent requirement for continuous research and development of more efficient shale technology.

7 Conclusion and Implications

Summarizing the experience in the United States, there are four takeaways for China and other countries who are anticipating to develop unconventional oil.

First, a forward-looking energy security strategy is necessary. The world oil crisis in the 1970s directly led the U.S. government to step on a long journey of "energy independence" (Wang 2014). Under the guidance of the strategic policy of "energy independence", the U.S. government encourages technological innovation and provides subsidies to support the development of shale oil industry, which has changed the plight and decline of oil exploitation, stabilized and improved the supply of the U.S. oil, thus weakened the Middle East's position as the "world oil and gas center". The U.S. has regained control of world oil and even the dominance of international energy in recent years. It has also triggered a worldwide boom of shale oil and gas. China is the largest energy consumption country in the world. From the perspective of long-term national interests, promoting the exploration and production of unconventional oil and gas can ensure energy security and independence, as well as improve the current predicament of high dependence on foreign oil. Therefore, early preparation and planning of energy security strategy by the government are very important.

Second, a pragmatic energy and environment strategy is essential. In order to deal with the worsening climate and environmental problems, it is urgent to reduce the total amount of carbon emissions. However, the promising renewable energy has been developing slowly for decades (in 2015, the renewable energy accounts for only 3% of the world's total energy consumption, and the proportion is only 8% even in European Union which is most environmental friendly region that encourages renewable development), so it is unable to undertake such a large number of emission reduction tasks in the short term. Without sacrifice of economic development, the United States has had an effective control of carbon emissions by changing the internal consumption structure of fossil fuels and replacing the seriously polluting coal with relatively clean oil and natural gas. In addition, the relevant regulatory policies, laws and regulations of the U.S. government also avoid environmental damage that might happen in the process of energy exploitation. Due to its resource endowment, coal plays a leading role in China's energy consumption (64% in 2015, compared with less than 20% in the rest of the world), which directly leads to the sharp deterioration of China's environment. However, this also implies that China has great potential for emission reductions if we find cleaner energy to replace coal. In a short term, the government should promote the development of unconventional oil and gas resources to replace coal. Meanwhile, it is necessary to support the development of renewable energy industry and increase the potential of medium and long-term emission reduction in China.

Third, government financial subsidies are useful. The success of the Shale Revolution of oil and gas in the United States cannot be separated from the financial-support policies of the government. Since the 1970s, the U.S. government has implemented a series of policies to encourage the development of alternative energy. The Energy Tax Act enacted on November 9, 1978 introduced tax incentives for alternative energy production. The Windfall Profit Tax Act was introduced in 1980, which provided subsidies for unconventional resources. In 1997, the United States continued to implement tax relief policies for unconventional energy. In the 21st century, the government kept on providing tax incentives and special subsidies for unconventional oil and gas production as well as relevant research innovation, ensuring the successful large-scale development of shale oil and gas.

Fourth, a market with diversified competition is of great significance. In the United States, there are about 8,000 enterprises in the field of oil and gas industry (Zeng et al. 2013). The highly opened market system encourages competition and prompts many SMEs to continuously carry out technological innovation. Many of them became professional companies that concentrated on one segment of the supply chain (Peng et al. 2016). Large oil and gas companies take advantage of their capital and market advantages to join the development of shale oil and gas industry through cooperation with SMEs, which further accelerates resource integration, reduces production costs and transaction costs, and improves the price competitiveness of shale oil and gas (Yin et al. 2013). The diversified access mechanism of investment subjects has gradually formed a good development mode: "SMEs promote technological innovation, professional companies provide professional services, large oil and gas companies integrate resources and realize large-scale development", which has greatly promoted the production of unconventional oil in the United States.

References

Chaudhary A S. Shale oil production performance from a stimulated reservoir volume[Z]. Texas A&M University, 2011.
Dong Chunling Rethinking the Shift of the Center of Gravity in Oil and Gas World: Based on an Assessment of the Shale Gas Revolution's Limitations [J]. Contemporary International Relations. 2014(2).
EIA. Annual Energy Outlook 2012: With Projections to 2035[R]. Energy Information Administration, 2012.
Etemad B, Luciani J, Bairoch P, et al. World Energy Production, 1800–1985[M]. DIANE Publishing Company, 1998.
Jaffe A M. The Americas, Not the Middle East, Will Be the World Capital of Energy[J]. Foreign Policy. 2011(188): 86–87.
Kolb R W. The natural gas revolution: At the pivot of the world's energy future[M]. FT Press, 2013.
Lang Yihuan, Wang Limao Evolution of Petroleum Geopolitical Patterns and China's Policy Response [J]. Resources science. 2008(12): 1778–1783.

Li Zongtian, Su Jianzheng, Zhang Rusheng Morden Fracturing Technology of Horizontal Well in Shale[M]. China Petrochemical Press, 2016.

Pena A, Gutierrez L, Archimio A. New treatment creates infinite fracture conductivity[J]. Exploration and Production. 2010, 10(38): 71–73.

Peng Yuanzheng, Dong Xiucheng Cause analysis and prevention of bearing bush wear offeed gas compressor for hydrogen production (2015–2016) [M]. China Petrochemical Press, 2016.

Shu Jianzhong Impact of the shale gas revolution on U.S. energy dominance [J]. International Review. 2014(5): 78–89.

Speight J G. Shale gas production processes[M]. Gulf Professional Publishing, 2013.

Sun Zhangtao, Tian Qianning, Wu Xishun etc. Advancements in global tight oil exploration and exploitation and the implications for China [J]. China Mining Magazine. 2015(9): 7–12.

Wang Lei, Wang Zhenxia The Impact of shale Gas Revolution on Economy of the United States and Countermeasures of China [J]. Energy of China. 2015, 37(5): 22–25.

Wang Zhuoyu From "Shale Gas Revolution" to "Energy Independence": Prospects, Impacts and Challenges [J]. Theory Monthly. 2014(3): 143–148.

Wu Zhengwan. Geopolitical Impact Analysis of American "Energy Independence" [J]. International Forum. 2014(4): 7–12.

Xu Xiaojie. Global Impact of U.S. Energy Independence Trend [J]. International Economic Review2013(2): 34–45.

Yin Shuo, Zhang Yaohui Analysis on the International Experience and China's Countermeasures of the Shale Gas Industry Development [J]. Reform. 2013(2): 28–36.

Zeng Shaojun, Yang Lai, Zeng Kaichao Status, Problems and Solutions to China's Shale Gas Development [J]. China Population Resources and Environment. 2013, 23(3): 33–38.

Zuckerman G. The frackers: The outrageous inside story of the new billionaire wildcatters[M]. Penguin, 2013.

Chapter 4
Current Situation, Challenges and Countermeasures of Shale Industry in China

Abstract Shale resources reserves and technologically recoverable resources are huge in China. With the increasing dependence of oil and gas on the outside world, the necessity of developing unconventional oil and gas (especially shale gas) has become increasingly prominent in China. The development of shale resources in China has been increasing since its first production in 2012. With breakthroughs in technology and continuous follow-up of laws, regulations and policies, China has achieved a good start in shale resource development. Developing shale oil and gas resources will have a far-reaching impact on the improvement of China's energy supply capacity and the optimization of energy structure. At present, there is still a big gap between the development of shale industry in China and the leading countries which have successfully carried out the Shale Revolution. There are also some obstacles in system, mechanism, environment and technology in the development of shale industry. This chapter summarizes the development conditions, current situation, future prospects and existing problems of shale industry in China, and puts forward policy recommendations for the development of shale industry on this basis.

Keywords Shale industry · Development status · Challenges and countermeasures

1 Introduction

In the structure of global energy consumption, the consumption of three fossil fuels including oil, coal and natural gas ranks among the top three of all energy types. As shown in Table 1, crude oil, coal and natural gas respectively account for 33%, 29% and 24% of global energy consumption in 2015, and these three fossil fuels constitute 86% of global energy consumption. Fossil fuels are the primary energy not only in developed countries such as the United States and European countries, but also in developing countries such as China and India. But unlike the United States and Europe, China relies heavily on coal rather than oil and gas. In 2015, the rate of China's coal consumption in the total energy consumption reached up to 64%, lifting the world's coal proportion in the total energy consumption from 19% to 29%. Coal performs not as good as oil and gas both in the aspect of carbon dioxide emission and

© Zhejiang University Press 2020
B. Gong, *Shale Energy Revolution*,
https://doi.org/10.1007/978-981-15-4855-0_4

Table 1 Energy consumption structure in various regions in 2015

	Crude oil (%)	Natural gas (%)	Coal (%)	Nuclear energy (%)	Hydropower (%)	Renewable energy (%)
World	33	24	29	4	7	3
China	19	6	64	1	9	2
United States	37	31	17	8	3	3
European Union	37	22	16	12	5	8
Others	37	30	20	3	8	2

the thermal efficiency[1]. Consequently, China's coal-based energy consumption structure has become one of the main issues in China's structural transformation, energy conservation and emission reduction in the context of the new normal of economy. In 2015, the "Work Plan for Strengthening Air Pollution Prevention and Control in Energy Industry" was published by National Energy Administration, which proposed to gradually reduce the proportion of coal consumption, and increase the proportion of natural gas and non-fossil fuels in energy consumption. Oil and gas are the most significant strategic resources in the world, which has been widely used in all areas and sectors in China. The "Outline of the 13th Five-Year Plan for National Economic and Social Development of the People's Republic of China" published by the State Council in March 2016 presented that China should profoundly promote the energy revolution and establish a clean, low-carbon, safe, and effective modern energy system. China's first Natural Gas Development White Paper, *China Natural Gas Development Report (2016)*, co-released by the National Energy Administration, the Development Research Center of the State Council and the Ministry of Land and Resource, has set the tone officially again by emphasizing that natural gas will be cultivated as the main energy resources in China.

China has long been in the situation of "lavish in coal, lack in oil and gas". As conventional high-quality oil and gas fields dried, the oil and gas self-sufficiency rate plummeted (Figs. 1 and 2). According to the data in *2018 Domestic and Foreign Oil and Gas Industry Development Report*, the dependence of foreign oil and gas in China were 70% and 45% in 2018, respectively, indicating that energy shortage and energy dependence are the most critical risk that China would confront in the future (Yu and Wu 2015). Britain's BP World Energy Outlook published in 2016 also predicted that China would soon exceed the United States and become the world's biggest oil consuming country and net energy importer. However, there exist two main problems in China's oil and gas import. First, most of the crude oil imported to China are from Middle East and Africa that are political instable. As a result, China

---

[1]In terms of carbon dioxide emission intensity, coal is 1.7 times that of natural gas, and 1.3 times that of crude oil. In terms of efficiency, take the thermal power generation as an example, its efficiency of energy use is merely about 35%, while that of natural gas could exceed 80%.

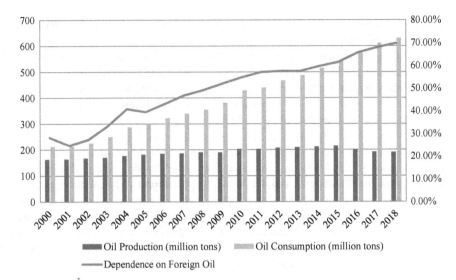

Fig. 1 Production, consumption and dependence of foreign oil in China. *Data source* National Bureau of Statistics, National Development and Reform Commission, "2018 Domestic and Foreign Oil and Gas Industry Development Report", "2017 Domestic and Foreign Oil and Gas Industry Development Report", "China Natural Gas Development Report (2017)", China Business Intelligence Network, China Economic Information Network

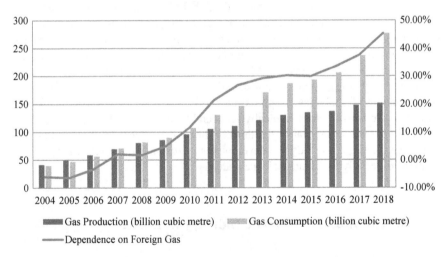

Fig. 2 Production, consumption and dependence of foreign gas in China. *Data source* National Bureau of Statistics, National Development and Reform Commission, "2018 Domestic and Foreign Oil and Gas Industry Development Report", "2017 Domestic and Foreign Oil and Gas Industry Development Report", "China Natural Gas Development Report (2017)", China Business Intelligence Network, China Economic Information Network

faces high risk of supply interruption, which highly threatened the energy security and supply in China. Second, in terms of transportation, most of China's imported crude oil was transported by international oil tankers, and they have no choice but to pass Malacca Strait. However, the situation is complex and the piracy is frequent in Indian Ocean, which brings challenge to our energy security as well. Nevertheless, it's worth noting that China has taken actions to deal with these problems: the Belt and Road initiative strengthened the trade relations of China with those oil and gas producers such as Russia and Iran, and explored diversified oil and gas origin and transportation methods; the opening of the Gwadar Port enables China to bypass the Malacca Strait, which opens an alternative channel to Europe and the Middle East and hence relieves the security problem of oil and gas import. While China's oil and gas import sources are broaden and guaranteed, domestic unconventional oil and gas resources, such as shale oil and shale gas, also accelerate the development process. The Shale Gas Development Plan (2016–2020) published in September 2016 has clearly signified that the exploration and production of unconventional oil and gas resources, especially shale gas, will be the key project and industry in China's "13th Five-Year Plan".

The U.S. is the first country to explore and produce the shale, accomplish technological breakthroughs and realize commercial production in the world. The success of the United States in the Shale Revolution promoted the recovery of the U.S. economy, added more than 1.7 million job opportunities, increased America's strategy chips in Middle East, enhanced America's global discourse on climate issues, and affected the whole country in many other aspects including economy, employment, geopolitics, natural and social environment. This huge revolution whipped by the U.S. has swept the global oil and gas market, triggering the upsurge of shale exploration and production in many countries like China, Russia and Canada. According to the results of geological exploration statistics from EIA, China's technically recoverable amount of shale gas is approximately 3.15 billion cubic meters (ranks the second in the world), and technically recoverable amount of shale oil is approximately 3.91 billion tons (ranks the third in the world). Hence, it is important and necessary for China to study the development status and future tendency of shale industry, especially the clean shale gas industry.

2   Current Situation of Shale Industry in China

In October 2009, China's first shale gas exploration project was launched in Chongqing; in November, the area of Fushun-Yongchuan was listed as China's first shale gas resource production project, which was jointly developed by China National Petroleum Corporation (CNPC) and Shell. As a result, China has become the third country that started the shale gas exploration and production after the U.S. and Canada. In order to collect more information about reserves, during the period of 2009–2012, Ministry of Land and Resource has conducted a national assessment of the reserves of shale gas and shale gas resources with a total investment of 660 million

RMB. Totally, the potential of shale gas resources in 41 basin areas, 87 assessment modules and 57 cold shale gas segments were evaluated. The discovered potential of shale gas geological resources is 134.44 trillion cubic meters, and the potential of recoverable resources is 25.09 trillion cubic meters (see Table 2). In 2013, the EIA predicted that the total amount of recoverable shale gas resources is 31.5828 trillion cubic meters in China (see Table 3). The latest evaluation result from the Ministry of Land and Resource in 2015 showed that, the total amount of national technically recoverable shale gas resources was 21.8 trillion cubic meters.

According to the statistics from Ministry of Land and Resource, the total amount of recoverable natural gas reserves is about 80 trillion cubic meters, within which conventional natural gas accounts for 32 trillion cubic meters and unconventional natural gas accounts for 48 trillion cubic meters. The shale gas accounts for a great proportion of unconventional recoverable resources and therefore the exploration and production of shale gas can prominently increase China's energy self-sufficiency rate. After the country's first production of 25 million cubic meters of shale gas in 2012, the country's output reached 200 million cubic meters in 2013. In 2014, production

Table 2 Distribution of China's shale gas resources estimated by ministry of land and resources

District name	Geological resources (trillion cubic meters)	Share (%)	Technical recoverable resources (trillion cubic meters)	Share (%)
Upper Yangzi, Yunnan, Guizhou and Guangxi	62.59	46.54	9.94	39.62
North and Northeast China	26.79	19.93	6.7	26.70
Mid-down Yangzi and Southeast China	25.16	18.72	4.64	18.49
Southwest China	19.9	14.81	3.81	15.19
Total	134.42	100	25.09	100

Table 3 Distribution of China's shale gas resources estimated by the U.S. energy information agency

Shale basin	Shale gas (trillion cubic meters)	Shale oil (trillion tons)
Sichuan Basin	17.7441	0
Yangzi Platform	4.2167	0
Jianghan Basin	0.7924	0.2857
North Jiangsu	1.2735	0.4286
Tarim Basin	6.0845	11.5714
Junggar Basin	1.0188	17.2857
Songliao Basin	0.4528	9.5714
Total	31.5828	39.1428

of shale gas further improved more than five times, to 1.3 billion cubic meters. As of 2014, China has 54 shale gas blocks that have prospecting rights, with a total investment of 20 billion RMB in the area of 170 thousand square kilometers. There are more than 20 domestic and foreign enterprises explore and produce share gas in 5 sedimentary basins and districts in 11 provinces.

Although the annual production increased to 4.5 billion cubic meters in 2015, China still failed to fulfill the development goal in the "12th Five-Year Plan" that the shale gas production should surpass 6.5 billion cubic meters in 2015. During the "12th Five-Year Plan", Sinopec took the lead in making a technological breakthrough in Fuling area, Chongqing, and achieved commercial production of shale gas with a production of 50 billion cubic meters in 2016 and 60 billion cubic meters in 2018. Furthermore, the official launch of "demonstration project for shale gas development in Fuling" during the "13th Five-Year Plan" will continuously improve the exploration and development system of shale gas, which has tremendous practical significance to the establishment of industry standards and demonstration base. Meanwhile, the Changning-Weiyuan National Shale Gas Demonstration Zone has achieved large-scale production as well. In 2016, the cumulative production of shale gas throughout the year has achieved 2.3 billion cubic meters, which is a double production of the previous year. In prediction, this demonstration base's production would climb to 80 billion cubic meters in 2020. Thanks to these two large shale gas projects, China's shale gas production increased rapidly. In 2016, the production increased to 7.9 billion cubic meters. On September 30, 2016, National Energy Administration released the *Shale Gas Development Plan (2016–2020)* urging that shale gas production should achieve 30 billion cubic meters in 2020, 80–100 billion cubic meters in 2030. Moreover, there has been a string of policies, regulations and standards intensively published and executed since 2011 (see Table 4). These policies guaranteed a rapid growth in China's shale gas industry, the production of shale gas further increased to 9.0 billion cubic meters in 2017 and then inclined to 10.9 billion cubic meters in 2018. It is estimated that the annual production of shale gas in China can reach 17 billion cubic meters in 2020. Although high growth rate has been witnessed in China's shale gas production, it is still difficult to achieve the target assigned in the *Shale Gas Development Plan (2016–2020)*.

Table 5 divides China's crude oil into four types, including "onshore conventional", "offshore conventional", "onshore unconventional" and "offshore unconventional", and reports the changes and trends of output for each of the four types from 1970 to 2040. The energy market is significantly affected by the economic cycle. In order to eliminate the deviation caused by fluctuations, this table compares the changes in the average value for each decade.[2] The data shows that: the annual production of unconventional oil resources increased more than 10 times: from 12 million barrels

---

[2]The data from the 1970s, 1980s, 1990s, and 2000s are the average values of the actual output per decade (e.g., the 1970s output was the average annual output of the decade from 1970 to 1979). The data of the 2010s is the actual values of 2010–2015 and the predicted values of 2016–2019. The data of the 2020s and 2030s are the average values corresponding to the predicted output for those two decades. The 2040 figure is the forecast for year 2040.

in 1970s to 160 million barrels in 2010s; the proportion of unconventional oil production to total oil production improved from 2% in 1970s to 11% in 2010s. From 1990s to the beginning of 21st century, the proportion of unconventional oil production fell from 10 to 9%, which was mainly caused by the surge of conventional oil production, both onshore and offshore, while unconventional oil production witnessed no

Table 4 Timeline of policies, regulations and standards for shale development

Release time	Context
June 2011	The Ministry of Land and Resources launched the first round of tenders for shale gas exploration rights
December 2011	The Ministry of Land and Resources identified shale gas as an independent mineral, which is invested and managed as individual minerals
March 2012	Published shale gas development plan (2011–2015), completed the resource potential survey, achieved major breakthrough in key technology
May 2012	The Ministry of Land and Resources released "Announcement on Investigation of Intention to Bid for Shale Gas Exploitation Rights"
October 2012	"The Notice on the Works Relative to Strengthen the Exploration and Production and the Supervision and Management of Shale Gas Resources" encourages all types of investment entities to enter the field of exploration and production, and shale gas extraction enterprises were granted 0.4 RMB subsidies per cubic meter shale gas produced
November 2012	"The Notice on the Introduction of Subsidies for the Development and Utilization of Shale Gas" points out that local government can properly provide subsidies using local public finance in accordance with the utilization of local shale gas
October 2013	"The Shale Gas Industrial Policy" exempts shale gas exploiting enterprises from the compensation fee for mineral resources and the usage fee of mineral rights, studies and introduces tax incentives such as resource tax, value-added tax and income tax; exempts imported self-use equipment of shale gas production which cannot be produced domestically (including technology imported with equipment) from customs duties in accordance with the relevant provisions
June 2014	"The Technical Specification for the Calculation and Evaluation of Shale Gas Resources/Reserves" sets uniform standards and basis for shale gas reserve calculation, resource forecasting and national registration statistics and management
April 2015	"The Notice on the Policy of Financial Subsidy for the Exploitation and Utilization of Shale Gas" stipulates that the subsidy is 0.3 RMB per cubic meter for 2016–2018 and 0.2 RMB per cubic meter for 2019–2020
September 2016	"The Shale Gas Development Plan (2016–2020)" aims to achieve shale gas production of 30 billion cubic meters in 2020 and 80–100 billion cubic meters of shale gas production by 2030
November 2016	"The National Mineral Resources Plan (2016–2020)" proposes to optimize the structure of mineral development and utilization, vigorously develop clean and efficient energy sources such as natural gas, coal seam gas, shale gas and geothermal energy

(continued)

Table 4 (continued)

Release time	Context
December 2016	The National Development and Reform Commission's "13th Five-Year Plan" for Natural Gas Development proposes to gradually cultivate natural gas into one of the main energy sources and build a modern natural gas industry system. Taking the southern sea phase as the focus of exploration, the application of horizontal wells and "factory" operation model, the comprehensive breakthrough of offshore shale gas efficiency development technology, to achieve substantial increase in output, to explore the potential of land-to-sea transition phase and land-based shale gas exploration and production, to find new core areas, and to lay the foundation for further production
February 2017	The "13th Five-Year Plan" for the Development of Modern Integrated Transportation System proposes the timely construction of gas storage and coal seam gas, shale gas and coal gas pipelines
May 2017	"13th Five-Year Plan" national oil and gas resources evaluation launched, this evaluation will include shale gas, oil shale and other unconventional oil and gas resources
June 2017	The General Office of the Central Committee of the Communist Party of China and the General Office of the State Council released the "Reform Program for the Transfer of Mining Rights", which proposed to build a "more comprehensive competition transfer, more perfect use of paid, more reasonable division of power, more appropriate supervision and services" mining rights transfer system. The Ministry of Land and Resources was responsible for oil, shale gas and other six minerals mining rights approval
July 2017	The National Development and Reform Commission and the Ministry of Commerce jointly issued "the Directory of Guidance for Foreign Investment Industries (revised in 2017)" to remove restrictions on foreign investment in a number of unconventional oil and gas exploration and production areas, including shale gas, and further open of mining industry to the public
April 2018	"The Notice of the Reduction of Resource Tax on Shale Gas" by the Ministry of Finance and the State Administration of Taxation proposed that from April 1, 2018 to March 31, 2021, the tax on shale gas resources (at the prescribed rate of 6%) will be reduced by 30%

growth. Offshore unconventional oil production has not started until the beginning of the 21st century but achieved rapid growth, and its production surpassed onshore unconventional production in 2010s.

In terms of the forecasts, the annual production of unconventional oil will increase from 160 million barrels to 216 million barrels in 2040. During the same period, the total oil production will decrease from 1503 million barrels a year to 1033 million barrels a year, which is a one-third cut. Therefore, the market share of unconventional oil will increase to 21% by 2040. Compared with the rapidly decreasing trend of conventional oil production (1343 million barrels a year in 2010s to 817 million barrels in 2040), the improvement in unconventional oil production slowed the rising speed of China's dependency of foreign oil. Furthermore, taking the onshore-offshore production structure into consideration, from 2010s to 2040, the offshore unconventional

Table 5 Changes in China's crude oil structure from 1970 to 2040

Classification	Time	Onshore		Offshore		Total	
		Output (million barrels)	Market share (%)	Output (million barrels)	Market share (%)	Output (million barrels)	Market share (%)
Conventional oil	1970s	497	97	1	0	498	98
	1980s	827	95	4	0	830	95
	1990s	938	85	56	5	994	90
	2000s	1042	80	150	11	1192	91
	2010s	1116	74	227	15	1343	89
	2020s	1004	76	200	15	1204	91
	2030s	812	73	135	12	947	85
	2040	669	65	148	14	817	79
Unconventional oil	1970s	12	2	0	0	12	2
	1980s	45	5	0	0	45	5
	1990s	107	10	6	1	113	10
	2000s	72	6	44	3	115	9
	2010s	48	3	112	7	160	11
	2020s	69	5	43	3	112	9
	2030s	144	13	19	2	163	15
	2040	205	20	11	1	216	21
Total	1970s	509	100	1	0	510	100
	1980s	872	100	4	0	875	100
	1990s	1045	94	62	6	1107	100
	2000s	1114	85	194	15	1307	100
	2010s	1164	77	339	23	1503	100
	2020s	1073	82	243	18	1316	100
	2030s	956	86	154	14	1110	100
	2040	874	85	159	15	1033	100

Data source Rystad Energy

oil production will start to decrease, which will be fully compensated by the rapid growth in onshore unconventional oil production. Besides unconventional oil, offshore conventional oil production is also likely to decrease in the future. The decline in offshore activities is possibly caused by some oil pollution incidents at sea, and the increased likelihood of maritime conflict driven by ascending complex geopolitical situation. Hence, to reduce the negative prospect of offshore oil exploitation, its environmental effect should attract more attention and its contamination should be reduced; in the meantime, we should strengthen the negotiations and consultations with neighboring countries, safeguard our territorial sovereignty and security, and enhance our ability to cope with the increasingly complex geopolitical environment.

These would be some significant measurements and potential growth points of the oil exploitation in China in the future.

Table 6 divides China's natural gas into four types, including "onshore conventional", "offshore conventional", "onshore unconventional" and "offshore unconventional", and reports the changes and trends of output for each of the four types from 1970 to 2040. For the same reason mentioned above, this table compares the changes in the average value for each decade as in Table 5. The data shows that: the annual production of unconventional gas resources surged 16 times: from 8 million barrels in the 1970s to 127 million barrels in the 2010s; the proportion of unconventional gas production to total gas resource production climbed from 17% in the 1970s to

Table 6 Changes in China's natural gas structure from 1970 to 2040

Classification	Time	Onshore		Offshore		Total	
		Output (million barrels)	Market share (%)	Output (million barrels)	Market share (%)	Output (million barrels)	Market share (%)
Conventional gas	1970s	38	83	0	0	38	83
	1980s	42	56	0	0	42	56
	1990s	59	53	12	11	71	64
	2000s	173	65	31	12	204	76
	2010s	304	63	54	11	358	74
	2020s	504	57	86	10	590	67
	2030s	475	46	90	9	564	54
	2040	426	33	95	7	521	41
Unconventional gas	1970s	8	17	0	0	8	17
	1980s	33	44	0	0	33	44
	1990s	40	36	0	0	40	36
	2000s	64	24	0	0	64	24
	2010s	127	26	0	0	127	26
	2020s	296	33	0	0	296	33
	2030s	473	46	0	0	473	46
	2040	762	59	0	0	762	59
Total	1970s	46	100	0	0	46	100
	1980s	75	100	0	0	75	100
	1990s	99	89	12	11	111	100
	2000s	237	88	31	12	268	100
	2010s	431	89	54	11	485	100
	2020s	799	90	86	10	886	100
	2030s	948	91	90	9	1037	100
	2040	1188	93	95	7	1283	100

Data source Rystad Energy

26% in the 2010s, and they are all produced onshore. Nowadays, although the total production of unconventional gas is lower than that of unconventional oil (127 million barrels vs. 160 million barrels), it can be seen that unconventional gas is more important in gas extraction than unconventional oil is in total oil extraction, in terms of the share of both in the extraction of their respective resources (26% vs. 11%). Thus, the importance of unconventional gas in total gas exploitation is more critical.

In terms of the forecasts, average annual production of unconventional gas will increase dramatically from the current 127 million barrels to 762 million barrels in 2040, while the production of conventional gas will achieve the peak level in the 2020s, and decrease slowly since then. With the co-effect of these two trends, the proportion of unconventional gas to total gas exploitation will reach 59% and exceed conventional gas to take on the dominant role of natural gas supplier. Besides, the average annual exploitation of unconventional gas will also exceed the unconventional oil in the 2030s (473 million barrels vs. 173 million barrels).

In terms of the entire structure of China's oil and gas production, the average annual production were 510 million barrels crude oil and 46 million barrels natural gas in 1970s, then they are increased to 1503 million barrels crude oil and 485 million barrels natural gas 2010s. During this period, although natural gas achieved higher growth rate (increased 11 times vs. 3 times), the total production of crude oil is still more than 3 times of natural gas in China. However, this situation will change in the future, as crude oil production is predicted to be 1033 million barrels and natural gas production is predicted to be 1283 million barrels in 2040. At that time, the production of natural gas will exceed crude oil, the structure of oil and gas production will get totally reversed. The unconventional oil and gas production in China is on the rise while the proportion of conventional resource is decreasing constantly. Hence, the shale resources will make a huge difference in improving China's energy supply and optimizing China's energy structure.

From an international aspect, being two significant oil and gas producers and consumers, China and the U.S. are prominently differed from each other. Tables 7 and 8 show their differences in output level and structure of crude oil and natural gas production, respectively. The average annual production of oil is 511 million barrels in China and 3859 million barrels in the United States in the 1970s; in the meanwhile, the average annual production of gas is 46 million barrels in China and 3505 million barrels in the United States. By the 2030s, the average annual production of oil will be 1110 million barrels in China and 5294 million barrels in the United States, whereas the average annual production of gas will be 1037 million barrels in China and 4770 million barrels in the United States. Although China has achieved significant growth in oil and gas production, the gap between China and the United State is still very large.

The wide gap of oil and gas production between China and the U.S. is also affected by the Shale Revolution. From the 1970s to the 2000s, the oil and gas production has decreased in the United States, whereas the oil and gas production has achieved tremendous growth in China. However, due to the Shale Revolution, the U.S. oil and gas production witnessed significant growth, and unconventional production played a very important role in this boom. On the one hand, U.S. annual oil production

Table 7   Comparison of oil production between China and the United States

Area	Time	1970s	1980s	1990s	2000s	2010s	2020s	2030s
The United States	Production (million barrels)	3859	3693	3127	2706	4081	6140	5294
	Market share of unconventional oil (%)	3	4	7	11	54	76	76
China	Production (million barrels)	511	876	1107	1307	1503	1315	1110
	Market share of unconventional oil (%)	2	5	10	9	11	9	15
Rest of the world	Production (million barrels)	16594	17549	20782	24801	25078	27537	28231
	Market share of unconventional oil (%)	3	4	4	5	9	12	19

Data source   Rystad Energy

increased from 2706 million barrels in 2000s to 4081 million barrels in 2010s, and its annual gas production increased from 3171 million barrels in 2000s to 4188 million barrels in 2010s. The share of unconventional resource in gas production increased from 33% in 2000s to 72% in 2010s, and the share of unconventional resource in oil production increased from 11% in 2000s to 54% in 2010s. Moreover, the market share of unconventional oil and gas will continuously increase to 76% and 84%, respectively, in the next decade. To summarize, conventional oil and gas production is declining rapidly, but the Shale Revolution is not only able to fully compensated that decline, but also dramatically increase the total oil and gas output.

During the same period, China's oil and gas production does not grow as fast as the United States, and the slower development of unconventional oil and gas industry is one of the major reasons. The share of unconventional resource in gas production increased slightly from 24% in 2000s to 26% in 2010s, and the share of unconventional resource in oil production increased slightly from 9% in the 2000s to 11% in the 2010s. In the next twenty years, the share of unconventional oil is expected to increase from 11 to 15%, while the share of unconventional gas is expected to increase from 26 to 46% in China. Therefore, the development of unconventional gas production in China is faster than its unconventional oil production as well as the development of unconventional gas production for the rest of the world, but still a significant gap with the United States. The share of unconventional oil in China is

Table 8 Comparison of gas production between China and the United State

Area	Time	1970s	1980s	1990s	2000s	2010s	2020s	2030s
The United States	Production (million barrels)	3505	2880	3083	3171	4188	5136	4770
	Market share of unconventional gas (%)	4	7	16	33	72	84	84
China	Production (million barrels)	46	75	111	268	485	886	1037
	Market share of unconventional gas (%)	17	44	36	24	26	33	46
Rest of the world	Production (million barrels)	4141	7330	10036	12929	14205	17728	20225
	Market share of unconventional gas (%)	2	2	2	2	6	11	18

Data source Rystad Energy

lower than the rest of the world. It is worth noting that the oil and gas production in the U.S. will summit in the 2020s and then slowly decrease, which provides a certain opportunity for China to catch-up, especially if the Shale Revolution succeeds in China.

3 Challenges of Shale Industry in China

3.1 Low Level of Technology and High Production Cost

Shale gas reservoir is a typical kind of "continuous" petroleum reservoir. The "continuous" petroleum reservoirs, especially the "continuous" gas reservoirs, are characterized by continuous but low gas production, steady production capacity, large reserves and low recovery rate. Generally, the recovery rate of conventional gas is over 60% while that of shale gas is only 5–60%. It's necessary to artificially modify this situation to increase production, which leads to large amount of R&D investment and high operating cost. Table 9 shows the comparison of some economic parameters in shale gas production between China and the United States. It is obvious that there still remains a huge distance between their competitiveness in the shale industry. For

Table 9 Comparison of shale gas development between China and the US in 2014

	The United States	China
Yield/(billion cubic meter)	272.7	1.3
number of share gas wells	>20000	>400
Cost of single wells/million RMB	~30	~83
Market share/%	40	1.02
Investment/billion RMB	630	20

Data source BP World Energy Statistics

instance, China's cost of a single well is about 3 times as much as the United States but the output of a single well in China is much less than the average level in the United States.

The geological conditions become the primary factor to affect the cost of shale production. Due to the lack of information on formation structure and reservoir structure, some shale gas wells were abandoned because they did not have enough development value under current technology level, which limited the output per well and therefore led to high unit drilling costs (Liu et al. 2016). The geological conditions of shale exploitation in China is far more severe and complex than in the United States due to deeper oil and gas reservoir in depth, the more diversified terrain differences, the more complex rock structure, the lower concentration of oil and gas reservoir, the higher construction difficulty and single well production cost. Besides, many shale production sites are near the urban areas and are lack of water but suffer from geological disasters quite often, so that large-scale production is easy (Yu and Wu 2015).

Technical difficulties are another critical factor to influence the cost of shale production. The early investment in shale exploration and production is for advanced technologies including horizontal well technology, hydraulic fracturing technology, micro-seismic monitoring technology, etc. If important technical breakthrough cannot be achieved or the imported technologies are not suitable to local production, previous investments will turn into huge sinking cost, resulting in net income loss. The U.S. has achieved very successful technology breakthrough, and therefore the unit shale gas production cost is merely 60% of conventional gas production cost over the same period, so that commercial production of shale gas is on the right track. China has just started research on shale gas drilling technology in recent years, but has achieved some improvements. For example, the cycle of horizontal drilling is constantly shortening from 150 days to 70 days even 46 days recently, and the cost of single horizontal drilling has reduced from 100 million RMB to 50–70 million RMB (Li et al. 2015). Moreover, shale drilling technology, hydraulic fracturing technology, rotating guidance technology, earth exploration technology and many other technologies have been produced domestically. Innovation of new fracking vehicles, mobile drilling rigs and other equipment, as well as shale gas "sweet point" prediction software, are well applied in shale gas exploration and production process (Huang 2016). Although great progress has been made, China's shale industry still has a weak foundation, especially in independent research and development. In addition, due to the difference in geological conditions, the imported advanced technologies and equipment cannot function very well, which reduces production and increases cost (Liu et al. 2016). Finally, the U.S. shale gas production technology attributes to the vitality and innovation of small and medium-sized enterprises, the core technology of shale oil and gas production in China, however, is in the hands of large state owned oil and gas companies. Limited access permission, insufficient development, and lack of innovation ability of domestic SMEs also impeded the technological advances in China's shale oil and gas industry.

3.2 Environmental Problems

The shale resources production can trigger some environmental risks. For instance, the use of hydraulic fracturing technology will consume large amount of water, although most of them can be recycled and reused, part of the fracking fluid would possibly leak into groundwater layer and cause contaminations (You et al. 2015). The chemistry medicines contained in these liquids, including sour acids, insecticides, crackers, etc., may cause severe environmental problems such as heavy metal and toxic substance issues if leaks occur.

Moreover, the process of shale gas production generates a certain amount of methane, whose greenhouse effect is 25 times that of carbon dioxide. It's analyzed that the methane emission rate during the shale gas drilling completion phase can be 190 times that of conventional gas production, once emitted, the greenhouse effect of shale gas production can be a big emission problem. Furthermore, the shale gas production requires large amount of lands for drilling, possibly lead to a waste of land resources, soil disturbance, sedimentation of pollutants and other negative impacts (Yang et al. 2015). Finally, the producing process can also cause noise pollution, damage of natural and human landscapes and even trigger earthquake.

3.3 Shortage in Infrastructure Construction

The gas pipelines construction and operation is an important component of shale gas industry. By the end of 2017, China has constructed and operated 74 thousand kilometers of gas pipelines, but the density of pipelines is only 7.3 m/km^2, which is only 1/8 of the density in the United States, 1/9 of the density in France, 1/10 of the density in Germany and 1/40 of the density in Austria. The inadequate pipeline network facilities have greatly hindered the shale gas transportation and the development of the whole industry. Besides, due to the lack of Compressed Natural Gas (CNG) and small Liquefied Natural Gas (LNG) facilities, transportation through pipelines is the major measure to bring natural gas from producers to consumers, which becomes a bottleneck restricting China's development of the shale gas industry. Take the biggest shale gas field in China, Fuling Demonstration Zone as an example. This field is located in the mountainous region at the intersection of Yangzi River and Wujiang River where transportation is extremely inconvenient. Within Fuling Demonstration Zone, there are 8 gas stations, 1 transmission station and 22 km of gas mainline with 1.5 million cubic meters of daily gas transmission capacity. However, if the pipeline network construction cannot be accelerated, the shortage in shale gas transportation capacity will impede improvement in output and the commercialization of production (Li and Wan 2015). In addition, China's shale gas resource is mainly in mountain and basin areas in the Midwest where terrain conditions are complex. This makes it difficult and costly to build pipeline networks. Such shortage in infrastructure construction has hindered the development of shale gas production.

3.4 Lack of Marketization

Marketization and commercialization are key to major breakthroughs in shale oil and gas development in the United States. More than 8,000 SMEs take part in shale gas exploration and production, and more than 85% of shale gas is produced by SMEs. The diversification of investment subjects, the technological innovation of SMEs and the financial supports from large enterprises jointly lead to the rapid growth of the shale resource industry in the United States. In contrast, it is the large state owned enterprises that dominate shale gas production in China. PetroChina, Sinopec and CNOOC have monopolized the upstream activities. The failure to introduce competition into the market, due to lack of SMEs and private companies, is the major factor that restricts and hinders the marketization, commercialization and rapid growth of China' shale gas industry. Moreover, the development of shale industry urges reform of the whole industry chain, that is to say, from opening of upstream exploration rights to the third-party access to pipe network construction in midstream, and then to price setting in downstream, a free market mechanism that encourages innovation and competition is a must-have.

3.4.1 Monopoly of Upstream Mining Rights and Prospecting Rights

In the United States, "Full Owner" of the land owns ownership of underground resources as well. In the meanwhile, on their private will, the landowner can divide the land property rights and mineral rights and sell them respectively. Thus, once oil and gas companies intend to explore an area, they should not only sign a lease with mineral holders, but also get a permission of surface use from the on-land rights owner. An important principle of ownership separation is the dominance of mineral rights, thus, the owner of the surface cannot prevent the mineral resources owner from carrying out the exploration and production of mineral resources (Huang 2016). In many U.S. states, to eliminate landlords hindering energy extraction, forced land leases are legalized with lands explored by landlords themselves or their tenants (Zuckerman 2014). Although the separation of rights may harm the interests of surface owners, the marketization and commercialization of mineral resources exploration and production is greatly encouraged.

According to the "Mineral Resources Law of the People's Republic of China", all mineral resources are state owned, this national ownership of surface and underground mineral resources cannot be changed or transferred. The central government of China makes plans on the development and production of important minerals. No one can do exploration and production without the permission of relevant authorities in the State Council. Thus, in China, the prospecting right and exploiting right of minerals are independent from each other, and they need to be obtained with payment to the state. Limited to application qualification and investigation scale, statistics from Ministry of Land and Resource show that 97% of all exploration and production in China are owned by the three biggest state-owned petroleum enterprises, including PetroChina, Sinopec and CNOOC. Moreover, it is difficult to withdraw or trade prospecting right and exploiting right in the market, which seriously hinders the marketization process of the oil and gas industry (Huang et al. 2016).

3.4.2 Operation Mechanism of Pipe Network in Midstream

The construction and operation of gas pipeline network plays an important role in shale gas industry. The construction of China's pipeline network is relatively lagged, and most of the existing pipelines were constructed for the downstream monopolists. Hence, there is no extra capacity open to any third party and private companies. Nowadays, 90% of all gas pipelines are in charge of PetroChina, which creates many conflicts of interest between various parties and PetroChina during shale gas transportation (Yang 2014).

3.4.3 Price Setting in Downstream

The energy price reform is one of the highlights of market-oriented reform of China's energy system. Take natural gas as an example, from "12th Five-Year Plan", its price has witnessed the change from cost-plus to alternative energy prices linking, from the establishment of ex-factory price to adjustment of station prices, and the merge of incremental gas price and stock gas price. As a consequence, gas price dropped to some extent, and the single price setting mode is diversified. However, under the circumstances of low international oil price and severe competition from alternative energies, the growth rate of gas demand has slowed down, the mode of "base sales on production" was less suitable than "base production on sales" in order to better balance market supply and demand (Huang et al. 2016). "Action Plan for Energy Development Strategy (2014–2020)" proposed that price reform should be promoted in oil, gas, and electricity market, competitive prices should be open gradually, gas wellhead prices and sale prices should be set by market, while oil and gas pipeline transmission price should set by the government (Huang 2016). Published by State Council in October 2015, "Several Opinions on Promoting the Price Mechanism Reform" has developed following principles for the market-based pricing mechanism reform in natural gas field: "control the middle and let go of both ends", promote diversified competition among market subjects, securely manage and gradually reduce cross-subsidies. It is necessary to untangle price issues of natural gas as soon as possible, liberalize natural gas sources and sales prices, and establish a mechanism of market-driven energy prices.

3.5 Inadequate Subsidies

In 2012, the Ministry of Land and Resources issued the "Shale Gas Development and Utilization Subsidy Policy" which sets standards on the amount of subsidies for shale gas production. China's subsidy standard for shale gas production is 0.4 RMB per cubic meter in 2012–2015, and will drop to 0.3 per cubic meter in 2016–2018 and 0.2 per cubic meter in 2019–2020. At the current stage, since shale gas does not have a cost advantage over conventional oil and gas resources, its development relies more on government support and preferential policies (Yue 2015). However, at present, there is only a single way to subsidize this industry and subsidy is very limited, while the tax reductions and subsidies towards investment in the industry are insufficient (Huang et al. 2016). Moreover, the difficulty of implementing policies in some places makes the actual benefits and incentives even less than regulated, thereby reducing the effectiveness of policies and motivation of investments, which hinders the technological progress and rapid growth of shale gas industry.

4 Policy Implications for Shale Industry in China

4.1 Improve Technology and Independent Innovation Capabilities

In the field of shale exploration and production, technological innovation has greatly improved the efficiency of horizontal well drilling, the cost of drilling has decreased significantly, the maximum length of horizontal wells has also increased rapidly, and the improvement of technology is the key to yield growth and cost reduction. The EIA report at the ECF International Shale Gas Forum on December 7, 2016 mentioned that rig and cutting tools, ground drilling equipment, directional well tools, and batch drilling technologies have helped oil producers increase drilling efficiency by more than 35% over the past eight years. The key laboratory in Sichuan Province have improved the daily production of the average well from 81,500 to 22,800 m^3 with the advanced technology, which effectively increases the output of natural gas wells.

The United States, is one of the most advanced countries in shale technology, when learning and studying from the United States, China not only needs to introduce the technology concept, equipment and talent, but also adjusts and updates these imported technologies based on local conditions so that these technologies can have the maximum impacts.

4.2 Environmental Protection in Shale Production

The exploration and production of shale resources may induce environmental risks, and therefore environmental protection has become an urgent task to realize the sustainable development of shale resources exploration and production. First, the government should increase R&D investment, innovate new technology, reduce the pollution components in fracturing liquid and develop environmental friendly fracturing process; improve the recycling system of water resources, enhance the reuse ratio of waste liquid; improve drilling and production tools to solve the problem of methane gas leakage. Second, the government also needs to strengthen environmental supervision, set up a unified regulatory institution, and accelerate environmental protection legislation. Third, enterprises are required to establish environmental awareness, improve social responsibility, and achieve clean production process.

4.3 Establish the Market Mechanism

The change of prospecting right from registration system to bidding system is the first step of upstream market-oriented reform. At present, China's exploration license for shale gas has been bid for two rounds, but due to high investment costs and other reasons, the exploration and production process is relatively slow (Wu and Yang 2015), and the third round of tenders are pending. Only by establishing and perfecting the trading system of exploration rights and introducing competition to avoid resource misallocation can we establish an effective exit mechanism for enterprises that do not have the competitiveness, attract more capital and investment to enter, and promote the rapid growth of the shale industry.

At present, China's social capital participation in shale production is mainly divided into two categories, including technical service type and capital service type (Huang et al. 2016), most of these social capitals do not have the ability to be listed, and they do not have a solid financial foundation. On the one hand, national and local governments can help small and medium-sized private enterprises to create conditions for registration and listing, or set up a shale industry development fund to invest in small but promising companies (Wu and Yang 2015). On the other hand, SMEs can increase their productivity by expanding their financing channels and improving their level of professional services through mergers and acquisitions with the three major oil Chinese companies, and cooperation with local governments (Huang et al.

2016). For example, PetroChina sets up a second "joint venture between enterprises and local governments" of shale gas exploration and production company, Sichuan shale gas exploration and production Co., Ltd., in late 2016. Different from the first "joint venture between enterprises and local governments" of shale gas exploration and production company, Sichuan Changning Natural Gas Development Co., Ltd. (Changning Company), PetroChina transformed from absolute to relative holding in the new company, with shareholders made up of PetroChina and local state-owned enterprises. Such changes not only reduce PetroChina's investment risk, but also promote local economic development.[3]

The United States Federal Energy Regulatory Commission (FERC) issued Order No. 636 - Restructuring of Pipeline Services in 1992, which requires pipeline companies to provide open access services and implement the principle of marketization of third-party access and operational pricing of the pipe network. The opening up of midstream oil and gas pipeline network activities is one of the most important reforms of the industry in China. In 2016, PetroChina initiated internal pipeline business realignment, separating pipeline transportation business from natural gas business to achieve the independence of respective operations. On March 19, 2019, the seventh meeting of the Central Committee for Comprehensive and Deepening Reform formally considered and adopted "Opinions on the Implementation of the Operation Mechanism Reform for the Oil and Gas Pipeline Network", which announced that China will form an oil and gas pipeline network company. The establishment of the new pipe network company will be conducive to achieve better interconnection, realize the separation of distribution and sales, and straighten out the oil and gas costs and price accounting. Allowing more market-oriented oil and gas production to enter the pipeline freely is conducive to the diversification of energy suppliers, and the liberalization of downstream sales market, which enables users to have more choices in the oil and gas services and further eliminates the barriers of private capital into the oil and gas market. Therefore, the establishment of the new pipe network companies is conducive to the activation of energy market competition.

4.4   Enhance Subsidy Supports

Drawing on the experience of the United States, the commercialization of the shale industry relies heavily on the government's subsidy supports. In recent years, China has achieved rapid growth in shale gas production, but the net profit per unit has not significantly increased, which still needs the government to play a great supporting role before the technologies are more sophisticated and competitive (Yue 2015). Confronting the problem of insufficient marketization in the upstream, midstream, and downstream of China's shale industry, the government subsidy policy should be clearer, and the quantity, scope and conditions of subsidies should be more scientific

---

[3] From the China Geological Survey, Oil and Gas Resources Research Center, "Shale Gas Dynamics" No. 22.

and reasonable, which can attract more social capital and lead to the healthy and promising shale industry.

4.5 Establish the Geological Information Database

The establishment of geological information database is a prerequisite for the development of shale industry. China has diverse nature of the terrain, complex geological conditions, immature geological exploration technology, and therefore the condition of shale resources have not yet been fully discovered and recorded (Gao et al. 2015). The U.S. Shale Revolution has dramatically changed the world oil and gas industry, but without complete geological data, reserves information, and sophisticated technology, the development of China's shale industry make no haste in order to avoid the waste of resources due to haphazard investment. Therefore, China should first encourage shale resources investigation and evaluation, enhance exploration efforts and supporting investment, establish and establish a high-quality and comprehensive geological information service database, and strive to reduce the natural risk and market investment risk of shale production (Geng et al. 2015).

5 Summary

China has long been in the situation of "lavish in coal, lack in oil and gas", and its energy consumption has heavily relied on coal for a long time. With the increasing negative impact of coal-based energy consumption structure, it is necessary to optimize the energy structure, reduce coal consumption, control crude oil consumption and encourage natural gas consumption. However, China has consumed much more crude oil and natural gas than it produced in recent years, which led to rapid increase in dependence of foreign oil and gas and caused serious challenges to China's energy security situation. Meanwhile, the success of the Shale Revolution in the United States has drawn many countries' attentions to the unconventional oil and gas resources, including China. As a result, it is of great importance to analyze the current situation of China's unconventional oil and gas industry and explore the pathways for catch-up. This chapter studies the development status and future trends of China's shale industry from three aspects, including current situation, existing challenges and countermeasures.

China's reserves and technically recoverable quantity of shale resources are huge, mainly located in the Sichuan Basin and Yangzi platform. Since the first production in 2012, China's shale gas production achieved rapid growth. At the same time, technologies in exploration and production have made breakthroughs continuously, which have greatly improved the productivity and efficiency and made China the third country in the world to achieve commercial production of shale gas. Since 2011, in order to boost the development of shale industry, China has issued many policies, regulations and standards, and has continuously improved the investment environment of the shale industry. To summarize, China has successfully launched the development of the shale industry and make fruitful achievements.

At present, China's unconventional gas production has increased 16 times compared with the production in the 1970s, the share of unconventional gas on total natural gas production increased from 19% in 1970s to 26% in 2010s. By 2040, unconventional gas production is expected to grow to 762 million barrels of oil equivalent, and will account for more than half of total gas production, making it the main force for natural gas production. At the same time, thanks to the large amount of shale gas production, China's natural gas production will exceed crude oil production, which builds a solid foundation to optimize energy structure and realizes the goal of "making natural gas China's main energy source". As the main unconventional natural gas resource, shale gas is the major driving force on improving China's energy supply capacity and energy structure. In terms of oil production, the exploitation of unconventional oil resources will also achieve some growth the next 20 years, which will partially compensate the decline in unconventional oil production.

Although China's shale industry has witnessed a good start and kept on improving, there is still a big gap between China and the United States in shale industry. In the United States, the proportion of unconventional gas is 72%, and the proportion of unconventional oil is 54%. In China, however, these two numbers are 26% and 11%, respectively. The good news is that China has paid much attention to the development of the shale industry: many investments have been made and many supporting policies have been enacted. If more successfully reforms and incentives can be introduced, China is able to catch up in the future in shale industry.

However, it is worth noting that there are still some institutional, technical and environmental problems that may hinder the development of China's shale industry, which can be concluded as follows: the low technical level, high exploitation costs, the potential risk of environmental damage, the insufficient infrastructure construction such as transportation network, low degree of marketization, and insufficient subsidies.

In the long term, satisfying energy demand and reducing dependence on foreign energy is the major targets for China's oil and gas industry and an important guarantee for China's energy security. China should try its best to accelerate the marketization reform of the whole industry, improve the pipeline network, energy storage system and other infrastructure, issue more good policies, increase financial subsidies, and strengthen environmental supervision to support the faster development of the shale industry.

References

Gao Yang, Luo Ling, Li Wenbo, et al. The analysis of the shale gas industry development in China [J]. China Mining Magazine, 2015(8):23–25.

Gregory Zuckerman. The Frackers: The Outrageous Inside Story of the New Billionaire Wildcatters [M]. China Renmin University Press, 2014.

Geng Xiaojin, You Shenggang, Wu Yanting, et al,. Study on the financial problems of shale gas industry and policies suggestion [J]. China Mining Magazine, 2015(10):68–71.

Huang Peihuang. Analysis on the U.S. Land Ownership and the Title Defects under the Sale and Purchase Agreement [J]. Petroleum & Petrochemical Today, 2016, 24(5):37–41.

Huang Xiaoyong, Xing Guangcheng, XieShujiang. Annual Development Report on World Energy (2016) [M]. 2016.

Li Shixiang, Wanpei. Study on Supportive Policy of Shale Gas Exploration in China— A Case Study on Fuling National Shale Gas Demonstration Center [J]. Natural Resource Economics of China, 2015, 28(7):44–47.

Li Xingru, Liu Yagai, Yu Changliang. Analysis on the Situation of China's Unconventional Natural Gas Exploration and Development [J]. Natural Resource Economics of China, 2015(8):64–67.

Liu Zihan, Guo Ju'e, Wang Shubin. The Research on the Learning Curve of Technology Engineering Implementation for Shale Gas Development in China [J]. Science and Technology Management Research. 2016,36(3): 118–122.

Wu Kan, Yang Shuwang. Cost Analysis and Financial Support Strategies on the Shale Gas Exploration and Development in China [J]. Journal of East China University of Science and Technology (Social Science Edition), 2015, 30(5):82–89.

Yang Hongbo, Pengmin, Zhang Yanming. Tax and Fee Policy of Shale Gas Resources Development Impact on Environment [J]. Ecological Economy(Chinese Edition), 2015, 31(12):70–73.

Yang Liening. The Impacts of Shale Gas on International Demand of Energy and China's Development Strategy [J]. China Business and Market, 2014, 28(4):117–121.

You Shenggang, Guoqian, Wu Yanting, & Zeng Chunlin. (2015). Water utilization of shale gas development: a case of Chongqing. China Mining Magazine, 2015, s1: 195–198.

Yu Guohe, Wu Qiaosheng. The strategic revelation in view of the new energy security according to the America experience of shale gas development [J]. China Mining Magazine. 2015(11): 1–4.

Yue Laiqun. Thoughts on the Issues of Shale Gas under the Background of Low Oil Prices [J]. Natural Resource Economics of China, 2015(10):13–17.

Part II
Micro Analysis of Global Oil and Gas Companies

Chapter 5
Multi-dimensional Interactions in the Oilfield Market: A Jackknife Model Averaging Approach of Spatial Productivity Analysis

Abstract This chapter develops a methodology to assess the productivity in oilfield service companies, taking multi-dimensional interactions (e.g., regions, segments, products etc.) into account. Firstly, various spatial models are utilized on 54 oilfield service firms to estimate the production function that separately accounts for cross-sectional dependence in business segment and geography, where the general spatial model (GSM) is found to be the most efficient. Secondly, two GSM models, one accounting for interactions in business segments and the other in geography, are combined in a Jackknife model averaging method to derive the aggregate production function of the oilfield market. Evidence of cross-sectional dependence and constant returns to scale are found, as well as positive spillover effects across firms. Moreover, the oilfield market had achieved high-speed growth in productivity since 2003, but experienced a significant crash in 2009 after the financial crisis and productivity has stagnated in recent years.

Keywords Multi-dimensional interactions · Spatial econometric model · Model averaging method · Global oilfield market

1 Introduction

Many present-day conglomerates have footprints in multiple nations or regions and generate multiple products in different segments, which has led to an increase in the study of multidivisional firms (Gong 2016; Piccolo et al. 2015), multi-product firms (De Loecker et al. 2016; Dupont et al. 2002), multinational firms (Crescenzi et al. 2014; Kedron and Bagchi-Sen 2012), and multi-segment firms (Maksimovic and Phillips 2002; Ortiz-Molina and Phillips 2011). As a result of these numerous footprints, the interactions and competition among firms within a given industry are multi-dimensional.

© Zhejiang University Press 2020   79
B. Gong, *Shale Energy Revolution*,
https://doi.org/10.1007/978-981-15-4855-0_5

Table 1 Multi-dimensional interactions between Schlumberger and Halliburton

Revenue	Exploration		Production		Subtotal	
	SLB	HAL	SLB	HAL	SLB	HAL
North America	A	I	B	J	E	M
Latin America	C	K	D	L	F	N
Subtotal	G	O	H	P	Q	R

The oilfield market is one such energy market, which can be divided into five segments in four regions.[1] It is the upstream of the petroleum industry to explore for and extract crude oil and natural gas. Among the 54 publicly traded oilfield firms in our dataset, there are 24 multi-segment multi-region firms that have footprints and face competition in multiple segments and regions. Hence, taking multi-dimensional interactions into account is necessary to conduct a productivity analysis of this market.

As an example, two leading oilfield firms in the market, Schlumberger (SLB) and Halliburton (HAL), both have footprints in the exploration and production segments in North America (NAM) and Latin America (LAM) markets. As shown in Table 1, ABCD are Schlumberger's revenues and IJKL are Halliburton's revenues in each region-segment market. The direct interactions should be in the same region for the same segment (i.e., A vs. I, B vs. J, C vs. K, and D vs. L). However, public firms usually do not release such detailed information. In many cases, they publish revenues by region and revenues by segment. In other words, Schlumberger releases EFGH, and Halliburton releases MNOP in their annual reports, which automatically sums to Schlumberger and Halliburton's overall revenue, Q and R, respectively. According to the detailed level of information, this chapter denotes ABCD and IJKL as the "first-best" data, EFGH and MNOP as the "second-best" data, and Q and R as the "third-best" data. It is worth noting that the "third-best" data are easy to get from financial reports, the "second-best" data are available in some cases, while the "first-best" data are unobserved in most cases.

Classic productivity analysis in the energy market only compares firms' total output (i.e., Q vs. R), which ignores the heterogeneity in different submarkets. Wolf (2009) compares the performance of 50 state-owned and private oil companies for 1987–2006, where the sum of oil and gas production is used as the unique output in order to estimate the production function of the oil and gas industry. Hartley and Medlock (2008) and Eller et al. (2011) emphasize several reasons to use revenue, rather than production, as the output in the petroleum industry, including that: (1) physical output measures may fail to capture the effect of subsidies, such as a lower domestic price as the result of political pressure on state-owned companies; (2) a

---

[1]Oilfield Market Report (OMR) by Spears divides the oilfield market into five segments, including: (1) exploration, (2) drilling, (3) completion, (4) production, and (5) capital equipment, downhole tools and offshore services (capital equipment, hereafter). OMR also separates the global market into four regions, including: (1) North America, (2) Latin America, (3) Europe, Africa, and Commonwealth of Independent States, and (4) Middle East and Asia.

natural way to aggregate the multiple outputs (crude oil and natural gas to refined outputs) is to measure their relative value at market prices; and (3) data limitations may be present as for many firms, revenue figures are more readily available than the physical outputs of different products. As a result, many scholars (Eller et al. 2011; Hartley and Medlock III 2013) use aggregated firm-level revenue (i.e., Q and R in Table 1) as the output when estimating the production function of the oil and gas industry. The utilization of "third-best" data as output is also witnessed in other energy markets. Abbott (2006) treats the amount of electricity consumed as the output when estimating the productivity of Australian state electricity sectors over the period of 1969–1999. Fallahi et al. (2011) study the productivity of 32 Iran's power electric generation management companies for 2005–2009 using net electricity produced as the output.

However, some economists use the extra information provided by the "second-best" data when available. Al-Obaidan and Scully (1992) study the international petroleum industry, and although firm-level revenue (i.e., Q and R in Table 1) is still employed as the unique output, revenues by segment and by region (i.e., EFGH and MNOP in Table 1) are utilized to calculate two control variables, including the vertical integration ratio and multi-nationality ratio. Thompson et al. (1996) introduces a multi-output multi-input model when studying the 14 US major oilfield companies in the 1980s and 1990s. The method puts multiple outputs, rather than one output, into the production function, which provides another way to use the "second-best" data. This is also widely used in the electricity distribution industry, where the electricity delivered/sold and the numbers of customers are the two outputs (Çelen 2013; Pérez-Reyes and Tovar 2009; Von Hirschhausen et al. 2006), as well as many non-energy markets, such as banking, airlines etc. Moreover, Gong (2016) suggests a third approach to use the "second-best" data, where the revenue by segment can affect the shape of the production function, which is assumed to be fixed in the aforementioned two approaches. Different segments have different production techniques, and therefore different production functions. Revenue by segment measures the frequency of using each production technique, and thereby decides the aggregate production function. Gong (2016) builds a varying/random coefficients production function to estimate the productivity of oilfield companies.

The second wave of studies derives more information from the "second-best" data, which is overlooked or unobserved by the first wave of studies that only use the "third-best" data. However, there are still two weaknesses in the second wave. First, the interactions and competition among firms are not introduced into the production function using the "second-best" data. Second, most studies only consider one-dimensional disaggregation (either segment-wide or region-wide), rather than the combination of the different dimensions.

On the one hand, interactions and competition exist in the same nation/region (E vs. M in North America and F vs. N in Latin America) since companies have to compete for inputs, such as labor and capital, which have endowment constraints within a region. On the other hand, interactions and competition exist in the same segment/product line (G vs. O in exploration and H vs. P in production) since the outputs target the same buyers. Therefore, conglomerates care about both market shares by region and by segment. Moreover, a company's output (sales) not only depends on its own inputs, but is also influenced by its competitors', as the supply of inputs in the same region and the demand for the same products are constrained.

The purpose of this chapter is to consider multi-dimensional interactions and competition in production analysis when only "second-best" data is available. In terms of the two aforementioned problems in the second wave of studies, this chapter tackles the first issue, the interactions of companies, by introducing spatial techniques, and further solves the second issue, the combination of multi-dimensional interactions, by introducing a model averaging method.

Spatial econometrics consists of econometric techniques dealing with interactions of economic units in space. The spatial weights matrices capture the interactions (distance) between individuals, which can be defined as geographical or economic characteristics. The first spatial weights matrix in this chapter measures the geographical distance among firms (i.e., how similar their business portfolios are by region). The second spatial weights matrix in this chapter measures the economic distance among firms (i.e., how similar their business portfolios are by segment).

The production function can be estimated using each of the two spatial weights matrices to capture the interaction in one dimension at a time. As a result, we have two candidates for the true data generating process (DGP), which leads to a model selection problem. This chapter uses the jackknife model averaging (JMA) method to assign a set of weights to both candidate models, rather than select a single model as the "best" or "true" model. This model averaging approach simultaneously considers the two-dimensional interactions (segments and regions) among conglomerates and can be generalized to higher dimension analysis, if necessary. To sum up, this chapter first uses spatial techniques to control interactions in each dimension separately and then uses the model averaging method to combine the multi-dimensional interaction effects.

There are three central contributions of this chapter: (1) introduces spatial techniques to control the interactions of companies, which is seldom applied in the energy market; (2) utilizes a model averaging method to combine multi-dimensional interactions among competitors, which is a new but important characteristic of the energy market; and (3) it is the first research to study the multi-dimensional interactions in the global oilfield market, which is a less studied energy market due to data limitation, but increasingly important because of the Shale Revolution.

Compared with the example in Table 1, the empirical part of this chapter focuses on 54 companies (rather than Schlumberger and Halliburton alone) in the global oilfield market from 2002 to 2014. In the first dimension, the market is divided into five segments (rather than exploration and production segments alone). In the second dimension, the global market is divided into four regions (rather than North America and Latin America alone). The major empirical findings are: (1) it is necessary to use spatial techniques to control the spatial dependence both segment-wide and region-wide in this market; (2) the jackknife approach derives even weights, indicating that the interactions in both dimensions are essential; (3) the total effects of the inputs sum to one, indicating constant returns to scale; (4) small but significant positive indirect effects are observed, which implies some spillover effects in the market; (5)

the spillover effects from other companies to a specific company are stable across firms; (6) the spillover effects of a particular company to other companies have some variation across firms, but the differences between small and big firms are negligible; and (7) the oilfield market had achieved high-speed growth in productivity since 2003, but experienced a significant crash in 2009 after the financial crisis and productivity has stagnated in recent years.

The remainder of the chapter is structured as follows. Section 2 introduces the two-step model. Section 3 studies the global oilfield market as an application. Section 4 concludes the chapter.

2 Model

2.1 Production Function

The production function is assumed to have a Cobb-Douglas functional form in this chapter. This subsection introduces and compares a non-spatial model and three types of spatial models to estimate the production function. The spatial weights matrices used to catch the multi-dimensional interactions among conglomerates are then constructed. Finally, the potential endogeneity problem in the production function is discussed.

2.1.1 Non-spatial Model

This chapters begins with a non-spatial production function, which is of the form:

$$y_{it} = X_{it}\beta + \varepsilon_{it}, \quad i = 1, \ldots, N; \, t = 1, \ldots, T, \tag{1}$$

where y_{it} is the output of the i-th unit at time t, X_{it} vectors the inputs plus the constant term, β vectors the parameters to be estimated, and ε_{it} is an i.i.d. disturbance term with zero mean and variance σ_ε^2.

Fixed or random effects models are typically used to control individual heterogeneity without the consideration of spatial/individual interactions in earlier panel data setups. According to the First Law of Geography by Tobler (1979), everything is related to everything else, but closer things are more related. If such cross-sectional dependence is overlooked or consciously ignored, we cannot derive efficient estimators and unbiased standard errors. Moreover, inferences about parameters of interest may be invalid due to the presence of cross-sectional dependence (Chudik and Pesaran 2013; Phillips and Sul 2003).

The spatial econometric model is one of the methods that deal with spatial interactions in regression models that address cross-section dependence explicitly. Many studies (Artis et al. 2012; Detotto et al. 2014; Eberhardt and Teal 2013) use spatial techniques in productivity analysis. This chapter introduces three types of spatial econometric approaches below to control the potential cross-sectional dependence.

2.1.2   The Spatial Autoregressive Model (SAR)

The most frequently encountered specification in spatial econometrics is the Spatial Autoregressive Model[2] (SAR) (Anselin 2013; Cliff and Ord 1973; LeSage and Pace 2009; Ord 1975). This model captures endogenous interaction effects, explaining the dependence between the dependent variable y of each unit. In other words, the value of y in one unit depends on the values of y in other units, resulting in the formulation of spillover effects.

$$y_{it} = \rho \sum_{j=1}^{N} \omega_{ij} y_{jt} + X_{it}\beta + \varepsilon_{it}, \tag{2}$$

or in matrix notation

$$Y = \rho WY + X\beta + E, \tag{3}$$

where ω_{ij} is the element of the spatial weights matrix W that measures the distance between i and j. ρ is a new unknown parameter that measures the magnitude of indirect effects.

2.1.3   The Spatial Error Model (SEM)

In the SAR model, the error term is assumed to be classical (i.e., an i.i.d. disturbance term with zero mean and variance σ_ε^2). However, the spatial influence (interaction effects) may come through the error terms rather than the dependent variable, which leads to the Spatial Error Model[3] (SEM) (Bivand 1984; Cliff and Ord 1973; LeSage and Pace 2009; Ripley, 1981):

$$y_{it} = X_{it}\beta + \varepsilon_{it}, \varepsilon_{it} = \lambda \sum_{j=1}^{N} \omega_{ij} \varepsilon_{jt} + u_{it}, \tag{4}$$

or in matrix notation

$$Y = X\beta + E, E = \lambda WE + X\beta + U, \tag{5}$$

---

[2]Spatial Autoregressive Model may be referred to as the Spatial Lag Model.
[3]Spatial Error Model may be referred to as the Spatial Autocorrelated Model.

where λ is a scalar spatial error parameter, U is white noise with zero mean and variance σ_u^2, and E is a spatially autocorrelated disturbance vector with constant variance and covariance terms specified by a fixed spatial weights matrix and a single coefficient λ:

$$E \sim N\left(0, \sigma_u^2 (I - \lambda W)^{-1}(I - \lambda W')^{-1}\right).$$

2.1.4 The General Spatial Model (GSM)

The combination of SAR and SEM is called the General Spatial Model (GSM). This model can capture endogenous interaction effects and the interaction effects among the error terms simultaneously. The full GSM model is

$$y_{it} = \rho \sum_{j=1}^{N} \omega_{ij} y_{jt} + X_{it}\beta + \varepsilon_{it}, \varepsilon_{it} = \lambda \sum_{j=1}^{N} \omega_{ij}\varepsilon_{jt} + u_{it}, \tag{6}$$

or in matrix notation

$$Y = \rho WY + X\beta + E, E = \lambda WE + X\beta + U \tag{7}$$

and can be written as

$$Y = (I - \rho W)^{-1} X\beta + (I - \rho W)^{-1}(I - \lambda W)^{-1} U.$$

Anselin et al. (2008) provide Lagrange Multiplier tests under a panel data setting to choose which model fits the data best. Moreover, we can also use AIC or BIC methods to select from SAR, SEM, and GSM.

2.1.5 Spatial Weights Matrices

Prior to the estimation of the above models, the spatial dependence structure between firms must be specified. This chapter constructs two spatial weights matrices, including the segment-wide weight matrix W_1 to describe whether firms do business in the same segment/product line and the region-wide weight matrix W_2 to describe whether firms do business in the same region.

The elements ω_{ij}^1 in W_1 and the elements ω_{ij}^2 in W_2 can be constructed as follows:

$$\omega_{ij}^1 = \frac{\# \text{ of segments that firm } i \text{ and } j \text{ both have business}}{\# \text{ of segments that firm } j \text{ has business}},$$

and

$$\omega_{ij}^2 = \frac{\text{\# of regions that firm } i \text{ and } j \text{ both have business}}{\text{\# of regions that firm } j \text{ has business}}.$$

It is easy to see that the elements ω_{ij}^1 and ω_{ij}^2f range from zero to one, and a larger value means that firms i and j have more overlapping business. Therefore, these numbers measure the intensity of interactions between the two companies. For panel data, this chapter takes the mean of each ω_{ij}^m across time to derive time-invariant elements of the spatial weights matrices. Moreover, these weights matrices are standardized by row.

2.1.6 Endogeneity Problem

One problem we often face in estimating a production function is endogeneity, as input choices are determined by some information that is observed by the company but unobserved by economists (Ackerberg et al. 2015) or other companies. The potential endogeneity problem in the production function can derive biased OLS estimates. Marschak and Andrews (1944) point out that this simultaneity problem is more crucial for inputs that change frequently, which is the case in the oilfield market, since the firms adjust inputs heavily and rapidly based on exploration and production (E&P) spending from the oil and gas firms. The massive volatility of energy prices forces companies to divest capital and cut headcount aggressively during recessions.

Olley and Pakes (1996) propose a set of two-step techniques to solve the endogeneity problem. In their model, observed investment is utilized to control for unobserved productivity shocks (efficiency). However, in practice, investment may be an invalid proxy, as some datasets have many missing investment data. Therefore, Levinsohn and Petrin (2003) extend the model by replacing investment with intermediate inputs as the proxy. However, as Ackerberg et al. (2015) emphasize, the coefficients of the exogenous inputs cannot be identified, since the collinearity problems exist in both models.

Another widely used method to solve the endogeneity problem is the instrumental variables (IV) approach. This chapter first uses the control function method to help test the exogeneity of each input using t-tests for the significance of the reduced form residuals (see details in Amsler et al. 2016). Then, a Two-Stage Least Square (2SLS) method is applied to solve the endogeneity problem in the linear Cobb-Douglas production function.[4] The potential instrument variables in the 2SLS include input prices[5] and lagged values of input use (Levinsohn and Petrin 2003). Blundell and

---

[4]If we face some nonlinear production function such as translog, the control function method can be applied. See details in Amsler et al. (2016).

[5]Levinsohn and Petrin (2003) suggest using input prices as instruments if the input market is perfectly competitive and hence the firms are price takers. Although there are the "Big Four" companies in the oilfield market, the four-firm concentration ratio is 26%, which is much lower than the upper bound of 40% for an industry to be considered effectively competitive (Collins and

Bond (2000) and Guan et al. (2009) emphasize using input levels lagged at least two periods, as they are valid instruments only if the lag time is long enough to break the dependence between the input choices and the serially correlated shock. In this chapter, robust results are derived when treating lag two and lag three input quantities as instruments, respectively. Lag two input quantities are therefore chosen, along with the input prices, to be the IVs so that the sample size is larger in the regression.

2.2 Model Averaging Methods

Different spatial weights matrices W provide different estimations of the production function. These two competing spatial weights matrices both include useful characteristics of the interaction effects. Therefore, some spatial interactions among units will be overlooked if we only use a general selection method to choose one of the two estimations, rather than a combination of the two.

This chapter needs to combine these estimations to capture more information and describe the true data generating process (DGP). In other words, a weight is assigned to every estimation according to its ability to explain the data, since both weight matrices specify the true DGP to some extent. As a result, the weighted average estimation fits the data the best. It is worth noting that if the weight of one estimation is zero, then the model averaging problem becomes a model selection problem. Thus, the model averaging procedure is a general method of model selection.

There are several weight-determination techniques in the literature. Buckland et al. (1997) proposed assigning weights based on an information criterion of the competing models:

$$w_m = \exp(-0.5 I_m) / \sum_{m \in M} \exp(-0.5 I_m), \ I_m = l - 2\log(L_m) \tag{8}$$

where w_m refers to the weight assigned to the m-th model, I_m is the information criterion of the m-th model, M is the set of all the competing models, and in this study, $M = (1, 2)$. l refers to some penalty function, and L_m refers to the maximized likelihood function for the m-th model. Assuming n is the number of observations and k is the number of unknown parameters, the information criterion is the AIC score if the penalty function is $l = 2k$ and the BIC score if the penalty function is $l = k \cdot \log(n)$. Equation (8) guarantees that the w_m sums to unity.

The information criteria-based approach is easy to utilize, but hard to test for effectiveness and quality improvement. Hansen and Racine (2012) proposed a jackknife-based model averaging method that is asymptotically optimal and approaches the

---

Preston 1968; Parker and Connor 1979). Therefore, the oilfield market is a competitive market. Moreover, the bargaining power of the price mainly belongs to the Exploration and Production (E&P) Spending firms who buy the services from oilfield companies. In summary, this chapter utilizes input prices as instruments because the oilfield market is competitive and the oilfield firms are lacking in bargaining power, if not perfectly competitive and pure price takers.

minimum expected square errors when the sample size approaches infinity. Essentially, the jackknife method aims to minimize a "leave-one-out" cross-validation criterion.

For each model m (using the spatial weights matrix m in this case), this chapter first derives the leave-one-out validation. More specifically, it derives the jackknife estimator of the dependent variable $\hat{y}^m = \left(\hat{y}_1^m, \ldots, \hat{y}_N^m\right)'$ where $\hat{y}_i^m$ is the fitted value of y_i after the i-th observation is removed in the regression process. When solving spatial panel data models, this chapter slightly revises the model to "leave-one-unit-out" validation. The jackknife estimator is then denoted as $\hat{y}^m = \left(\hat{y}_1^m, \ldots, \hat{y}_N^m\right)'$ where $\hat{y}_i^m$ vectors the fitted values for unit i across time after all the observations of the i-th unit are deleted.

The weights w_m are assumed to be non-negative and sum to one, so the space $\Omega_M = \left(w \in R^M : w_m \geq 0, \sum_{m=1}^{M} w_m = 1\right)$. The jackknife weights $w^* = \left(w_1^*, \ldots, w_M^*\right)$ are achieved by minimizing the cross validation criteria over weight space:

$$w^* = \underset{w=(w_1,\ldots,w_M)\in\Omega_M}{\mathrm{argmin}} \quad CV_n(w) = \frac{1}{n}\hat{e}(w)'\hat{e}(w) \qquad (9)$$

where

$$\hat{e}(w) = y - \sum_{m=1}^{M} w_m \hat{y}^m.$$

Here $\sum_{m=1}^{M} w_m \hat{y}^m$ is the weighted average of the jackknife estimator, leaving $\hat{e}(w)$ as the weighted average residual.

Finally, the model averaging spatial production function has the form:

$$y_{it} = \sum_{m=1}^{M} w_m^* \left(\rho_m \sum_{j=1}^{N} \omega_{ij}^m y_{jt} + X_{it}\beta_m + \varepsilon_{it}^m\right), \varepsilon_{it}^m = \lambda_m \sum_{j=1}^{N} \omega_{ij}^m \varepsilon_{jt}^m + u_{it}^m. \qquad (10)$$

Whether ρ_m and λ_m are equal to zero depends on the selection among SAR, SEM, and GSM, according to the data.

3 An Empirical Application

3.1 Background of the Global Oilfield Market

The oilfield market, also called the oil and gas service industry, is a complex network that involves specialized technology in the upstream of the petroleum industry. Companies in the oilfield market provide the infrastructure, equipment, intellectual property and services needed to explore for and extract crude oil and natural gas. Most major integrated oil and gas companies, such as Exxon and Shell, choose to rent or buy part of the necessary equipment from these oilfield service firms. The oil and gas companies have been widely studied (Berk and Rauch 2016; Ramos and Veiga 2011; Sabet and Heaney 2016), but only a few studies (Haggerty et al. 2014; Phan et al. 2014) focus on oilfield service firms. The oilfield market generated total revenues of over $400 billion in 2014, a significant portion of which comes from the exploration and production (E&P) spending of oil and gas companies.

As conventional oil and gas resources are now being exhausted, oil and gas companies are currently paying more attention to unconventional oil and gas, offshore production and aging reservoirs to maintain a steady supply. The exploration and production of such unconventional resources require more activities and services from the oilfield market. The Shale Revolution, especially driven by the technology of Hydraulic Fracturing and Directional Drilling, dramatically reshaped the oilfield market and has resulted in a 10% compound annual growth rate (CAGR) over the past decade.

The Oilfield Market Report (OMR) by Spears & Associates provides the segment-level revenue and region-level revenue for each company, which can then provide the segment-wide and region-wide spatial weights matrices, respectively. More information about the OMR is given in Appendix 1. Figure 1 provides the average revenue

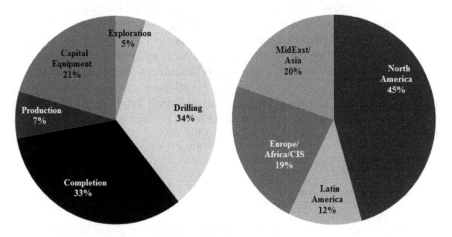

Fig. 1 Average revenue share by segment and by region in 2014

Table 2 Revenue share by segment and by region among top oilfield firms in 2014

Unit in billion $	Schlumberger		Halliburton		Baker Hughes		Weatherford	
Total revenue	48.0	(100%)	31.4	(100%)	22.7	(100%)	15.5	(100%)
(1) By segment								
Exploration	3.9	(8%)	0.8	(2%)	–	–	–	–
Drilling	20.7	(43%)	12.3	(39%)	8.7	(38%)	5.0	(32%)
Completion	20.0	(42%)	17.7	(56%)	9.5	(42%)	7.2	(46%)
Production	3.2	(7%)	0.7	(2%)	4.6	(20%)	3.0	(19%)
Capital equipment	0.2	(0.5%)	–	–	–	–	0.4	(3%)
(2) By region								
North America	17.8	(37%)	16.3	(52%)	13.1	(58%)	7.4	(48%)
Latin America	7.7	(16%)	3.5	(11%)	2.0	(9%)	2.2	(14%)
Europe/Africa/CIS	12.0	(25%)	6.6	(21%)	4.1	(18%)	3.3	(21%)
MidEast/Asia	10.6	(22%)	5.0	(16%)	3.4	(15%)	2.6	(17%)

share by segment and by region in 2014. Based on the first pie chart in Fig. 1, the Drilling and Completion segments are the biggest segments; each contributes to around one-third of the total sales, followed by the Capital Equipment segment, which generates 21% of total revenue, while the Production and Exploration segments are the smallest segments. The second pie chart in Fig. 1 shows that North America provides almost half of the global revenue.

There are four diversified oilfield firms (the "Big Four"): Baker Hughes (BHI), Halliburton (HAL), Schlumberger (SLB) and Weatherford (WFT). Table 2 lists the revenue share by segment and by region among these four oilfield firms in 2014, which can help generate an interaction table analogous to Table 1. The revenue share by segment data shows that: (1) BHI has a footprint in three segments, HAL and WFT both do business in four segments, and SLB covers all five segments; (2) all four companies have massive investments in drilling and completion segments; (3) BHI and WFT also pay significant attention to the production segment; and (4) these integrated companies are not interested in the capital equipment segment, as they do not have significant outputs in this second-largest segment, as shown in Fig. 1. The revenue share by region data shows that: (1) all four companies are active in all four regions; (2) BHI and HAL rely heavily on the North American market; and (3) SLB and WFT are relatively international in terms of business distribution across different regions.

3.2 Data Description

This chapter analyzes the spatial production function in the global oilfield market using deflated revenue as the output, the number of employees as the first input, and capital as the second input. OMR provides revenue data by segment and by region, which helped to construct balanced panel data with 54 × 13 = 702 firm-year observations over a thirteen-year period from 2002 to 2014.

This chapter contains the annual overall revenue, the number of employees, and the total capital for the 54 public firms during the same period from Thomson ONE, Bloomberg and FactSet. This study adopted the widely used unified perpetual inventory method (PIM) in Berlemann and Wesselhöft (2014) to adjust the capital data, which is explained in Appendix 2.

A company's overall revenue (collected from Thomson ONE, Bloomberg and FactSet) is not always equal to its total revenue in the oilfield market (collected from OMR). In some cases, the former may be larger because the company may have business other than oilfield services. In other cases, the former could be smaller, since the OMR adds the acquired firm's revenue to the mother firm's revenue, even in the years before acquisition, in order to build a balanced panel. This study utilizes the input proportionality assumption suggested by Foster et al. (2008) to calculate the labor and capital employed in the oilfield market for each firm.

Table 3 summarizes the firm-level input and output employed in the oilfield market after data adjustment. Average revenues increased more than four-fold, from $1.075 billion in 2002 to $4.648 billion in 2014. In the labor market, the average number of employees almost doubled, from 6,573 in 2002 to 12,550 in 2014, which shows a large amount of new employment in this market. In the capital market, the amount of average capital in 2014 was more than four times the level it was in 2002, from $0.821 billion to $3.488 billion. To sum up, both revenues and input (costs) increased dramatically from 2002, which was very likely driven by the Shale Revolution. The capital productivity was stable across time, since capital and revenue had the same growth rate, whereas labor productivity increased significantly, as the growth rate of employment was lower than that of revenue.

Table 4 reports the number of companies and average revenue in each of the five segments and four regions. There are only nine companies in the Exploration segment; five are specialized firms and four are integrated firms. The Production segment is the other segment with a small number of competitors; one specialized firm and twelve integrated firms are active in the segment. The Exploration and Production segments are the two smallest segments, not only because they have the

Table 3 Oilfield market summary statistics at firm-level

Variables	2002		2006		2010		2014	
	Mean	St. dev.	Mean	St. dev.	Mean	St. dev.	Mean	St. dev.
Revenue (billion $)	1.075	(1.983)	2.354	(4.039)	2.921	(5.118)	4.648	(8.395)
Labor (thousands)	6.573	(11.949)	8.513	(14.586)	9.625	(17.442)	12.55	(21.276)
Capital (billion $)	0.821	(1.402)	1.43	(2.508)	2.224	(3.333)	3.488	(4.430)

Table 4 Oilfield market summary statistics at division-level in 2014

	Single-division firms		Multi-divisional firm		Total	
	# of firm	Revenue	# of firm	Revenue	# of firm	Revenue
(1) By segment						
Exploration	5	0.61	4	2.29	9	1.36
Drilling	8	2.27	20	3.41	28	3.09
Completion	1	0.25	24	3.42	25	3.30
Production	1	1.15	12	1.42	13	1.40
Capital equipment	10	1.84	19	1.75	29	1.78
(2) By region						
North America	10	0.85	42	2.53	52	2.20
Latin America	–	–	37	0.79	37	0.79
Europe/Africa/CIS	–	–	42	1.37	42	1.37
MidEast/Asia	–	–	40	1.24	40	1.24

least number of companies, but also because the average revenue for these firms is also low, standing at 1.36 and 1.4 billion, respectively. On the contrary, Drilling and Completion are the two biggest segments, as there are more companies in these two segments (28 and 25, respectively) and their average revenue is greater than 3 billion. The difference between Drilling and Completion is that the former segment has eight specialized companies with a considerable amount of revenue, while the latter segment is dominated by integrated firms. The Capital Equipment segment includes ten specialized firms and nineteen integrated firms, making it the biggest segment in terms of population. However, the market share of this segment of the oilfield market is smaller than the Drilling and Completion segments, due to the smaller size of companies, at an average production of 1.78 billion. In terms of the geographical divisions, North America has ten single-region firms and 42 multi-region firms, while the other three regions are all dominated by multi-region companies. To summarize, multidivisional firms have advantages in most submarkets both segment-wide and region-wide. Such advantages are witnessed not only in the number of active firms, but also in the average revenue for these firms. The nested competition reflected in Table 4 implies the importance and necessity of taking multi-dimensional interactions of oilfield companies into consideration.

3.3 Empirical Results

Firstly, we need to test the cross-sectional dependence. This chapter adopts Pesaran's CD test (Pesaran 2004) and the Breusch-Pagan LM test (Breusch and Pagan 1980) for the oilfield panel data. Pesaran's CD test generates a z value of 44.3 (corresponding to a p-value < 2.2e−16) and the Breusch-Pagan LM test generates a chi-square of

4757.5 (corresponding to a p-value < 2.2e−16). Both tests reject the null hypothesis and support the existence of cross-sectional dependence. Therefore, spatial analysis is necessary, as ignoring spatial dependency yields inefficient, biased and inconsistent estimates in cross-unit panels.

Secondly, this chapter decides whether the individual effects should be treated as fixed or random by using the following tests: (1) the Baltagi, Song and Koh LM test (Baltagi et al. 2003) and (2) the Hausman test for spatial panel data models (Millo and Piras 2012). The Baltagi, Song and Koh LM test gives a p-value of around 0.96 using W_1 and W_2 as the spatial weights matrix (alternative hypothesis: random effects). The Hausman test gives a chi-square value of 850.45 and 170.62 using W_1 and W_2 as the spatial weights matrices, respectively (alternative hypothesis: one model is inconsistent). As a result, both tests suggest using the fixed effects model.

Thirdly, we need to choose the "best" model among SAR, SEM and GSM. This study explores the relative fit of three spatial models using a likelihood ratio test, or by comparing AIC values. Given a set of candidate models for the data, the preferred model is the one with the smallest AIC value. Therefore, AIC rewards goodness of fit (as assessed by the likelihood function), but also includes a penalty, as the number of estimated parameters increases. Table 5 reports the estimation results of SAR, SEM and GSM with W_1 and W_2 as the spatial weights matrices, respectively.

Table 5 shows that the GSM has lower AIC scores than SAR and SEM and fits the oilfield data best in both spatial weights matrices cases. Therefore, this chapter chooses to include both a spatial lag of the dependent variable and spatial autoregressive disturbances in the spatial production function.

The model averaging weights obtained using the jackknife criterion in Eq. (9) is 0.47719 for GSM (W_1) and 0.52281 for GSM (W_2). LeSage and Pace (2009) suggest reporting the average of the direct effects and the average of the indirect effects for

Table 5 Estimation Results

Determinants	SAR		SEM		GSM	
	W_1	W_2	W_1	W_2	W_1	W_2
log(Labor)	0.743***	0.735***	0.730***	0.740***	0.742***	0.738***
	(0.016)	(0.017)	(0.016)	(0.017)	(0.015)	(0.016)
log(Capital)	0.206***	0.199***	0.206***	0.212***	0.207***	0.199***
	(0.016)	(0.016)	(0.016)	(0.016)	(0.015)	(0.016)
Intercept	0.674***	−1.979***	−0.850***	−0.973***	0.633***	−2.352***
	(0.010)	(0.098)	(0.093)	(0.083)	(0.084)	(0.082)
ρ	−0.272***	0.191**	−	−	−0.266***	0.251***
	(0.047)	(0.084)	−	−	(0.039)	(0.073)
λ	−	−	−0.179	−0.999**	−0.509***	−0.999**
	−	−	(0.150)	(0.451)	(0.167)	(0.479)
AIC score	704.9	732.6	736.3	722.4	696.9	711.7

Notes Significant at: * 10, ** 5 and *** 1 percent; Standard error in parentheses

Table 6 Direct/indirect/total elasticity and internal/external/total returns to scale

Effects	Estimates	Effects	Estimates	Effects	Estimates
log (Labor)		log (Capital)		Returns to scale	
Total	0.795***	Total	0.217***	Total	1.012
	(0.074)		(0.028)		(0.080)
Direct	0.742***	Direct	0.203***	Internal	0.945***
	(0.016)		(0.016)		(0.022)
Indirect	0.053**	Indirect	0.014**	External	0.067***
	(0.022)		(0.006)		(0.023)

Notes Significant at: * 10, ** 5 and *** 1 percent; Standard error in parentheses

each input. Therefore, this study first calculates the average effects for each model and then takes the weighted average of each model's average level using the jackknife weights. Table 6 reports the direct, indirect and total effects estimates, as well as internal, external and total returns to scale (RTS) defined by Glass et al. (2016). The direct effects are computed by averaging the diagonal elements of $(I - \rho W)^{-1}\beta$, while the indirect effects are computed by averaging the row sums of the off-diagonal elements of $(I - \rho W)^{-1}\beta$. The total effects are the sum of the direct and indirect effects. The direct effects of labor and capital are 0.742 and 0.203, respectively. The indirect effects appear to be 0.053 and 0.014, which are 6.7% and 6.5% of their own total effects for labor and capital, respectively. The small but significantly positive indirect effects indicate the existence of spillover effects in the global oilfield market. Finally, this chapter calculates the internal, external and total RTS. The total RTS shows evidence of constant returns to scale, but the internal and external RTS do not.

Compared with the average indirect effects of labor and capital in Table 6, this chapter is more interested in the indirect effects (spillover effects) for each oilfield company. Following LeSage and Pace (2009), this chapter estimates the spillover effects from other companies to a specific company and the spillover effects of a particular company to all other companies for all 54 firms in Table 7 and Table 8, respectively. On the one hand, Table 7 shows that the spillover effects of increasing one unit of factor inputs in all other firms are very similar firms, where the labor spillover effects range from 0.047 to 0.054 with a standard deviation of 0.002 and the capital spillover effects range from 0.012 to 0.014 with a standard deviation of 0.0005. On the other hand, Table 8 shows that the spillover effects of increasing one unit of factor inputs in a particular firm to all other companies have some variation across the firms. The effects of one's labor on other firms range from 0.016 to 0.064 with a standard deviation of 0.011 and the effects of one's capital on other firms range from 0.004 to 0.016 with a standard deviation of 0.003. Furthermore, the average spillover effects of labor and capital for the 27 big firms are 0.0526 and 0.0135, while those for the 27 small firms are 0.0516 and 0.0131. Therefore, the differences in spillover effects between small and big firms are negligible. In summary, the relatively lower variations in the spillover effects from other companies to a specific

Table 7 The aggregated spillover effects from all other companies

Company name	Indirect effects		Company name	Indirect effects	
	Labor	Capital		Labor	Capital
Akita Drilling Ltd	0.052	0.013	Noble Drilling	0.052	0.013
Atwood Oceanics Inc	0.052	0.013	NOV	0.053	0.014
Baker Hughes	0.053	0.014	Oceaneering Int'l	0.053	0.014
Bourbon	0.052	0.013	Oil States Int'l	0.053	0.014
Calfrac Well Svs Ltd.	0.053	0.014	Parker Drilling	0.053	0.014
CGGVeritas	0.052	0.013	Pason Systems	0.052	0.013
China Oilfield Services	0.053	0.014	Patterson-UTI Energy	0.053	0.014
Core Labs	0.052	0.013	Petroleum Geo-Svs	0.047	0.012
Dawson Geophysical	0.047	0.012	Precision Drilling	0.053	0.014
Diamond Offshore	0.052	0.013	Pulse Seismic	0.047	0.012
Dril-Quip	0.053	0.014	Rowan Companies	0.052	0.013
ENSCO	0.052	0.013	RPC	0.053	0.014
Ensign Resource Svs	0.053	0.014	Saipem SPA	0.053	0.014
Exterran Holdings	0.053	0.014	SBM Offshore	0.053	0.014
FMC Technologies	0.053	0.014	Schlumberger	0.054	0.014
Fred. Olsen Energy	0.053	0.014	Schoeller-Bleckmann	0.052	0.013
Fugro	0.052	0.013	Subsea 7 S.A.	0.052	0.013
GE Oil & Gas	0.053	0.014	Superior Energy Svs	0.053	0.014
Gulf Island Fabrication	0.052	0.013	Technip	0.053	0.014
Halliburton	0.053	0.014	TESCO Corp.	0.053	0.014
Helmerich & Payne	0.052	0.013	Tetra Technologies	0.053	0.014
ION Geophysical Corp.	0.047	0.012	TGS-NOPEC	0.047	0.012
Key Energy Services	0.053	0.014	Tidewater	0.052	0.013
Logan International Inc.	0.053	0.014	Trican Well Svs Co.	0.053	0.014
McDermott	0.052	0.013	Unit Corporation	0.052	0.013
Nabors Industries	0.053	0.014	Weatherford	0.053	0.014
Newpark Resources	0.053	0.014	Bristow Group Inc.	0.052	0.013

company and the relatively higher variations in the spillover effects of a particular company to other companies are consistent with those found in Han et al. (2016).

Another aim of the chapter is to estimate the growth in Total Factor Productivity (TFP), which shows the progress of the oilfield market across time. Figure 2 shows the TFP as well as TFP growth rate of the oilfield market over the period of 2002–2014. The oilfield market achieved tremendous growth from 2003 to 2008, where five out of the six years had a two-digit growth rate. Then, the negative effect of the 2007–2009 financial crisis on the oilfield market was witnessed, as the growth rate in TFP fell to −22.7% in 2009. However, the oilfield market recovered quickly and

Table 8 The aggregated spillover effects to all other companies

Company name	Indirect effects		Company name	Indirect effects	
	Labor	Capital		Labor	Capital
Akita Drilling Ltd	0.059	0.015	Noble Drilling	0.059	0.015
Atwood Oceanics Inc	0.059	0.015	NOV	0.049	0.013
Baker Hughes	0.042	0.011	Oceaneering Int'l	0.054	0.014
Bourbon	0.063	0.016	Oil States Int'l	0.058	0.015
Calfrac Well Svs Ltd.	0.052	0.013	Parker Drilling	0.058	0.015
CGGVeritas	0.056	0.014	Pason Systems	0.063	0.016
China Oilfield Services	0.056	0.014	Patterson-UTI Energy	0.052	0.013
Core Labs	0.063	0.016	Petroleum Geo-Svs	0.035	0.009
Dawson Geophysical	0.035	0.009	Precision Drilling	0.042	0.011
Diamond Offshore	0.059	0.015	Pulse Seismic	0.035	0.009
Dril-Quip	0.054	0.014	Rowan Companies	0.059	0.015
ENSCO	0.059	0.015	RPC	0.039	0.010
Ensign Resource Svs	0.042	0.011	Saipem SPA	0.064	0.016
Exterran Holdings	0.016	0.004	SBM Offshore	0.043	0.011
FMC Technologies	0.054	0.014	Schlumberger	0.049	0.013
Fred. Olsen Energy	0.064	0.016	Schoeller-Bleckmann	0.063	0.016
Fugro	0.063	0.016	Subsea 7 S.A.	0.063	0.016
GE Oil & Gas	0.044	0.011	Superior Energy Svs	0.049	0.013
Gulf Island Fabrication	0.063	0.016	Technip	0.054	0.014
Halliburton	0.044	0.011	TESCO Corp.	0.064	0.016
Helmerich & Payne	0.059	0.015	Tetra Technologies	0.052	0.013
ION Geophysical Corp.	0.035	0.009	TGS-NOPEC	0.035	0.009
Key Energy Services	0.031	0.008	Tidewater	0.063	0.016
Logan International Inc.	0.054	0.014	Trican Well Svs Co.	0.052	0.013
McDermott	0.063	0.016	Unit Corporation	0.059	0.015
Nabors Industries	0.049	0.013	Weatherford	0.049	0.013
Newpark Resources	0.052	0.013	Bristow Group Inc.	0.063	0.016

obtained two-digit growth for three years in a row from 2010 to 2012. Over the next two years, however, the oilfield market was faced with the TFP stagnation.

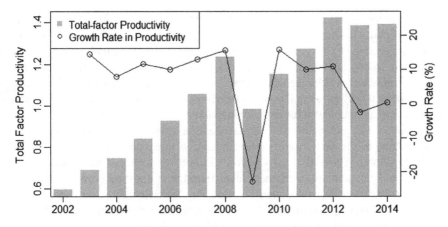

Fig. 2 Total factor productivity and TFP growth of the oilfield market for 2002–2014

4 Conclusion

This chapter uses spatial techniques to estimate productivity of the oilfield market, where a spatial weights matrix controls for segment-wide competition among firms. However, oilfield companies not only compete in the same segments, but also in the same regions. Therefore, another spatial weights matrix can control the region-wide competition among firms. The model averaging method is then utilized to consider segment-wide competition and region-wide competition simultaneously by giving weights to different spatial weights matrices.

Theoretically, this chapter tackles two problems that have been overlooked in literature related to the energy market, including the interactions of companies and the combination of multi-dimensional interactions among firms within the same industry. Empirically, this is the first research to study double-dimensional interactions in the global oilfield market, and provides evidence for the necessity to control these interactions.

At the micro-level or firm-level, evidence of positive spillovers and constant returns to scale were found. Thus, the balanced development across segments, regions and companies should be encouraged. Moreover, this chapter finds that the differences in spillover effects between small and big firms are negligible. Therefore, the government cannot pay attention and provide resources exclusively to the big companies or the state-owned enterprises. The development of the small oilfield companies is equally important to the entire market as the effect from the big oilfield companies. Finally, moderate mergers and acquisitions will not have a significant influence on production, due to the constant returns to scale and relatively stable spillover effects across firms.

At the macro-level or market-level, the oilfield market had achieved high-speed growth in productivity since 2003, which verifies the technology progress brought about by the Shale Revolution. However, the market also experienced a significant crash in 2009 due to the financial crisis. Therefore, systemic financial risks and severe volatility in energy prices should be monitored and prevented to maintain the productivity of the oilfield market, which guarantees the stable supply of oil and gas to support economic growth. Finally, productivity stagnation was observed in recent years. Continuous developments of current techniques, such as hydraulic fracturing and horizontal drilling, as well as the innovation of new shale techniques, are the key to achieving another boom for the oilfield market.

Segment-wide and region-wide interactions also exist across the entire petroleum industry due to the existence of international and integrated conglomerates, such as ExxonMobil, Shell, BP and Chevron. Future research can study the multi-dimensional interactions in the petroleum industry if the "second-best" data are available. The other important energy market, the electricity sector, is mainly a local market, rather than a global market. However, multi-dimensional interactions can still be considered within a nation or region, particularly if some utilities own multiple power plants or use various energy sources to generate electricity.

Appendix 1: OMR Data Introduction

This study uses data from the Oilfield Market Report (OMR) by Spears & Associates. This report provides revenue information of the global oilfield equipment and service markets. Spears & Associates began tracking the oilfield market in 1996 and publishes its OMR year by year. Every time, the report not only releases new data for the current year, but also updates previously published data. Most numbers in the OMR are estimates developed by Spears through five sources: public company reports (about 100 firms), published information, interviews (about 2,000 discussions), trade shows, and site visits.

There are many advantages of this OMR dataset. Firstly, this report brings estimations under the same criteria for all the firms in the industry. Different firms have different segmentations in their financial reports, so direct use of their revenue declarations by product line from SEC filings is not wise. Secondly, this dataset is widely used by most firms and clients in the field. Thirdly, Spears has investigated the numbers through five sources mentioned above to confirm its estimations in the past twenty years. Lastly, the OMR is updated annually, which revises any incorrect numbers according to the newest information.

In this chapter, two waves of the OMR (2011 and 2015) are used to generate firm-level data from 2002 to 2014. OMR2011 includes firm-level revenue by segment from 2002 to 2011, and OMR2015 includes firm-level revenue by segment from 2005 to 2014.

The combined OMR contains share and size analysis for five segments from approximately 600 companies working around the world. OMR gives detailed revenue by segment for 275 companies, 114 of which are public firms that publish

complete financial information. Within those 114 public firms have revenue by segment information, 54 of them have complete revenue by region data from 2002 to
2014. Therefore, this chapter uses a balanced panel with $54 \times 13 = 702$ observations.

Appendix 2: Estimating Capital Stocks by Perpetual Inventory Method

The perpetual inventory method (PIM) is the most widely used method to impute
capital stocks in many productivity analyses and is adopted in many statistical offices.
Berlemann and Wesselhöft (2014) review three types of PIM including the steady-
state approach, the disequilibrium approach, and the synthetic time series approach.
Then, they combine these three approaches into a unified approach in order to prevent the drawbacks of the various methods. Their approach follows the procedure
proposed by de la Fuente and Doménech (2006).

The PIM defines capital stock of a company as an inventory of investments. The
aggregate capital stock falls in the depreciation rate per period. Hence, the capital
stock in period t is a weight sum of the history of the capital stock investment:

$$K_t = \sum_{i=0}^{\infty} (1 - \delta)^i \cdot I_{t-(i+1)}$$

However, a complete time series of past investments from day one is not available
for many firms. Thomson ONE, Bloomberg, and FactSet only cover the recent portion
of investment history. Suppose the investment can only be tracked back to period t_1,
then the current capital stock can be estimated by using

$$K_t = (1 - \delta)^{t-t_0} \cdot K_{t_0} + \sum_{i=0}^{t-1} (1 - \delta)^i \cdot I_{t-(i+1)} \tag{2.1}$$

Therefore, the information needed to calculate capital stock includes a time series
of investment $I_{t-(i+1)}$, the rate of depreciate δ, and the initial capital stock K_{t_0}. Firstly,
de la Fuente and Doménech (2006) propose smoothing the time-series investment
data since the economies are on their adjustment path towards equilibrium rather
than staying in a steady state most of the time. Therefore, this study smooths the
observed capital expenditure (investment) using a regression $I_{it} = \alpha_i + \beta_1 t + \epsilon$ for
each firm. Secondly, this study follows the lead of Kamps (2006) and uses time-
varying depreciation schemes, which seems to be the most plausible variant. The
time-variant smooth depreciation rate can be estimated as the fitted value of the
regression $\delta_t = \alpha + \beta_2 t + \epsilon$. This study collects a given firm's annual depreciation
and total capital data to calculate the depreciation rate in accounting and uses this
information to run the regression. Finally, the initial capital stock at time t_0 can be

calculated from the investment I_{t_1}, the long-term investment growth rate g_I, and the estimated depreciation rate δ: $K_{t_0} \approx I_{t_1}/(g_I + \delta_{t_1})$, where the growth rate g_I is β_1 and the investment I_{t_1} is the fitted value in the same regression. Similar to the method used in Berlemann and Wesselhöft (2014), this study assumes all the years before t_1 without desegregated data have the same constant depreciation rate as year t_1. But for all the recent years that we have investment data, the depreciation rate is time variant. Therefore, Eq. (2.1) becomes:

$$K_t = \prod_{i=t_1}^{t}(1 - \delta_i)I_{t_1}/(g_I + \delta_{t_1}) + \sum_{i=0}^{t-1} \prod_{j=t-(i+1)}^{t-1} (1 - \delta_j)I_{t-(i+1)}$$

In our empirical study, t is 2014 for most companies that are still active while t_1 presents the first year of investment data and varies across firms.

References

Abbott M. The Productivity and Efficiency of the Australian Electricity Supply Industry. Energy Economics. 2006, 28 (4):444–454.
Ackerberg D.A., Caves K., and Frazer G. Identification Properties of Recent Production Function Estimators. Econometrica. 2015, 83 (6):2411–2451.
Al-Obaidan A.M., and Scully G.W. Efficiency Differences between Private and State-Owned Enterprises in the International Petroleum Industry. Applied Economics. 1992, 24 (2):237–246.
Amsler C., Prokhorov A., and Schmidt P. Endogeneity in Stochastic Frontier Models. Journal of Econometrics. 2016, 190 (2):280–288.
Anselin L. Spatial Econometrics: Methods and Models: Springer Science & Business Media, 2013.
Anselin L., Le Gallo J., and Jayet H. Spatial Panel Econometrics. In The Econometrics of Panel Data. Springer, pp. 625–660, 2008.
Artis M.J., Miguelez E., and Moreno R. Agglomeration Economies and Regional Intangible Assets: An Empirical Investigation. Journal of Economic Geography. 2012, 12 (6):1167–1189.
Baltagi B.H., Song S.H., and Koh W. Testing Panel Data Regression Models with Spatial Error Correlation. Journal of Econometrics. 2003, 117 (1):123–150.
Berk I., and Rauch J. Regulatory Interventions in the Us Oil and Gas Sector: How Do the Stock Markets Perceive the Cftc's Announcements During the 2008 Financial Crisis? Energy Economics. 2016, 54:337–348.
Berlemann M., and Wesselhöft J.-E. Estimating Aggregate Capital Stocks Using the Perpetual Inventory Method–a Survey of Previous Implementations and New Empirical Evidence for 103 Countries–. Review of Economics/Jahrbuch für Wirtschaftswissenschaften. 2014, 65 (1).
Bivand R. Regression Modeling with Spatial Dependence: An Application of Some Class Selection and Estimation Methods. Geographical Analysis. 1984, 16 (1):25–37.
Blundell R., and Bond S. Gmm Estimation with Persistent Panel Data: An Application to Production Functions. Econometric Reviews. 2000, 19 (3):321–340.
Breusch T.S., and Pagan A.R. The Lagrange Multiplier Test and Its Applications to Model Specification in Econometrics. The Review of Economic Studies. 1980, 47 (1):239–253.
Buckland S.T., Burnham K.P., and Augustin N.H. Model Selection: An Integral Part of Inference. Biometrics. 1997, 53 (2):603–618.
Çelen A. Efficiency and Productivity (Tfp) of the Turkish Electricity Distribution Companies: An Application of Two-Stage (Dea&Tobit) Analysis. Energy Policy. 2013, 63:300–310.

Chudik A., and Pesaran M.H. A Review and Comparison of Tests of Cross-Section Independence in Panels. In B.H. Baltagi ed. The Oxford Handbook on Panel Data. Oxford University Press, 2013.

Cliff A.D., and Ord J.K. Spatial Autocorrelation. Pion Ltd., Lonéon. 1973.

Collins N.R., and Preston L.E. Concentration and Price-Cost Margins in Manufacturing Industries: Univ of California Press, 1968.

Crescenzi R., Pietrobelli C., and Rabellotti R. Innovation Drivers, Value Chains and the Geography of Multinational Corporations in Europe. Journal of Economic Geography. 2014, 14 (6):1053–1086.

de la Fuente A., and Doménech R. Human Capital in Growth Regressions: How Much Difference Does Data Quality Make? Journal of the European Economic Association. 2006, 4 (1):1–36.

De Loecker J., Goldberg P.K., Khandelwal A.K., and Pavcnik N. Prices, Markups, and Trade Reform. Econometrica. 2016, 84 (2):445–510.

Detotto C., Pulina M., and Brida J.G. Assessing the Productivity of the Italian Hospitality Sector: A Post-Wdea Pooled-Truncated and Spatial Analysis. Journal of Productivity Analysis. 2014, 42 (2):103–121.

Dupont D.P., Grafton R.Q., Kirkley J., and Squires D. Capacity Utilization Measures and Excess Capacity in Multi-Product Privatized Fisheries. Resource and Energy Economics. 2002, 24 (3):193–210.

Eberhardt M., and Teal F. No Mangoes in the Tundra: Spatial Heterogeneity in Agricultural Productivity Analysis. Oxford Bulletin of Economics and Statistics. 2013, 75 (6):914–939.

Eller S.L., Hartley P.R., and Medlock K.B. Empirical Evidence on the Operational Efficiency of National Oil Companies. Empirical Economics. 2011, 40 (3):623–643.

Fallahi A., Ebrahimi R., and Ghaderi S. Measuring Efficiency and Productivity Change in Power Electric Generation Management Companies by Using Data Envelopment Analysis: A Case Study. Energy. 2011, 36 (11):6398–6405.

Foster L., Haltiwanger J., and Syverson C. Reallocation, Firm Turnover, and Efficiency: Selection on Productivity or Profitability? The American Economic Review. 2008, 98 (1):394–425.

Glass A.J., Kenjegalieva K., and Sickles R.C. Returns to Scale and Curvature in the Presence of Spillovers: Evidence from European Countries. Oxford Economic Papers. 2016, 68 (1).

Gong B. 2016. "Efficiency and Productivity Analysis of Multidivisional Firms." Dissertation, Rice University.

Guan Z., Kumbhakar S.C., Myers R.J., and Lansink A.O. Measuring Excess Capital Capacity in Agricultural Production. American Journal of Agricultural Economics. 2009, 91 (3):765–776.

Haggerty J., Gude P.H., Delorey M., and Rasker R. Long-Term Effects of Income Specialization in Oil and Gas Extraction: The Us West, 1980–2011. Energy Economics. 2014, 45:186–195.

Han J., Ryu D., and Sickles R. How to Measure Spillover Effects of Public Capital Stock: A Spatial Autoregressive Stochastic Frontier Model. In Spatial Econometrics: Qualitative and Limited Dependent Variables. Emerald Group Publishing Limited, pp. 259–294, 2016.

Hansen B.E., and Racine J.S. Jackknife Model Averaging. Journal of Econometrics. 2012, 167 (1):38–46.

Hartley P., and Medlock K.B. A Model of the Operation and Development of a National Oil Company. Energy Economics. 2008, 30 (5):2459–2485.

Hartley P.R., and Medlock III K.B. Changes in the Operational Efficiency of National Oil Companies. The Energy Journal. 2013, 34 (2):27–57.

Kamps C. New Estimates of Government Net Capital Stocks for 22 Oecd Countries, 1960–2001. IMF Staff Papers. 2006, 53 (1):120–150.

Kedron P., and Bagchi-Sen S. Foreign Direct Investment in Europe by Multinational Pharmaceutical Companies from India. Journal of Economic Geography. 2012:lbr044.

LeSage J.P., and Pace R.K. Introduction to Spatial Econometrics (Statistics, Textbooks and Monographs): CRC Press, 2009.

Levinsohn J., and Petrin A. Estimating Production Functions Using Inputs to Control for Unobservables. The Review of Economic Studies. 2003, 70 (2):317–341.

Maksimovic V., and Phillips G. Do Conglomerate Firms Allocate Resources Inefficiently across Industries? Theory and Evidence. The Journal of Finance. 2002, 57 (2):721–767.

Marschak J., and Andrews W.H. Random Simultaneous Equations and the Theory of Production. Econometrica, Journal of the Econometric Society. 1944:143–205.

Millo G., and Piras G. Splm: Spatial Panel Data Models in R. Journal of Statistical Software. 2012, 47 (1):1–38.

Olley G.S., and Pakes A. The Dynamics of Productivity in the Telecommunications Equipment Industry. Econometrica. 1996, 64 (6):1263–1297.

Ord K. Estimation Methods for Models of Spatial Interaction. Journal of the American Statistical Association. 1975, 70 (349):120–126.

Ortiz-Molina H., and Phillips G.M. Real Asset Illiquidity and the Cost of Capital. Journal of Financial and Quantitative Analysis. 2011.

Pérez-Reyes R., and Tovar B. Measuring Efficiency and Productivity Change (Ptf) in the Peruvian Electricity Distribution Companies after Reforms. Energy Policy. 2009, 37 (6):2249–2261.

Parker R.C., and Connor J.M. Estimates of Consumer Loss Due to Monopoly in the Us Food-Manufacturing Industries. American Journal of Agricultural Economics. 1979:626–639.

Pesaran M.H. "General Diagnostic Tests for Cross Section Dependence in Panels." Institute for the Study of Labor (IZA). 2004.

Phan D., Nguyen H., and Faff R. Uncovering the Asymmetric Linkage between Financial Derivatives and Firm Value—the Case of Oil and Gas Exploration and Production Companies. Energy Economics. 2014, 45:340–352.

Phillips P.C., and Sul D. Dynamic Panel Estimation and Homogeneity Testing under Cross Section Dependence. The Econometrics Journal. 2003, 6 (1):217–259.

Piccolo S., Tarantino E., and Ursino G. The Value of Transparency in Multidivisional Firms. International Journal of Industrial Organization. 2015, 41:9–18.

Ramos S.B., and Veiga H. Risk Factors in Oil and Gas Industry Returns: International Evidence. Energy Economics. 2011, 33 (3):525–542.

Ripley B.D. Spatial Statistics: Wiley Series in Probability and Mathematical Statistics. New York. 1981.

Sabet A.H., and Heaney R. An Event Study Analysis of Oil and Gas Firm Acreage and Reserve Acquisitions. Energy Economics. 2016.

Thompson R.G., Dharmapala P., Rothenberg L.J., and Thrall R.M. Dea/Ar Efficiency and Profitability of 14 Major Oil Companies in U.S. Exploration and Production. Computers and Operations Research. 1996, 23 (4):357–373.

Tobler W. Cellular Geography. In Philosophy in Geography. Springer, pp. 379–386, 1979.

Von Hirschhausen C., Cullmann A., and Kappeler A. Efficiency Analysis of German Electricity Distribution Utilities–Non-Parametric and Parametric Tests. Applied Economics. 2006, 38 (21):2553–2566.

Wolf C. Does Ownership Matter? The Performance and Efficiency of State Oil Vs. Private Oil (1987–2006). Energy Policy. 2009, 37 (7):2642–2652.

Chapter 6
The Shale Technical Revolution—Cheer or Fear? Impact Analysis on Efficiency in the Global Oilfield Service Market

Abstract The shale technical revolution has reshaped the oil and gas industry dramatically but also controversially as it affects existing energy policies as well. Many related policies, such as the fracking tax in the U.S. and the shale subsidies policy in China, depend heavily on whether or not the innovation is commercially successful. This chapter develops a two-step approach to evaluate the effect of the revolution on efficiency in the global oilfield service (OFS) market, which can be divided into five segments. In the first step, a new semiparametric model is introduced to evaluate firm-level technical efficiencies assuming segment-specific production functions for each of the five segments. In the second step, this study tests if companies acquiring directional drilling (DD) and/or hydraulic fracturing (HF) techniques can maintain efficiency. The empirical results show that practicing just one of the techniques will decrease efficiency. However, combining the two can produce significant spillover effects and improve efficiency. Therefore, innovation and integration are both crucial for the OFS market. Some policy implications are also discussed.

Keywords Stochastic frontier analysis · Semiparametric model · Global oilfield service market · Multidivisional firms · Shale technical revolution

1 Introduction

The oilfield service (OFS) market, or oil and gas service industry, is a complex process that involves specialized technology at each step of the oil and gas supply chain. Companies in the OFS market provide the infrastructure, equipment, intellectual property, and services needed to explore and extract crude oil and natural gas. Therefore, this market is the upstream of the petroleum industry. The global OFS market has a total market capitalization of over $4 trillion, generating total revenues over $400 billion in 2014.[1]

---

[1]Data from 2015 Oilfield Market Report (OMR) by Spears.

© Zhejiang University Press 2020
B. Gong, *Shale Energy Revolution*,
https://doi.org/10.1007/978-981-15-4855-0_6

The Shale Revolution, which benefited mainly from new technologies in hydraulic fracturing and directional drilling, has resulted in a 10% compound annual growth rate (CAGR) for the OFS market over the past decade. As conventional oil and gas resources are now being exhausted, oil and gas companies are currently paying more attention to unconventional oil and gas, offshore production, and aging reservoirs to maintain a steady supply. Therefore, the revolution is also called an unconventional revolution.

Hydraulic Fracturing (HF) is a well stimulation technique in which rock is fractured by a pressurized liquid. The process involves the high-pressure injection of "fracking fluid" (primarily water containing sand or other chemical additives) into a wellbore to create cracks in the deep-rock formations through which natural gas, petroleum, and brine will flow more freely. Directional Drilling (DD) is the practice of drilling non-vertical wells, and it includes the popular horizontal drilling. This technology can hit some targets that cannot be reached by vertical drilling and can drain a broad area from a single drilling pad. The combining of two technologies, HF and DD, has led to the Shale Revolution. Some rock units that were unproductive when drilled vertically can become fantastic producers of oil and/or gas. The magic of converting worthless shales into productive reservoir rocks occurs in many locations, such as the Barnett Shale of Texas, the Fayetteville Shale of Arkansas, the Marcellus Shale of the Appalachian Basin, the Bakken Formation of North Dakota, and the Haynesville Shale of Louisiana and Texas. Figure 1 illustrates the hydraulic fracturing and directional drilling activities.

The Oilfield Market Report (OMR) by Spears divides the OFS industry into five macro segments: (1) exploration, (2) drilling, (3) completion, (4) production, and (5) capital equipment, downhole tools and offshore services (capital equipment, hereafter). OMR reports segment-level revenue for the 114 public firms in the field, where 68 firms are single-division and 56 firms are multidivisional.[2] These five macro segments can be further divided into 32 micro-market segments, including Hydraulic Fracturing (under "completion" segment) and Directional Drilling (under "drilling" segment). Based on OMR, the total revenue of the entire OFS market increased by 183% from 2005 to 2015, while the HF segment and the DD segment increased by 395% and 287% respectively during the same period, which implies that these two techniques are leading the development of the entire market.

On the one hand, the Shale Revolution is generating massive revenues for OFS companies and is producing sufficient energy supplies. Many people cheer the low energy prices and the mitigation of the energy shortage. On the other hand, the new innovations also require huge amounts of investment, such as labor and capital inputs as well as Research and Development (R&D) spending, which is feared for the related financial risk, sustainability, and low input-output ratio.[3] It is difficult to estimate the profitability of the new techniques in practice. Public firms report total inputs and

---

[2]28 firms do business in two segments, 10 firms are active in three segments, seven firms have footprints in four segments, and only one firm covers all five segments.
[3]The Shale Revolution is also criticized for climate reasons. The oil and gas from shale is "worse than coal" for the climate since there is greater leakage of methane to the atmosphere in unconventional wells. Moreover, while a high supply of oil and gas decreases energy prices, it discourages the

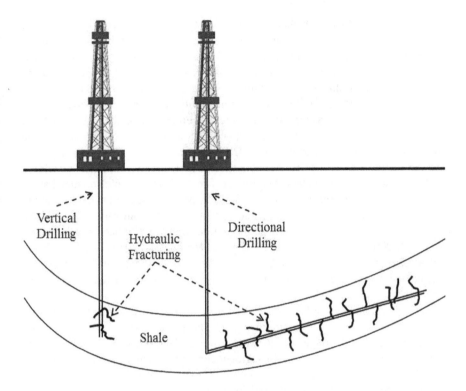

Fig. 1 Diagram of hydraulic fracturing and directional drilling

outputs, and possibly segment/division-level outputs, but not segment/division-level inputs. Therefore, it is hard to get cost information for a specific activity or segment to calculate the actual breakeven price for unconventional oil and gas.[4] As a result, whether the innovation is commercially successful is unknown.

But many energy policies depending on whether hydraulic fracturing and directional drilling techniques are earning or losing. For example, what should the tax rate of the fracking tax in the U.S. be? What subsidies should the Chinese government offer to encourage shale resource exploration and extraction? How should the renewable energy policy be adjusted to compete with shale oil and gas?

---

development of renewable energy. However, this chapter only focuses on analyzing the economic impact of the revolution from companies' perspectives.

[4]Although some firms report a breakeven price, many of them are wide ranges rather than fixed numbers. The veracity of the reported prices is also suspect since many firms adjust their price ranges frequently and continue to produce when the market price drops far below their reported breakeven prices. Sometimes even the companies themselves find it difficult to calculate the profitability of a certain program/segment because of the joint inputs and spillover effects. Remember, oilfield is a complex process that involves many steps in the energy supply chain.

This chapter evaluates whether the innovation has a positive or negative effect on firm-level efficiency using a two-step approach. If firms can maintain or even increase efficiency with hydraulic fracturing and directional drilling programs, it implies that these businesses are at least as competitive and profitable as traditional oil and gas businesses, which will reshape geopolitics and the global energy market.

Managi et al. (2004, 2006) study the productivity and efficiency of the offshore Gulf of Mexico oil and gas production, using data envelopment analysis (DEA) and stochastic frontier analysis (SFA), respectively. Thompson et al. (1996) analyze the efficiency of 14 major companies in the US oilfield market, using a non-parametric DEA for the period 1980–1991. Non-academic reports on this market are generated by advisory service firms such as Deloitte[5] and Ernst & Young,[6] which predict that the companies will be more efficient in the future. But all the academic and non-academic studies fail to consider the multidivisional structure of the companies and the pure effect of new shale technologies. The oil and gas industry has been better studied (e.g., Wolf 2009; Eller et al. 2011; Hartley and Medlock III 2013) using efficiency analysis. However, their focus is the difference between National Oil Companies and International Oil Companies (i.e., the effect of ownership), rather than the effect of the new shale technologies.

The OFS market is complex and can be divided into multiple segments, each using different technologies and hence following different production functions. In the first step, a semi-varying coefficient stochastic frontier model is introduced to estimate the firm-level efficiency with this multi-segment concern, which standard productivity and efficiency analysis overlooked or chose to ignore. Then, this chapter explores whether hydraulic fracturing and directional drilling have a significant effect on a firm's overall technical efficiency.

This study makes three central contributions. Firstly, the semiparametric production function considers the multi-segment characteristics of a market with multidivisional firms. Secondly, this study focuses on OFS companies, which experience much more volatility than oil and gas companies but are seldom studied.[7] Thirdly, this chapter estimates the impact of the Shale Revolution on efficiency, which provides essential messages to companies for their operational decisions and strategies as well as to governments for their policies and management.

The empirical results show that: (1) the production function is indeed segment-variant, which supports the validation of the multi-segment assumption considered; (2) the output elasticity of labor is consistent, while the output elasticity of capital varies greatly across segments; (3) the average firm-level efficiency for the OFS market is about 0.4, and the distribution is positively skewed; (4) having a footprint

---

[5]https://www2.deloitte.com/content/dam/Deloitte/uk/Documents/energy-resources/deloitte-uk-energy-and-resources-outlook-for-oilfield-services.pdf.

[6]http://www.ey.com/Publication/vwLUAssets/EY-review-of-the-UK-oilfield-services-industry-January-2017/$FILE/EY-Review-of-the-UK-oilfield-services-industry-January-2017.pdf.

[7]The productivity and efficiency of oilfield firms is studied much less than oil and gas companies for two reasons: the complex multi-segment characteristics and the lack of segment-level data. This chapter uses a very unique dataset to capture the multi-segment characteristics. The empirical result confirms the necessity of doing so.

in just a hydraulic fracturing or just a directional drilling business can decrease efficiency, but combining the two generates positive spillover effects; (5) all the findings above are robust when either a Cobb-Douglas or Transcendental Logarithmic production form is adopted.

The remainder of the chapter is structured as follows. Section 2 introduces the model. Section 3 provides data descriptions. Empirical results are presented and analyzed in Sect. 4. Section 5 gives conclusion and policy implications.

2 Model

This model includes two steps. Firstly, a stochastic frontier model is used to estimate firm-level aggregated production function as well as efficiency. Secondly, the derived efficiency is regressed on dummy variables of hydraulic fracturing and directional drilling as well as other variables.

2.1 Step One: Production Function and Technical Efficiency

This subsection develops a partial linear semiparametric varying coefficient stochastic frontier model ("Varying Frontier") to estimate the aggregated production function for multidivisional firms and further predicts firm-level efficiency with multi-segment concern.

2.1.1 Stochastic Frontier Analysis

Stochastic frontier production function model equals the deterministic frontier production function plus a symmetric random error variable, which is independently and simultaneously proposed by Aigner et al. (1977) and Meeusen and Van den Broeck (1977) in the form

$$\ln Y_i = x_i'\beta + v_i - u_i, \quad i = 1, \dots, N,$$

where Y_i is the output of firm i, x_i is the vector of inputs typically in logarithms, v_i accounts for measurement errors and other sources of non-systematic statistic noise, and u_i is a non-negative random variable representing technical inefficiency (the distance to the frontier).

The stochastic frontier literature in the early 1980s mainly consists of analyses for cross-sectional data. v_i is usually assumed to follow a normal distribution that is independent of each u_i while u_i is assumed to follow a variety of distributions including half-normal distribution (Aigner et al. 1977), normal truncated distribution (Stevenson 1980), and gamma distribution (Greene 1990). Given panel data, Schmidt and Sickles (1984) proposed panel stochastic frontier model in the form

$$\ln Y_{it} = \alpha + x_{it}'\beta + v_{it} - u_i = \alpha_i + x_{it}'\beta + v_{it}, \quad i = 1, \ldots, N, t = 1, \ldots, T. \tag{1}$$

Then fixed effects or random effects methods can be used to estimate α_i under different conditions. Other estimators can be found in Cornwell et al. (1990), Kumbhakar (1990), Battese and Coelli (1992), Lee and Schmidt (1993), Kneip et al. (2003), and Sickles (2005).

2.1.2 Weight Index and Multi-segment Concern

One industry may have multiple segments. For example, the global OFS market has five segments, including exploration and production. Since the technologies utilized in exploration and production are different, the production function is segment-specific. For a multidivisional firm who has footprints in multiple segments, different production technologies are used to convert inputs to outputs. Therefore, the aggregated production function for this firm is not equal to any of the segment-specific production functions, but a combination of them. This chapter attempts to estimate the aggregated production function for multidivisional firms and then derives firm-level efficiency.

Since multidivisional firms use different production technologies, some weight index is needed to estimate the aggregated production function with multi-segment concern. The revenue share by segment/division for firm i at time t, θ_{it}, is an eligible weight to capture the heterogeneity in technologies since it indexes the proportion of business using each of the segment-specific techniques. In other words, θ_{it} measures the frequency of using every segment-specific technology in a multidivisional firm. Imagine a "M inputs – N products/segments – T periods" industry, $\theta_{it} = (\theta_{i1t}, \theta_{i2t}, \ldots, \theta_{iMt})$ where $\theta_{ijt} = \frac{R_{ijt}}{\sum_{J=1}^{N} R_{ijt}}; \forall j = 1, 2, \ldots, N$ and R_{ijt} is the revenue for firm i in segment/division j at time t.

As a standard single frontier model, Eq. (1) ignores the heterogeneity in production technologies across segments. The next subsection adds θ_{it} into the stochastic frontier model to estimate the aggregated production function when firms may have different technologies in their portfolio and use them at different frequencies.

2.1.3 General Model

Equation (1) presents a linear production model and can be generalized to

$$Y_{it} = f(X_{it}; \beta_0) \cdot \exp(\tau Z) \cdot \exp(v_{it}) \cdot \exp(-u_i), \tag{2}$$

where Y_{it} is the aggregated output of individual i at time t; $X_{it} = \left(X_{it}^1, X_{it}^2, \ldots X_{it}^M\right)$ vectors the M types of inputs; $f(X_{it}; \beta_0) \cdot \exp(\tau Z)$ is the production frontier over time, where $f(X_{it}; \beta_0)$ is the time-invariant part of the production function, $\beta_0 = (\beta_{01}, \beta_{02}, \ldots \beta_{0M})$ is a vector of technical parameters to be estimated. Z vectors a group of year dummy variables, controls the production frontier change over time and τ vectors the coefficients of the year dummy variables; $\exp(v_{it})$ is the stochastic component that describes random shocks affecting the production process, where v_{it} is assumed to be normally distributed with a mean of zero and a standard deviation of σ_v, and $TE_i = \exp(-u_i)$ denotes the technical efficiency defined as the ratio of observed output to maximum feasible output. $TE_i = 1$ or $u_i = 0$ shows that the i-th individual allocates at the production frontier and obtains the maximum feasible output at time t, while $TE_i < 1$ or $u_i > 0$ provides a measure of the shortfall of the observed output from the maximum feasible output. This study uses the popular "Error Components Frontier" (Battese and Coelli 1992) with time-invariant efficiencies to estimate u_i and TE_i.

Again, imagine a "M inputs – N products/segments – T periods" industry. The revenue share by segment θ_{it} is introduced to capture the heterogeneity in total revenue and production technologies. This chapter uses θ_{it} as a weight index and adds it into the aggregated production function:

$$Y_{it} = f(X_{it}; \beta_0, \theta_{it}) \cdot \exp(\tau Z) \cdot \exp(v_{it}) \cdot \exp(-u_i). \qquad (3)$$

The effect of the business portfolio θ_{it} can be either dependent or independent with the rest of the production function. If it is independent (i.e., $f(X_{it}; \beta_0, \theta_{it}) = f(X_{it}; \beta_0) \cdot m(\theta_{it})$), then a transfer to the traditional multiproduct stochastic frontier analysis is possible, where one product is a function of all inputs and all other products. Adams et al. (1999) and Liu (2014) use such a canonical regression to check the efficiency of the banking industry with multiple outputs and inputs, where these two papers model $f(X_{it}; \beta_0)$ nonparametrically and parametrically, respectively. This study assumes a Cobb-Douglas form and set a production function where θ_{it} is independent with $f(X_{it}; \beta_0)$

$$\ln Y_{it} = r(\theta_{it}) + \sum_{k=1}^{M} \beta_k\left(\ln X_{it}^k\right) + \tau Z + v_{it} - u_i, \qquad (4)$$

where $r(\theta_{it})$ is a nonparametric functions of θ_{it}. Although the intercept $r(\theta_{it})$ is a nonparametric functions of θ_{it} rather than a constant α as in Eq. (1), the core of production function $f(X_{it}; \beta_0)$ is still segment-invariant, which is a strong assumption. Therefore, the frontier estimated by Eq. (4) is called "Single Frontier".

This chapter focuses on the other situation, where θ_{it} can directly affect the production function through their effects on the technical parameters. This model is inspired by the smooth/varying coefficient model (see Hastie and Tibshirani 1993) and therefore called the varying production frontier, where the coefficients are nonparametric functions of some "threshold" variables (θ_{it} in this case).

$$Y_{it} = f\left(X_{it}; \beta_0' = r(\theta_{it})\right) \cdot \exp(\tau Z) \cdot \exp(v_{it}) \cdot \exp(-u_i). \tag{5}$$

Equation (5) allows the change in aggregated production function when revenue share θ varies. For example, if a multidivisional firm has major business in segment A and minor business in segment B, then the aggregated production function of this firm is likely to be closer to the production function in segment A, as this company uses production technology from this segment more frequently. Since using multiple technologies jointly can lead to nonlinear spillover effects caused by shared R&D investment, joint inputs, and so on, we cannot simply take the weighted average of the segment-specific production functions. Hence, a nonparametric function $r(\cdot)$ is used to control the nonlinear combination of technologies.

2.1.4 Semi-varying Coefficient Model

Productivity and efficiency analysis is dominated by two approaches: the parametric stochastic frontier analysis (SFA) and the nonparametric deterministic data envelopment analysis (DEA). Each method has its own strengths and drawbacks: stochastic frontier analysis is suitable for noisy data, but requires the priori assumption of an explicit functional form; data envelopment analysis does not require specified functional form, but does not allow for statistical noise since no stochastic component is included. In recent years, many new semiparametric and nonparametric stochastic frontier techniques have been applied to narrow the gap between SFA and DEA. Such development results in new methods to better model the aggregated production function for multidivisional firms who use multiple production technologies.

Fan et al. (1996) propose a semiparametric method that allows for statistical noise and does not need to specify the functional form of the production frontier. Their approach, known as semiparametric frontier analysis, has the form

$$y = f(x) + \epsilon = f(x) + \mu + v - u \tag{6}$$

where $f(x)$ is a semi- or nonparametric production function. Similar to parametric stochastic frontier analysis, u is a non-negative technical inefficiency term and v is a statistical noise term. μ is a constant that guarantees the expected value of ϵ equals zero. Therefore, $\epsilon = \mu + v - u$ is the disturbance term with a zero mean.

In practice, the semiparametric model is solved in two steps: in the first step, the semi- or nonparametric regression $y = f(x) + \epsilon$ is run to retrieve the residuals $\hat{\epsilon}$; in the second step, the residual is decomposed as $\hat{\epsilon} = \mu + v - u$ using normal stochastic frontier model where $\hat{\epsilon}$ is the dependent variable and a constant is the only independent variable. Henningsen and Kumbhakar (2009) adopt this approach in their applied study on Polish farms, where they use logarithmic output and input quantities for three reasons: (1) the elasticities are easier to interpret; (2) the observations are more equally distributed when using constant bandwidths; and (3) the usual specification of the production function is easier to adopt.

As Henningsen and Kumbhakar (2009) point out, the nonavailability of software used to prevent applied studies to widely use this approach. This restriction has disappeared in recent years. Take R as an example, the "np" package (Hayfield and Racine 2008), the "gam" package (Hastie and Tibshirani 1990), or the "gamlss" package (Stasinopoulos and Rigby 2007) can be used in the first step and the "frontier" package (Coelli et al. 2012) can be used in the second step.

This section uses the varying coefficient model (VCM) for the production function $f(x)$ in Eq. (6). Hastie and Tibshirani (1993) first introduce VCM in the form

$$Y = X_1 r_1(\theta_1) + \ldots + X_p r_p(\theta_p) + \epsilon$$

where $\theta_1, \ldots, \theta_p$ change the coefficients of the $X_1, \ldots, X_p$ through unspecified functions $r_1(\cdot), \ldots, r_p(\cdot)$. The coefficients are nonparametric functions that are not constant, hence the name "varying/smooth coefficient model". VCM is initially applied to model time-variant coefficient functions in censored data in survival analysis.

In production analysis, environmental factors can only affect the frontier neutrally if treated as independent variables (X). Some varying coefficient stochastic frontier analysis treats the environment factors as θ_i and allows their effect on the frontier to be non-neutrally. R&D Spending is such an environmental factor that is believed to affect the frontier directly. Other examples of such "threshold" variables include tax rate, firm size, firm age, etc. (Kumbhakar and Sun 2013).

Zhang et al. (2012) develop a varying coefficient production function to study China's high technology industry, where panel data spanning the period 2000–2007 is used. Sun and Kumbhakar (2013) estimate stochastic production frontier in a Norwegian forest using a cross-section of 3,249 active forest owners. Both of these studies use R&D-varying coefficient production functions. However, they use an average production function, not a stochastic frontier model.

This section generates a partial linear semi-varying coefficient stochastic frontier analysis to model the OMR panel data for the OFS market where the revenue distribution by segment θ can directly affect the technical parameters and the frontier has a Cobb-Douglas (C-D) form.

$$\ln Y_{it} = \alpha + r_1(\theta_{it})\ln L_{it} + r_2(\theta_{it})\ln K_{it} + \tau Z + v_{it} - u_i \tag{7}$$

where Y_{it}, L_{it}, and K_{it} are the output, number of employees, and capital employed for firm i at time t, respectively.

There are two nonparametric approaches to estimate the $r_1(\cdot)$ and $r_2(\cdot)$ in Eq. (7): the kernel-based method (Fan and Huang 2005; Fan and Li 2004; Hu 2014; Su and Ullah 2006; Sun et al. 2009) and the spline-based method (Ahmad et al. 2005; Hastie and Tibshirani 1993). Fan and Zhang (2008) think that kernel smoothing methods are more reasonable, as the varying coefficient model is a local linear model, while Kim (2013) argues that spline methods are more attractive for their flexibility to involve multiple smoothing parameters. However, both methods have some disadvantages: the former may suffer from the "curse of dimensionality" and the latter may encounter computational challenges, since the number of spline basis functions can be large.

Since there are five variables in θ_{it} that will cause a "curse of dimensionality", this study selects the penalized B-spline approach to estimate the production function. It is assumed that the inefficiency term is time-invariant (u_i) so that the Least Square Dummy Variable (LSDV) can be used to derive a fixed effect estimator. Appendix 1 provides reasons to adopt time-invariant firm-level efficiency in this study. Lu et al. (2008) present results on the strong consistency and asymptotic normality for penalized B-spline estimators of such a varying coefficient model.

This chapter uses the two-step approach in Henningsen and Kumbhakar (2009) to estimate Eq. (7): (1) a penalized B-spline method is used to derive consistent coefficients and predict the residuals in the first step; (2) then, a normal stochastic frontier analysis is used where $\hat{\epsilon}$ is the dependent variable and a constant is the only independent variable. This chapter also develops a varying coefficient stochastic frontier analysis where the production function has a Transcendental Logarithmic (T-L) form to check the robustness of the varying coefficient model.

2.1.5   Endogeneity Problem

Endogeneity is a big issue in production function since input choices are determined by some information that are available by the firms (Ackerberg et al. 2015), which is unavailable by outsiders such as economists. Marschak and Andrews (1944) point out this simultaneity problem is more significant for inputs that adjust rapidly. OFS market is a typical example where the decisions of the companies depend heavily and frequently on exploration and production (E&P) spending from the oil and gas firms and the business cycles. The massive volatility forces companies to divest capital and cut headcount aggressively when the oil price goes down. The potential endogeneity problem in the production function can lead to biased OLS estimates.

One of the solutions to an endogeneity problem is using a set of two-step techniques, advocated by Olley and Pakes (1996). This method uses observed investment to "control" for unobserved productivity shocks (efficiency). Levinsohn and Petrin (2003) extend the idea by using intermediate inputs instead of investment to solve the simultaneity issue as investment is an invalid proxy in many datasets where significant amounts of observations have zero or missing investment. However, as Ackerberg et al. (2015) note, both of the models suffer from the collinearity problems so that the coefficients of the exogenous inputs cannot be identified.

Since the intermediate data is not available in the dataset, this chapter uses the most widely used instrumental variables (IV) estimation to solve the endogeneity problem. Recently, Amsler et al. (2016) introduce how to use instrumental variables method in stochastic frontier analysis when the production adopts Cobb-Douglas (C-D) and Transcendental Logarithmic (T-L) form, respectively. On the one hand, they applied a Corrected Two-Stage Least Square (C2SLS) to solve the endogeneity problem in C-D stochastic frontier model.[8] On the other hand, they suggest using the

---

[8]For C2SLS, the first step is to estimate the model by 2SLS and derive the residuals using the instruments. In the second step, these 2SLS residuals are decomposed using the maximum likelihood

control function method in T-L stochastic frontier model. Moreover, they introduce a method to reduce the number of instrument variables needed.[9]

Following Amsler et al. (2016), this study uses the C2SLS method for the linear C-D production function and the control function method for the nonlinear T-L production. The control function method can also test the exogeneity of the inputs using t-tests for the significance of the reduced form residuals (see detail in Amsler et al. 2016). The potential instrument variables include input prices and lagged values of input use (Levinsohn and Petrin 2003). However, lagged values of inputs are valid instruments only if the lag time is long enough to break the dependence between the input choices and the serially correlated shock. Blundell and Bond (2000) and Guan et al. (2009) both emphasize the input levels lagged at least two periods can be valid instruments. This study uses lag two and lag three input quantities as instruments respectively and get robust results. Therefore, input price and lag two input quantities are selected to be the instruments so that more observations can be pooled into the regression.

2.2 Step Two: Impact of the Shale Revolution

The Shale Revolution has mainly occurred in hydraulic fracturing and directional drilling. This chapter explores the effect of hydraulic fracturing and directional drilling activities on firm-level efficiency using Eq. (8).

$$T E_i = \beta_0 + \beta_1 \cdot H F_i + \beta_2 \cdot D D_i + \beta_3 \cdot H F_i \cdot D D_i + \beta_4 \cdot R_i + \beta_5 \cdot M_i \qquad (8)$$

where $T E_i$ is the technical efficiency for firm i, $H F_i$ is the dummy variable of companies who has hydraulic fracturing business, $D D_i$ is the dummy variable of companies who has directional drilling business, R_i refers the revenue for firm i in logarithms to control the size of the company, and M_i is the dummy variable of multidivisional firms who have footprints in multiple segments. Equation (8) also includes the interaction between $H F_i$ and $D D_i$ to estimate the potential spillover effects of the two technologies.

---

method, just as in classic stochastic frontier analysis. A somewhat similar two-step procedure is built by Guan et al. (2009).

[9]For example, suppose two inputs, labor and capital, are both endogenous. At least five instruments are needed since all of the two inputs, their square terms, and their interaction are endogenous in the T-L production function. However, under some additional assumptions, consistent estimators can be obtained using only two control functions, not five. This point has been made by some economists, including Blundell and Powell (2004), Terza et al. (2008), and Wooldridge (2010). See detailed discussion in Amsler et al. (2016).

3   Data

This chapter applies Eq. (7) in the OFS market using deflated revenue as the output, number of employees[10] as the first input, and capital as the second input. Division-level revenue data from 1997 to 2014 for each of the 114 public firms are collected from the three waves of the OMR (2000, 2011, and 2015) dataset. Appendix 2 introduces this report, the method employed to combine the three waves of data, and the detailed segmentation of the OFS market.

Data on the annual overall revenue, the number of employees, and total capital for the 114 public firms during same period is collected from Thomson ONE, Bloomberg, and FactSet. The total capital is the accounting capital, which is the sum of equity and long-term debt. This study adjusts the capital data following the unified perpetual inventory method (PIM) in Berlemann and Wesselhöft (2014), which is widely used in productivity analysis. Appendix 3 explains this data-generating process. Since the labor and capital data are the year-end values, the values at periods t and $t + 1$ are averaged to get the average value at period $t + 1$.

The overall revenue of a firm is not always equal to the total revenue in the OFS market as reported by the OMR. In some cases, the former may be larger because the company has some business outside the OFS market. On the other hand, the former could be smaller, as the OMR adds the acquired firm's revenue to the mother firm's revenue even in the years before acquisition. The input proportionality assumption suggested by Foster et al. (2008) is used to adjust the labor and capital used in the OFS market. Finally, the Bureau of Labor Statistics publishes the Producer Price Index (PPI) by North American Industry Classification System (NAICS) division. The output price indices deflate the revenue, which can be regarded as output.

Since input prices are selected as instruments to solve endogeneity problem, this chapter also collects labor price and capital price: (1) the labor price is the total labor cost divided by the number of employees. Many international firms have compensation cost information, but North American firms have no such information published. This chapter sets the labor price of each North American firm to its corresponding NAICS division average. The later information is available in the Labor Productivity and Cost (LPC) Database from the Bureau of Labor Statistics; (2) the capital price is the sum of the depreciation rate and interest rate. (i) Thomson ONE, Bloomberg, and FactSet offer depreciation and capital data, which can derive the depreciation rate. (ii) the interest rate can be estimated by a capital asset pricing model (CAPM).

---

[10]There are contractors (non-fulltime employees) working in the OFS field that are not included in the number of employees. We cannot find the number of these contractors in each firm, let alone their working hours to transfer them into the number of Full Time Equivalent (FTE) employees. Actually, this is a problem happens in many industries, where the companies' financial reports only provide the number of employees rather than the number of FTE employees. The existing studies usually use number of employees to be the proxy of total labor force. In order to reduce the potential bias, this chapter uses Cobb-Douglas production function so that the result is not skewed as long as the ratio of employees and non-FTE employees has no large variation across firms.

Table 1 Oilfield market summary statistics

Variables	Unit	1997	2001	2005	2009	2014
Average revenue	$ 1 · 10^9	0.97	1.02	1.33	1.7	2.78
Average number of employees	1 · 10^3	5.78	5.63	5.64	5.86	7.5
Average labor price	$1,000	50.7	54.7	69.6	81.7	95.9
Average capital	$ 1 · 10^9	0.61	0.68	1.17	1.39	2.51
Average capital price	%	18.9	21.3	20.2	20.7	21.2

The needed firm-level beta[11], the risk-free rate, and the expected market return are all available in Thomson ONE, Bloomberg, and FactSet.

Table 1 summarizes firm-level input and output in the OFS market. Average revenues increased almost three-fold, from $0.97 billion in 1997 to $2.78 billion in 2014. In the labor market, the average number of employees was around 5,750 from 1997 to 2009 and then jumped to 7,500 in 2014, which shows a large amount of new employment after the 2007–2009 financial crisis. The average wage almost doubled in the period of 1997 to 2014. In the capital market, the price of capital is very stable, while the amount of capital in 2014 was more than four times the level it was in 1997. To sum up, both revenues and costs increased dramatically from 1997, which was very likely driven by the Shale Revolution. Based on the dataset, this chapter can build a "2 inputs – 5 products/segments – 16 periods" model[12] for the OFS market.

4 Estimation Results

This empirical study applies the described models to public firms in the global OFS market. This study estimates production frontiers and firm-level efficiencies in the first step and then predicts the impact of the Shale Revolution on efficiency in the second step.

4.1 Production Frontiers

The "Varying Frontier" model in Eq. (7) cannot derive constant coefficients of the production function that are directly comparable with those in the "Single Frontier" model in Eq. (4). Therefore, this study visualizes the varying effects of labor and capital on output in the "Varying Frontier" model. Figure 2 illustrates the range

---

[11] In finance, the beta of an investment or a company is a measure of the risk arising from exposure to general market movements as opposed to idiosyncratic factors. The market portfolio of all investable assets has a beta of unity.

[12] In regression, the data in 1997 and 1998 are only used as instrument variables to control heterogeneity. Therefore, time t in Eq. (7) refers to 1999–2014 in the empirical study.

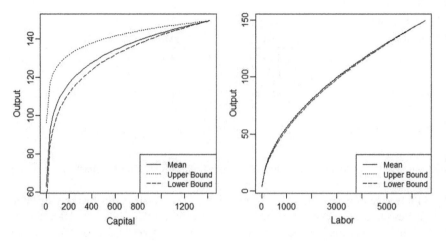

Fig. 2 The range of the production frontier in the "Varying Frontier" method

of such varying effects for firms with different business portfolios, which reveals the variation of the aggregated production function under the "Varying Frontier" method. It is clear that the capital effect varies greatly when technologies in different segments are utilized at different frequencies. However, the labor productivities in different segments are very robust. The varying effects support the validation of the segment-specific production assumption.

Figure 3 calculates the average effects of the varying coefficients in the "Varying Frontier" model and compares them with those in the "Single Frontier" model. The average effects of labor in the "Varying Frontier" model are a little less concave than the fixed labor elasticity in the "Single Frontier" model. A similar finding applies to the effect of capital.

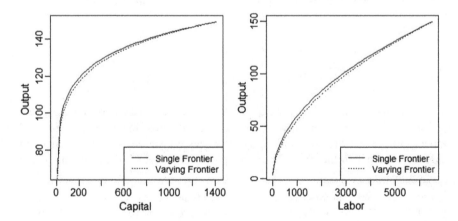

Fig. 3 Effect of capital and labor on output in various methods

Figure 4 further compares the two models by showing the "Output-Labor-Capital" relations graphically using 3D images and contour graphs. Overall, the comparisons again show that the average effects of the varying coefficients in the "Varying Frontier" model are a little less concave than the constant effects in the "Single Frontier" model, but the difference is not very significant.

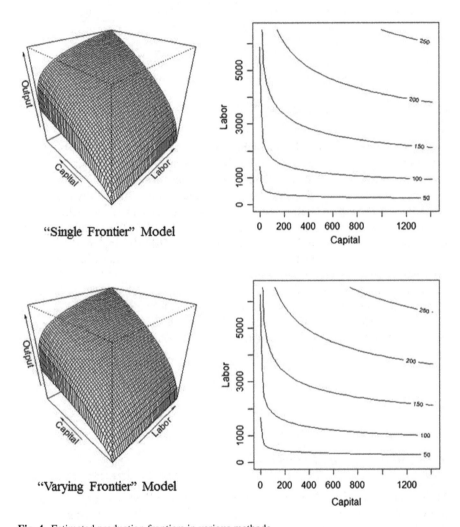

Fig. 4 Estimated production frontiers in various methods

Table 2 Technical efficiency statistics

	Single frontier		Varying frontier	
	C-D model	T-L model	C-D model	T-L model
Mean	0.27	0.32	0.43	0.42
Minimum	0.06	0.07	0.16	0.16
25% quantile	0.14	0.18	0.29	0.27
50% quantile	0.21	0.26	0.40	0.37
75% quantile	0.34	0.40	0.52	0.49
Maximum	1.00	1.00	1.00	1.00

4.2   Technical Efficiency

Table 2 summarizes the distribution of the efficiency scores in the OFS market. Since the difference is witnessed between the "Single Frontier" model and the "Varying Frontier" model, this chapter adds the estimation when the production function takes Transcendental Logarithmic (T-L) form for further comparisons. In practice, this chapter drops the top and bottom 2.5% of the estimations to eliminate outliers.

The average efficiency level of the industry is around 0.3 in the "Single Frontier" model and around 0.4 in the "Varying Frontier" model. The "Varying Frontier" model provides more robust estimation than the "Single Frontier" model when assuming different functional forms of the production frontier.

Table 3 presents the distribution of firms by technical efficiency scores, which is classified into four efficiency class intervals. For each of the efficiency class intervals and the overall average estimated technical efficiency scores, the lower and upper bounds of 95% Confidence Interval (CI) are obtained by using a bootstrap technique, called Efron's nonparametric bias-corrected and accelerated (BCa) method, with 10,000 replications (Briggs et al. 1999). It also supports that the efficiency estimated by the "Varying Frontier" model is higher than the one estimated by the "Single Frontier" model.

4.3   Impact of the Shale Revolution

The most important question this chapter seeks to answer is whether or not investing in hydraulic fracturing and directional drilling is a good strategy. Especially after the oil price crash in 2014, should we still consider these expensive innovations? In other words, should the Shale Revolution be cheered or feared, especially in the downturn?

Table 3 Technical efficiency class interval

Eff. range	Single frontier				Varying frontier			
	C-D model		T-L model		C-D model		T-L model	
	Firm #	Mean (95% CI)	Firm #	Mean (95% CI)	Firm #	Mean (95% CI)	Firm #	Mean (95% CI)
≤0.3	73	0.17 (0.15–0.18)	65	0.19 (0.17–0.21)	30	0.23 (0.22–0.24)	31	0.22 (0.21–0.23)
0.3–0.5	23	0.38 (0.36–0.41)	24	0.38 (0.36–0.41)	47	0.39 (0.38–0.41)	52	0.39 (0.38–0.41)
0.5–0.75	8	0.62 (0.58–0.67)	14	0.61 (0.58–0.65)	20	0.58 (0.56–0.61)	14	0.60 (0.57–0.62)
>0.75	3	0.89 (0.76–0.97)	4	0.93 (0.88–0.98)	10	0.91 (0.86–0.95)	10	0.88 (0.84–0.93)
Total	107	0.27 (0.23–0.31)	107	0.32 (0.28–0.36)	107	0.43 (0.40–0.47)	107	0.42 (0.38–0.46)

Table 4 Efficiency regression result in 2013

$\widehat{TE}_i$	Single frontier		Varying frontier	
	C-D model	T-L model	C-D model	T-L model
HF_i	−0.051	−0.040	−0.123**	−0.136**
	(0.076)	(0.080)	(0.057)	(0.056)
DD_i	−0.087	−0.092	−0.087**	−0.084**
	(0.057)	(0.063)	(0.041)	(0.040)
$HF_i \cdot DD_i$	0.166	0.123	0.182**	0.194**
	(0.110)	(0.116)	(0.083)	(0.082)
R_i	0.078***	0.092***	0.130***	0.126***
	(0.011)	(0.012)	(0.009)	(0.009)
M_i	−0.007	−0.002	0.0002	0.006
	(0.033)	(0.035)	(0.025)	(0.025)
Intercept	−0.246***	−0.291***	−0.427***	−0.421***
	(0.072)	(0.075)	(0.059)	(0.058)
R^2	0.42	0.46	0.73	0.72

Note Significant at: * 10, ** 5 and *** 1 percent; Standard error in parentheses

This study uses data in 2013 to estimate Eq. (8) since 113 companies are active this year, which is the largest cross-sectional data in the panel.[13] There are nine companies that only have hydraulic fracturing techniques, four companies that only have directional drilling techniques, and seven companies that utilize both hydraulic fracturing and directional drilling techniques. Table 4 reports the estimated results, which is the second step regression after estimating the efficiency.

Two things are consistent in all the four columns: (1) larger firms have advantages over smaller firms in terms of efficiency since the coefficient of R_i is always positive and significant[14]; and (2) other things being equal, multidivisional firms on average have neither an advantage nor a disadvantage in efficiency over single-division firms in the OFS market since the coefficient of M_i is statistically and economically insignificant.

The impact of the Shale Revolution on the "Single Frontier" estimated efficiency is not significant. With the multi-segment concern in the "Varying Frontier" model, however, this impact is both statistically and economically significant. According to the results in the C-D model (column 3 in Table 4), investing in only hydraulic fracturing or only directional drilling will lower a firm's overall efficiency when other things, including firm size, are equal. In other words, if a company has limited

---

[13]The oil price dropped at 2014, which had significant impact on firms' entry and exit decisions. The oilfield market peaked around 2013 as the stock prices of many oilfield companies hit all-time high, so does the number of firms in the field due to the profitability of the market.

[14]This result is consistent with the opinion of Schlumberger's CEO Paal Kibsgaard, who said in the 4Q2104 Earnings Call that scale is essential to drive performance in the oilfield market. The industry-leading size and integration capabilities are key competitive advantages.

resources and cannot expand quickly, it is not a good idea to divest the current business to support innovation in one of hydraulic fracturing and directional drilling. Entering into hydraulic fracturing alone will, on average, have a 12.3% points decrease in efficiency, while entering into directional drilling alone will, on average, have an 8.7% points decrease in efficiency. Since the traditional segments of the OFS are saturated, it is hard to increase market share dramatically in those segments. If a company has sufficient funding in hydraulic fracturing, it has to generate 95% more revenue in order to keep the current efficiency. In other words, a company has to double its revenue in a year so that the benefit from economies of scale can fully compensate the cost of innovating hydraulic fracturing. If investing in directional drilling, this company would also need to increase by two-thirds in revenue to achieve breakeven. This result makes sense because these technologies are innovated to extract oil and gas from the more complex and less productive reservoirs, which involve massive sunk costs and operating costs, and hence it is very difficult to break even.

Does that mean that the Shale Revolution should be feared and companies need to get rid of their investments? The coefficient of the interaction between hydraulic fracturing and directional drilling is significantly positive, which indicates the existence of spillovers of the combination. For a company that is already engaging in hydraulic fracturing, adding directional drilling to the portfolio can increase efficiency by 9.5% points. For a company that is already engaging in directional drilling, adding hydraulic fracturing to the portfolio can increase efficiency by 5.9% points. Although adding both technologies will still decrease efficiency by 2.8% points for companies that had not previously been engaging in either practice, the breakeven revenue growth is 22%. This growth rate requirement means that each of the two businesses only needs to contribute 11% of the company's sales, which is achievable and much lower than adding hydraulic fracturing alone (95%) and directional drilling alone (67%). This result supports the theory that combining hydraulic fracturing and directional drilling is crucial to the success of the Shale Revolution. The positive spillover effects of the combination can compensate for the massive investment.

As the first robustness check, this chapter repeated the second-step regression using the T-L model derived efficiency as the dependent variable in the fourth column in Table 4, which derives very close numbers, as analyzed above using the C-D model derived efficiency (column 3). As the second robustness check of our results, Table 5 lists the estimated results of the C-D Varying Frontier Model using 2010, 2011, 2012, and 2013, respectively. The results are pretty consistent over time.

4.4 More Discussions on Single and Varying Frontier Models

In the single frontier model, the unique frontier is the highest frontier among all the frontiers in the varying frontier model. Therefore, the efficiency level derived in the single frontier setting must be lower or equal to the one derived in the varying frontier setting, which is verified in Tables 2 and 3. For example, the median efficiency is 0.21

Table 5   Efficiency regression results of the C-D varying frontier model over time

$\widehat{TE}_i$	2010	2011	2012	2013
HF_i	−0.139**	−0.142**	−0.138**	−0.123**
	(0.058)	(0.056)	(0.055)	(0.057)
DD_i	−0.075*	−0.110***	−0.103***	−0.087**
	(0.041)	(0.040)	(0.037)	(0.041)
$HF_i \cdot DD_i$	0.192**	0.211***	0.195**	0.182**
	(0.080)	(0.077)	(0.075)	(0.083)
R_i	0.126***	0.131***	0.135***	0.130***
	(0.009)	(0.009)	(0.009)	(0.009)
M_i	0.003	−0.002	0.005	0.0002
	(0.026)	(0.025)	(0.024)	(0.025)
Intercept	−0.348***	−0.398***	−0.453***	−0.427***
	(0.054)	(0.055)	(0.056)	(0.059)
R^2	0.74	0.75	0.75	0.73

Note Significant at: * 10, ** 5 and *** 1 percent; Standard error in parentheses

for single frontier model and 0.4 for varying frontier model when C-D production function is adopted.

On the one hand, single frontier assumption is invalid logically, as different segments have different production process and use different techniques, which leads to different frontiers. Such invalid assumption of single frontier can lead to biased estimation of efficiency and biased impacts of new techniques sequentially, which reflects on the inaccurate magnitude of the coefficients in the first two columns of Table 4.

On the other hand, the firm-level efficiencies are lack of variations in the single frontier setting, which lead to lower R square and more insignificant coefficients when served as dependent variable. If we look at the coefficients of the new techniques and their interaction term in the first two columns of Table 4, their signs also imply negative effect of either techniques alone and positive spillover effects, as are predicted in the varying frontier model. But due to the lack of variation in efficiency, all the three coefficients are insignificant. Therefore, we cannot provide confident predictions as the one given in varying frontier setting.

To sum, the invalid single frontier assumption can lead to inaccurate magnitude and significance of the coefficients in the second-step regression.

5 Conclusion and Policy Implications

This chapter develops a two-step approach to estimate the impact of the Shale Revolution on firm-level efficiency and investment strategy regarding hydraulic fracturing and directional drilling. Stochastic frontier analysis is applied to derive firm-level efficiency in the first step. The second step regresses the efficiency on indicators of hydraulic fracturing and directional drilling as well as other variables.

The empirical results show that: (1) it is necessary to take multi-segment assumptions into consideration by introducing the revenue share by segment θ; (2) labor elasticity is stable while capital elasticity varies greatly across segments as per the varying coefficient model; (3) investing in only one of the two technologies in the Shale Revolution is likely to lower the overall efficiency of the company; (4) the combining of hydraulic fracturing and directional drilling produces positive spillover effects, which can compensate for the massive cost and maintain efficiency; (5) more cooperation, alliances, mergers, and acquisitions among experts of the two techniques should be encouraged.

Considering the less endowed reservoirs that the new technologies are working on, the Shale Revolution has so far been an economic success. OFS companies have the incentive to continue investing, even if there is a fracturing tax. Setting aside the environmental concern,[15] government could encourage the Shale Revolution since it increases oil and gas recoverable reserves, mitigates the energy shortage, and decreases energy prices. More cooperation, alliances, mergers, and acquisitions among hydraulic fracturing companies and directional drilling companies are also good ideas to share the huge amount of investment and produce spillover benefits. More specifically, there are two policy implications.

Firstly, this chapter finds that the efficiency enhancement is possible by introducing the new techniques. The empirical results show that these unconventional oil and gas techniques can be either cheer or fear, depending on the investment behavior. The positive spillover effects between hydraulic fracturing and directional drilling is the key to improve efficiency. Therefore, energy policies should be adjusted to encourage more cooperation, mergers and acquisitions among experts of the two techniques in order to achieve the spillover effects, such as the one between Mitchell Energy and Devon Energy, in line with anti-trust laws.

Secondly, either of the two techniques alone leads to lower efficiency. Therefore, the government should help decrease the "entry fee" (e.g., the R&D costs) to encourage more entrants. This is even more important currently, as lower break-even price is required in order to survive in the world with low oil price. Policies to lower the cost can help unconventional shale companies (mainly in the USA) to compete with OPEC members. The government can provide some information sharing platforms to release basic data and knowledge of shale resources, and encourage the cooperation among different companies and institutions.

---

[15]Although innovation to make these techniques more environmentally friendly is necessary, it does not fall within the scope of the present chapter.

This study discovers evidence of the competitiveness of the techniques engendered by the Shale Revolution, which provides information for policy makers and companies. Future studies can focus on the environmental effect of the Shale Revolution and analyze the social welfare change brought about by these innovations. Moreover, scholars can study how energy policies should be changed to face this competitive entrant in the energy market. Finally, although the varying coefficient model is a semiparametric method and more flexible than the standard parametric method, it still has a rigid functional assumption, such as the C-D and T-L forms. How to relax this assumption would be an interesting field to explore.

Appendix 1: Reasons to Adopt Time-Invariant Efficiency

In Eq. (7), the efficiency term, u_i, is time-invariant. Then, the dependent variable of Eq. (8) (TE_i) is time-invariant as well, since $TE_i = \exp(-u_i)$.

Whether to use time-variant or time-invariant efficiency is a problem that we cannot ignore. Many scholars have studied time-variant technical efficiency. Cornwell et al. (1990) introduced both the within estimator (CSSW) and the generalized least squares estimator (CSSG), where they assumed the firm effects of α_i with $\alpha_{it} = \theta_{i1} + \theta_{i2}t + \theta_{i3}t^2$. Sickles (2005) later examined various specifications of the time-variant firm effect α_{it} modeled in other research, including $\alpha_{it} = \gamma(t)\alpha_i = \left[1 + \exp(bt + ct^2)\right]^{-1}\alpha_i$ (Kumbhakar 1990), $\alpha_{it} = \eta_{it}\alpha_i = \exp[-\eta(1 - T)]\alpha_i$ (Battese and Coelli 1992), $\alpha_{it} = \theta_t\alpha_i$ (Lee and Schmidt 1993), and the general factor model $\alpha_{it} = c_{i1}g_{1t} + c_{i2}g_{2t} + \ldots + c_{iL}g_{Lt}$ (Kneip 1994; Kneip et al. 2003, 2012).

This chapter tested the difference if time-variant efficiencies are allowed but find no significant difference. Take one of the most popular method (Battese and Coelli: $\alpha_{it} = \exp[-\eta(1 - T)]\alpha_i$) as an example, the estimation of η is -0.002 with a p-value of 0.7553, which implies η is economically and statistically insignificant. Since η is insignificantly different from 0, $\alpha_{it} = \exp[-\eta(1 - T)]\alpha_i \approx \alpha_i$. In other words, the change in efficiency for a company is negligible. Therefore, we can use time-invariant efficiency.

Although the productivity (Total-Factor Productivity, or the frontier of the industry) changes dramatically across time because of the financial crisis, technical revolution, and other events, the firm-specific technical efficiencies are pretty robust according to my own experience after working in one of the largest OFS companies analyzing competitors in the OFS market. The robustness in efficiency is mainly because companies' reactions are very fast in this industry. OFS market is heavily affected by energy price and economic cycle. When the market is down, companies will sell asset, hold cash, and cut headcount immediately, which guarantees the stability of the efficiency.

To sum up, both the statistical results and my observation of the industry imply that time-invariant efficiency is a valid assumption. The adoption of time-variant efficiencies will lead to negligible difference but cost more degrees of freedom.

Appendix 2: OMR Data Introduction and Adjustment

This study uses data from the Oilfield Market Report (OMR) by Spears & Associates. This report details the global oilfield equipment and service markets associated with five macro-segments: exploration, drilling, completion, production, and capital equipment. Spears & Associates began tracking the OFS market in 1996 and publish its OMR annually. Each year, the report not only releases new data for the current year, but also updates previously published data. Most numbers in the OMR are estimates developed by Spears through five sources: public company reports (about 100 firms), published information, interviews (about 2,000 discussions), trade shows, and site visits.

There are several advantages of using the OMR dataset. Firstly, this report brings estimations under the same criteria. Different firms have different segmentations, so direct use of their revenue declarations by product line from their financial reports is not wise. Secondly, this dataset is widely used by most firms and clients in the field. Thirdly, Spears has investigated the numbers through many sources to confirm its estimations in the past twenty years. Lastly, the OMR is updated each year, which alters any incorrect numbers according to the newest information.

In this study, three versions of the OMR (2000, 2011, and 2015) are used to collect firm-level data from 1997 to 2014, which is denoted as OMR1997–2014. OMR2000 includes firm-level revenue by segment from 1997 to 2000, OMR2011 includes firm-level revenue by segment from 1999 to 2011, and OMR2015 includes firm-level revenue by segment from 2005 to 2014. Since different waves of data have different market divisions, this study uses the market segmentation of OMR2015 and adjusts the other two datasets to acquire statistically comparable numbers.

The revision in OMR2000 consist of (1) the "Mud Logging" segment being renamed as the "Surface Data Logging" segment; (2) the "Field Processing Equipment" segment being removed from the market; (3) the "Offshore O&M Services/Contracting" segment being added to the "Offshore Contract Drilling" segment; and (4) the "Production Logging" segment being added to the "Wireline Logging" segment. Moreover, the "Casing & Cementation Products" segment in both OMR2000 and OMR2011 is added to the "Completion Equipment & Services" segment. Finally, the "Pressure Pumping Service" segment in both datasets is divided into the "Cementing" and "Hydraulic Fracturing" segments.

The OMR1997–2014 contains share and size analysis for 32 micro-market segments within the 5 macro-segments from approximately 600 companies working around the world. OMR1997–2014 gives detailed revenue by segment for 275 companies, 114 of which are public firms that publish complete financial information annually. The other 300 smaller companies have been added to "Others" in the report. The detailed segmentation is as follows:

(I)   Exploration segment includes (1) Geophysical Equipment & Services;
(II) Drilling segment includes (2) Cementing, (3) Casing & Tubing Services, (4) Directional Drilling Services, (5) Drill Bits, (6) Drilling & Completion Fluids, (7) Inspection & Coating, (8) Land Contract Drilling, (9) Logging-While-Drilling, (10) Offshore Contract Drilling, (11) Oil Country Tubular Goods, (12) Solids Control & Waste Management, (13) Surface Data Logging;
(III) Completion segment includes (14) Completion Eqpt & Services, (15) Coiled Tubing Services, (16) Hydraulic Fracturing, (17) Productions Testing, (18) Rental & Fishing Services, (19) Subsea Equipment, (20) Surface Equipment, (21) Wireline Logging;
(IV) Production segment includes (22) Artificial Lift, (23) Contract Compression Services, (24) Floating Production Services, (25) Specialty Chemicals, (26) Well Servicing; and
(V)   Capital Equipment, Downhole Tools & Offshore Services segment includes (27) Downhole Drilling Tools, (28) Petroleum Aviation, (29) Offshore Construction Services, (30) Rig Equipment, (31) Supply Vessels, and (32) Unit Manufacturing.

Appendix 3: Estimating Capital Stocks Using Perpetual Inventory Method

The perpetual inventory method (PIM) is the most widely employed approach to estimate capital stocks in many statistical offices. Berlemann and Wesselhöft (2014) review the three PIM approaches used most frequently in the literature, consisting of the steady state approach, the disequilibrium approach, and the synthetic time series approach. After comparing the advantages and disadvantages of those three methods, they are able to combine them into a unified approach in order to prevent the drawbacks of the various methods. Their approach follows the procedure proposed by de la Fuente and Doménech (2006).

The PIM interprets a firm's capital stock as an inventory of investments. The aggregate capital stock falls in the depreciation rate per period. Therefore, the capital stock in period t is a weight sum of the history of the capital stock investment:

$$K_t = \sum_{i=0}^{\infty}(1 - \delta)^i \cdot I_{t-(i+1)}$$

However, a complete time series of past investments from day one is not available for many companies. Thomson ONE, Bloomberg, and FactSet only cover the recent portion of investment history. Suppose the investment can only be tracked back to period t_1, then the current capital stock can be estimated by using

$$K_t = (1 - \delta)^{t-t_0} \cdot K_{t_0} + \sum_{i=0}^{t-1}(1 - \delta)^i \cdot I_{t-(i+1)} \qquad (3.1)$$

Therefore, the information needed to calculate capital stock includes a time series of investment $I_{t-(i+1)}$, the rate of depreciate δ, and the initial capital stock K_{t_0}. Firstly, de la Fuente and Doménech (2006) propose smoothing the time-series investment data since the economies are on their adjustment path towards equilibrium rather than staying in a steady state most of the time. Hence, this study smooths the observed capital expenditure (investment) using a regression $I_{it} = \alpha_i + \beta_1 t + \epsilon$ for each firm. Secondly, this study follows the lead of Kamps (2006) and uses time-varying depreciation schemes, which seems to be the most plausible variant. The time-variant smooth depreciation rate can be estimated as the fitted value of the regression $\delta_t = \alpha + \beta_2 t + \epsilon$. This study collects a given firm's annual depreciation and total capital data to calculate the depreciation rate in accounting and use this information to run the regression. Finally, the initial capital stock at time t_0 can be calculated from the investment I_{t_1}, the long-term investment growth rate g_I, and the estimated depreciation rate δ: $K_{t_0} \approx I_{t_1}/(g_I + \delta_{t_1})$, where the growth rate g_I is β_1 and the investment I_{t_1} is the fitted value in the same regression. Similar to the method used in Berlemann and Wesselhöft (2014), this study assumes all the years before t_1 without desegregated data have the same constant depreciation rate as year t_1. But for all the recent years that we have investment data, the depreciation rate is time variant. Therefore, Eq. (3.1) becomes:

$$K_t = \prod_{i=t_1}^{t}(1 - \delta_i)I_{t_1}/(g_I + \delta_{t_1}) + \sum_{i=0}^{t-1} \prod_{j=t-(i+1)}^{t-1} (1 - \delta_j)I_{t-(i+1)}$$

In our empirical study, t is 2014 for most companies that are still active while t_1 presents the first year of investment data and varies across firms.

References

Ackerberg D.A., Caves K., and Frazer G. Identification Properties of Recent Production Function Estimators. Econometrica. 2015, 83 (6):2411–2451.

Adams R.M., Berger A.N., and Sickles R.C. Semiparametric Approaches to Stochastic Panel Frontiers with Applications in the Banking Industry. Journal of Business & Economic Statistics. 1999, 17 (3):349–358.

Ahmad I., Leelahanon S., and Li Q. Efficient Estimation of a Semiparametric Partially Linear Varying Coefficient Model. Annals of Statistics. 2005, 33 (1):258–283.

Aigner D., Lovell C.A., and Schmidt P. Formulation and Estimation of Stochastic Frontier Production Function Models. Journal of Econometrics. 1977, 6 (1):21–37.

Amsler C., Prokhorov A., and Schmidt P. Endogeneity in Stochastic Frontier Models. Journal of Econometrics. 2016, 190 (2):280–288.

Battese G.E., and Coelli T.J. Frontier Production Functions, Technical Efficiency and Panel Data: With Application to Paddy Farmers in India: Springer, 1992.

Berlemann M., and Wesselhöft J.-E. Estimating Aggregate Capital Stocks Using the Perpetual Inventory Method–a Survey of Previous Implementations and New Empirical Evidence for 103 Countries–. Review of Economics/Jahrbuch für Wirtschaftswissenschaften. 2014, 65 (1).

Blundell R., and Bond S. Gmm Estimation with Persistent Panel Data: An Application to Production Functions. Econometric Reviews. 2000, 19 (3):321–340.

Blundell R.W., and Powell J.L. Endogeneity in Semiparametric Binary Response Models. The Review of Economic Studies. 2004, 71 (3):655–679.

Briggs A.H., Mooney C.Z., and Wonderling D.E. Constructing Confidence Intervals for Cost-Effectiveness Ratios: An Evaluation of Parametric and Non-Parametric Techniques Using Monte Carlo Simulation. Statistics in medicine. 1999, 18 (23):3245–3262.

Coelli T., Henningsen A., and Henningsen M.A. "Package 'Frontier'." Technical Report, R. 2012.

Cornwell C., Schmidt P., and Sickles R.C. Production Frontiers with Cross-Sectional and Time-Series Variation in Efficiency Levels. Journal of Econometrics. 1990, 46 (1):185–200.

de la Fuente A., and Doménech R. Human Capital in Growth Regressions: How Much Difference Does Data Quality Make? Journal of the European Economic Association. 2006, 4 (1):1–36.

Eller S.L., Hartley P.R., and Medlock K.B. Empirical Evidence on the Operational Efficiency of National Oil Companies. Empirical Economics. 2011, 40 (3):623–643.

Fan J., and Huang T. Profile Likelihood Inferences on Semiparametric Varying-Coefficient Partially Linear Models. Bernoulli. 2005, 11 (6):1031–1057.

Fan J., and Li R. New Estimation and Model Selection Procedures for Semiparametric Modeling in Longitudinal Data Analysis. Journal of the American Statistical Association. 2004, 99 (467):710–723.

Fan J., and Zhang W. Statistical Methods with Varying Coefficient Models. Statistics and its Interface. 2008, 1 (1):179.

Fan Y., Li Q., and Weersink A. Semiparametric Estimation of Stochastic Production Frontier Models. Journal of Business & Economic Statistics. 1996, 14 (4):460–468.

Foster L., Haltiwanger J., and Syverson C. Reallocation, Firm Turnover, and Efficiency: Selection on Productivity or Profitability? The American Economic Review. 2008, 98 (1):394–425.

Greene W.H. A Gamma-Distributed Stochastic Frontier Model. Journal of Econometrics. 1990, 46 (1):141–163.

Guan Z., Kumbhakar S.C., Myers R.J., and Lansink A.O. Measuring Excess Capital Capacity in Agricultural Production. American Journal of Agricultural Economics. 2009, 91 (3):765–776.

Hartley P.R., and Medlock III K.B. Changes in the Operational Efficiency of National Oil Companies. The Energy Journal. 2013, 34 (2):27–57.

Hastie T., and Tibshirani R. Varying-Coefficient Models. Journal of the Royal Statistical Society. Series B (Methodological). 1993, 55 (4):757–796.

Hastie T.J., and Tibshirani R.J. Generalized Additive Models: CRC Press, 1990.

Hayfield T., and Racine J.S. Nonparametric Econometrics: The Np Package. Journal of Statistical Software. 2008, 27 (5):1–32.

Henningsen A., and Kumbhakar S. Semiparametric Stochastic Frontier Analysis: An Application to Polish Farms During Transition. In European Workshop on Efficiency and Productivity Analysis (EWEPA) in Pisa, Italy, June. 2009 pp.

Hu X. Estimation in a Semi-Varying Coefficient Model for Panel Data with Fixed Effects. Journal of Systems Science and Complexity. 2014, 27 (3):594–604.

Kamps C. New Estimates of Government Net Capital Stocks for 22 Oecd Countries, 1960–2001. IMF Staff Papers. 2006, 53 (1):120–150.

Kim Y.-J. A Partial Spline Approach for Semiparametric Estimation of Varying-Coefficient Partially Linear Models. Computational Statistics & Data Analysis. 2013, 62:181–187.

Kneip A. Nonparametric Estimation of Common Regressors for Similar Curve Data. The Annals of Statistics. 1994:1386–1427.

Kneip A., Sickles R., and Song W. On Estimating a Mixed Effects Model with Applications to the U.S. Banking Industry. Mimeo, Rice University. 2003.

Kneip A., Sickles R.C., and Song W. A New Panel Data Treatment for Heterogeneity in Time Trends. Econometric Theory. 2012, 28 (03):590–628.

Kumbhakar S.C. Production Frontiers, Panel Data, and Time-Varying Technical Inefficiency. Journal of Econometrics. 1990, 46 (1):201–211.

Kumbhakar S.C., and Sun K. 2013. "Estimation of a Flexible Stochastic Cost Frontier Model with Environmental Factors Subject to Economic Constraints." Paper presented at European Economic Association & Econometric Society 2013 Parallel Meetings. Gothenburg, Sweden, 26 – 30 August 2013.

Lee Y.H., and Schmidt P. A Production Frontier Model with Flexible Temporal Variation in Technical Efficiency. The measurement of productive efficiency: Techniques and applications. 1993:237–255.

Levinsohn J., and Petrin A. Estimating Production Functions Using Inputs to Control for Unobservables. The Review of Economic Studies. 2003, 70 (2):317–341.

Liu J. 2014. "Essays on Productivity and Panel Data Econometrics." Doctoral Thesis, Rice University. http://hdl.handle.net/1911/77201.

Lu Q., Yang C., and Li J. Rural-Urban Migration, Rural Household Income and Sustainable Development in Rural Areas of China. Chinese Journal of Population, Resources and Environment. 2008, 06 (02):70–73.

Managi S., Opaluch J.J., Jin D., and Grigalunas T.A. Stochastic Frontier Analysis of Total Factor Productivity in the Offshore Oil and Gas Industry. Ecological Economics. 2006, 60 (1):204–215.

Managi S., Opaluch J.J., Jin D., and Grigalunas T.A. Technological Change and Depletion in Offshore Oil and Gas. Journal of Environmental Economics and Management. 2004, 47 (2):388–409.

Marschak J., and Andrews W.H. Random Simultaneous Equations and the Theory of Production. Econometrica, Journal of the Econometric Society. 1944:143–205.

Meeusen W., and Van den Broeck J. Efficiency Estimation from Cobb-Douglas Production Functions with Composed Error. International Economic Review. 1977, 18 (2):435–444.

Olley G.S., and Pakes A. The Dynamics of Productivity in the Telecommunications Equipment Industry. Econometrica. 1996, 64 (6):1263–1297.

Schmidt P., and Sickles R.C. Production Frontiers and Panel Data. Journal of Business and Economic Statistics. 1984, 2 (4):367–374.

Sickles R.C. Panel Estimators and the Identification of Firm-Specific Efficiency Levels in Parametric, Semiparametric and Nonparametric Settings. Journal of Econometrics. 2005, 126 (2):305–334.

Stasinopoulos D.M., and Rigby R.A. Generalized Additive Models for Location Scale and Shape (Gamlss) in R. Journal of Statistical Software. 2007, 23 (7):1–46.

Stevenson R.E. Likelihood Functions for Generalized Stochastic Frontier Estimation. Journal of Econometrics. 1980, 13 (1):57–66.

Su L., and Ullah A. Profile Likelihood Estimation of Partially Linear Panel Data Models with Fixed Effects. Economics Letters. 2006, 92 (1):75–81.

Sun K., and Kumbhakar S.C. Semiparametric Smooth-Coefficient Stochastic Frontier Model. Economics Letters. 2013, 120 (2):305–309.

Sun Y., Carroll R.J., and Li D. Semiparametric Estimation of Fixed Effects Panel Data Varying Coefficient Models. Advances in Econometrics. 2009, 25:101–129.

Terza J.V., Basu A., and Rathouz P.J. Two-Stage Residual Inclusion Estimation: Addressing Endogeneity in Health Econometric Modeling. Journal of health economics. 2008, 27 (3):531–543.

Thompson R.G., Dharmapala P., Rothenberg L.J., and Thrall R.M. Dea/Ar Efficiency and Profitability of 14 Major Oil Companies in U.S. Exploration and Production. Computers and Operations Research. 1996, 23 (4):357–373.

Wolf C. Does Ownership Matter? The Performance and Efficiency of State Oil Vs. Private Oil (1987–2006). Energy Policy. 2009, 37 (7):2642–2652.

Wooldridge J.M. Econometric Analysis of Cross Section and Panel Data: MIT press, 2010.

Zhang R., Sun K., Delgado M.S., and Kumbhakar S.C. Productivity in China's High Technology Industry: Regional Heterogeneity and R&D. Technological Forecasting and Social Change. 2012, 79 (1):127–141.

Chapter 7
Different Behaviors in Natural Gas Production Between National and Private Oil Companies: Economics-Driven or Environment-Driven?

Abstract This chapter investigates firm-level efficiency in the petroleum industry during the period 2009–2015. A Jackknife model averaging method and two stochastic frontier models are utilized to estimate the input-output relation more accurately. The derived efficiency is then decomposed to predict the effect of various efficiency determinants with an emphasis on gas ratio and ownership. A significantly negative effect of natural gas ratio (in production portfolio) on efficiency is found for both National Oil Companies (NOCs) and privately-owned International Oil Companies (IOCs). This finding implies that the decline in natural gas ratio for IOCs is economics-driven, and the incline in gas ratio for NOCs is environment-driven. Therefore, the environmental objective is the NOCs' third non-commercial objective, alongside subsidizing below-market energy prices and offering excessive employment, as found in the literature. Governments may consider the transfer of subsidies from low energy prices to clean energy promotion, which leads to energy saving and emissions reduction.

Keywords Oil and gas companies · Efficiency analysis · Stochastic frontier · Natural gas ratio · Ownership structure

1 Introduction

Given the severe pollution of coal and the slow growth of renewable energy, an abundant production of natural gas guarantees the supply of electricity under some requirements of emissions reduction, and hence balances the sustainable development of environment and economy. Therefore, coal and renewables are the competing sources of natural gas from a consumers' perspective. Many studies (Robinson et al. 2013; Simsek and Simsek 2013; Wei et al. 2010) analyze the characteristics of these sources economically and environmentally. However, the major competitor to natural gas, from a producers' perspective, is crude oil, as petroleum enterprises decide the share of oil and gas in their production portfolio, which to some extent determines the supply of natural gas. Since natural gas produces fewer emissions than crude oil and coal, improving the share of gas production in petroleum industry benefits the environment from two perspectives. On the one hand, natural gas can be utilized to directly replace coal in electricity generation. On the other hand, gas is an alternative to oil in the transportation sector, which causes up to 40% CO_2 emission reductions (Hekkert et al. 2005).

Using data on 54 large petroleum firms, this chapter finds that the average share of natural gas in portfolio decreased from 42.69% in 2009 to 40.96% in 2015, which implies that gas production might be less effective than oil production. In order to prove that such a decline in the gas ratio is economics-driven, the impact of natural gas share on firm-level efficiency needs to be estimated. In the little research that studies the efficiency of oil and gas firms, the focus is the difference between National Oil Companies (NOCs) and privately-owned International Oil Companies (IOCs) (i.e., the effect of ownership), and no one has studied the impact of natural gas ratio. Hartley and Medlock (2008) argue the major difference between IOCs and NOCs is that the IOCs focus on a commercial objective, while the NOCs have a wider range of non-commercial objectives due to political pressure. If the decline in gas ratio is economics-driven, as we expected, a sharper fall should be observed among IOCs, since they pay more attention to economic performance. This chapter finds that the gas ratio decreased from 45.86% in 2009 to 42.18% in 2015 for IOCs, which further supports our hypothesis. However, an incline in gas ratio from 35.18 to 38.06% for NOCs is observed during the same period, which is either the result of political pressure for environmental reasons or the different effects of gas ratio on IOCs and NOCs.

This chapter aims to investigate the effect of gas ratio on firm-level efficiency for large petroleum companies and to check whether this effect is different in NOCs and IOCs. In the first step, this chapter uses the Jackknife model averaging method and two stochastic frontier analysis (SFA) to estimate the input-output relation and derive firm-level efficiency, the robustness of which is checked using a data envelopment analysis (DEA) and the adjustment of input categories. Then, the efficiency scores are decomposed using an efficiency determination equation to predict the effect of gas ratio for NOCs and IOCs. The potential endogeneity problems in both SFA and efficiency decomposition are carefully checked and addressed.

There are three central contributions of this chapter to the studies of the petroleum industry: (1) the stochastic frontier models used allow non-monotonic time-varying efficiency, which better captures the fluctuations in economy than the frontier models used in the literature; (2) a model averaging method is introduced to combine the advantages of paramedic and semi-parametric estimation of efficiency; and (3) to our knowledge, this is the first study to estimate the efficiency of petroleum companies after the financial crisis, and the first to address the effect of gas ratio. Moreover, the empirical results show that the effect of gas ratio on efficiency is significantly negative and indifferent between IOCs and NOCs, which implies the decline in gas ratio for IOCs is economics-driven, and the incline in gas ratio for NOCs is environment-driven. This chapter suggests governments replacing price subsidy with clean energy promotion, which leads to energy saving and emissions reduction.

The remainder of the chapter is structured as follows. Section 2 reviews related literature. Section 3 introduces the model. Section 4 describes the data employed. Empirical results are presented and policy implications are given in Sect. 5. Section 6 draws a conclusion.

2 Literature Review

Although the petroleum industry is an important market in the world, very little research to date has studied the productivity and efficiency of oil and gas companies (Eller et al. 2011; Hartley and Medlock III 2013; Wolf 2009). Al-Obaidan and Scully (1992) use both deterministic and stochastic frontier analysis (SFA) on cross-sectional data of 44 oil and gas companies to estimate the efficiency. They use assets as the capital input, number of employees as the labor input, and either revenue or physical products as the output to estimate firm-level efficiency, and find NOCs are less efficient than IOCs. Thompson et al. (1996) study the efficiency of 14 major petroleum enterprises in the U.S. oilfield market, using a non-parametric DEA for the period 1980–1991. Gong (2017) introduces spatial techniques into the production function to capture the interactions among oil and gas service companies and then derive total factor productivity (TFP). Gong (2018) evaluates the impacts of new shale techniques (hydraulic fracturing and directional drilling) on SFA-derived firm-level efficiency in the global oilfield service industry. It is worth noting that the last three papers study oilfield service firms rather than petroleum enterprises.

Instead of using firm-level data, Managi et al. (2004) analyze the productivity and efficiency of the offshore Gulf of Mexico oil and gas industry, using well-level and field-level data in a DEA model. A similar dataset is utilized by the same group of scholars in Managi et al. (2006), who adopt a SFA model with the Battese-Coelli (BC) estimator so that time-varying efficiency can be derived. In these two studies, quantities of oil and gas production are used as output variables.

Hartley and Medlock (2008) provide three reasons to use revenue rather than production as output to estimate firm-level efficiency. Firstly, physical output such as oil and gas produced may fail to catch the impact of subsidies (e.g., a lower domestic price) as the result of political pressure on NOCs. Secondly, a usual method to aggregate the multiple products (e.g., oil and gas) is to calculate their relative value at market prices. Thirdly, revenue figures are usually easier to collect than the quantities of various products. Empirically, Wolf (2009) shows the strong correlation between physical outputs and revenue in oil and gas companies. Recent literature (Eller et al. 2011; Hartley and Medlock III 2013) prefers to use revenue as the output in estimating the efficiency of the oil and gas companies.

In terms of inputs employed for petroleum firms, Al-Obaidan and Scully (1992) use only assets and number of employees. Wolf (2009) adds the sum of oil and gas reserves as the third input to produce oil and gas. Although total assets are kept as an input because they cover other capital than the reserves, Wolf (2009) emphasizes that total assets reflect accounting rather than economic value, which might be severely distorted by inflation. Therefore, Eller et al. (2011) remove total assets from the input portfolio and further separate oil reserves and gas reserves as two different inputs. Finally, Hartley and Medlock III (2013) add refining capacity as an input on the top of the input portfolio in Eller et al. (2011). This chapter follows Hartley and Medlock III (2013) by including number of employees, oil reserves, gas reserves, and refining capacity as the four inputs, since this avoids the distortion of total assets mentioned in Wolf (2009), but considers the two most crucial assets including reserves and refining capacity.

Besides inputs and outputs, the last important thing to be decided is the econometrical method that captures the input-output relation. SFA and DEA are the two most widely used methods to estimate firm-level efficiency given inputs and outputs. SFA is a parametric method that allows a stochastic term to control the noise, but requires assumption of the functional form. DEA is a nonparametric linear programming method that relaxes the rigid functional assumption but does not account for statistical noise. They are also the main competing models in the efficiency analysis of the petroleum industry. As mentioned above, Managi et al. (2004) and (2006) employ DEA and SFA to study the offshore Gulf of Mexico oil and gas industry using the same dataset, respectively. Moreover, both DEA and SFA are utilized in Eller et al. (2011) and Hartley and Medlock III (2013). This chapter uses different SFA models to estimate firm-level efficiency and a DEA model to check its robustness.

However, the key interest in the literature is the effect of ownership on efficiency. Hartley and Medlock (2008) present a model of NOCs and find that they have a wider range of non-commercial objectives, such as domestic consumer surplus and employment. Political pressure forces them to provide domestic subsidy by below-market energy prices and excessive employment, which raises input-output ratio and reduces efficiency. Many scholars (Al-Obaidan and Scully 1992; Eller et al. 2011; Hartley and Medlock III 2013; Wolf 2009) study the difference between NOCs and IOCs, and find that the former group is less efficient than the latter, empirically. Al-Obaidan and Scully (1992) find NOCs on average are only 63–65% as efficient as IOCs. Wolf (2009) also claims that NOCs are 20–30% less efficient than private oil companies. Eller et al. (2011) and Hartley and Medlock III (2013) further introduce an efficiency decomposition equation as a second-step regression after SFA or DEA, aiming to estimate the effect of ownership when other things are equal. Both these studies find a significantly lower efficiency level of NOCs than IOCs. This chapter also decomposes efficiency to predict the impact of efficiency determinants more accurately, but with an emphasis on natural gas ratio instead of ownership.

3 Methodology

3.1 Efficiency Measurements

The main approach used by this chapter to measure efficiency is stochastic frontier analysis, which was initially proposed by Aigner et al. (1977) and Meeusen and Van den Broeck (1977). Given cross-sectional data, a stochastic frontier production function model equals the deterministic frontier production function plus a symmetric random error variable in the form

$$Y_i = f(X_i) \cdot TE_i \cdot \exp(v_i), \tag{1}$$

where Y_i is the output of firm i, and X_i is the vector of inputs and other regressors. $f(\cdot)$ is the function that decides the frontier, which provides the highest attainable output given inputs. TE_i measures the technical efficiency from 0 to 100%. v_i is the stochastic part that accounts for measurement errors, which is typically assumed to follow a normal distribution. Assuming Cobb-Douglas form of the production function $f(\cdot)$ and taking the log of Eq. (1) gives the form

$$y_i = x_i'\beta - u_i + v_i, \tag{2}$$

where y_i is the output of firm i in logarithms, x_i is a vector of inputs and other regressors in logarithms, and $u_i = -\log(TE_i)$ is a non-negative random variable since $0 < TE_i \leq 1$. The efficiency can be derived by $TE_i = \exp(-u_i)$.

Schmidt and Sickles (1984) propose a stochastic frontier model under a panel data setting when efficiency is assumed to be fixed over time.

$$y_{it} = \alpha + x_{it}'\beta - u_i + v_{it} = \alpha_i + x_{it}'\beta + v_{it}, \tag{3}$$

Then fixed effects or random effects methods can be used to estimate α_i under different conditions, since Eq. (3) is the standard form of the panel data model.

However, the efficiency of a company, or the distance between its actual production and the industry's best practice, is likely to vary across time. Therefore, some scholars developed new methods to allow a time-variant efficiency in the form

$$y_{it} = \alpha + x_{it}'\beta - u_{it} + v_{it} = \alpha_{it} + x_{it}'\beta + v_{it}. \tag{4}$$

Based on Eq. (4), Battese and Coelli (1992) propose the error components specification with time-varying efficiencies

$$u_{it} = \exp(-\eta(t - T)) \cdot u_i, \tag{5}$$

where $u_{it} \sim N^+\left(\mu, \sigma_\mu^2\right)$ is a truncated normal distribution. However, the BC estimator has a monotonicity constraint on efficiency. If η is positive, u_{it} is increasing over time for every firm i, which refers to decreasing efficiency over time. Similarly, negative η and zero η can lead to increasing efficiency and fixed efficiency for all firms, respectively. Moreover, the efficiency changes at the same speed across firms and time, as the change rate $\exp(-\eta)$ is firm-invariant and time-invariant. As a result, this model applies to periods with stable micro and macroeconomic environment, such as the period 2002–2004 in Eller et al. (2011) and most of the period 2001–2009 in Hartley and Medlock III (2013).

This chapter studies efficiency changes over the period 2009–2015, during which the petroleum industry gradually gained momentum after the 2007–2009 financial crisis, then experienced another price crash in 2014. The BC estimator may fail to describe both the up and down of the market due to the monotonicity restriction. Hence, this chapter introduces two other SFA models that can better capture the non-monotonic fluctuations in the economy that affect efficiency.

Cornwell et al. (1990) propose a quadratic time-varying intercept of all firms on the basis of Eq. (4)

$$\alpha_{it} = \theta_{i1} + \theta_{i2}t + \theta_{i3}t^2, \tag{6}$$

where the quadratic function of time can catch the fluctuation in efficiency affected by business cycles. This Cornwell-Schmidt-Sickles (CSS) model can be solved by a within estimator, which is denoted as CSSW, if the individual effects are assumed to be correlated with the exogenous regressors. Otherwise, the Generalized Least Squares (GLS) estimator, which is denoted as CSSG, is preferred. A Hausman-Wu test can be adopted to choose between CSSW and CSSG.

Kneip et al. (2012) assume that firm-level efficiency is influenced by a set of time-varying factors, and hence model it by a linear combination of some basis functions. More specifically, this Kneip-Sickles-Song (KSS) model assumes the individual effects in Eq. (4) follow

$$u_{it} = \sum_{r=1}^{L} \theta_{ir} g_r(t), \tag{7}$$

where $g_1(t), \ldots, g_L(t)$ are the basis functions, and $\theta_{i1}, \ldots, \theta_{iL}$ are the coresponding parameters. The KSS estimator is derived by semiparametric techniques, which is more flexible than the paraemtric BC and CSS estiamtors. In fact, the KSS model is a general setting that nests both BC and CSS models. On the one hand, the BC model is a special case of KSS when $g_1(t) = \exp(-\eta(t - T)) / \sqrt{\frac{1}{T} \sum_{s=1}^{T} \exp(-\eta(t - T))^2}$ and $L = 1$. On the other hand, the CSS model can be nested in the KSS model when the polynomila functions are the basis functions and $L = 3$.

Endogeneity can be an issue in the CSS and KSS models, since some information witnessed by the petroleum enterprises that is employed in their decision-making process is unobserved to scholars (Ackerberg et al. 2015). Olley and Pakes (1996) and Levinsohn and Petrin (2003) deal with the problem by using observed investment or intermediate inputs to control for unobserved productivity shocks. Their approaches, however, oftentimes suffer from the collinearity problems and hence lead to inpausible results in empirical applications (Ackerberg et al. 2015). This chapter chooses the most widely used instrumental variables (IV) method with the endogeneity concern. The control function method introduced in Amsler et al. (2016) is adopted to check whether the inputs are endogenous or exogenous, where lagged input quantities, as suggested in Levinsohn and Petrin (2003) and Gong (2018), are employed as instruments. If any input is confirmed to be endogenous, the Corrected Two-Stage Least Square (C2SLS) method recommended in Amsler et al. (2016) can be used to correct the bias.

3.2 Model Averaging Method

There is a tradeoff between the parametric CSS model and the semiparametric KSS model. If the true data generating process (DGP) is close to the assumption in the parametric model (i.e., $\alpha_{it} = \theta_{i1} + \theta_{i2}t + \theta_{i3}t^2$), the CSS estimator outperforms the KSS estimator. However, the KSS estimator is preferred if the rigid assumption of the functional form in CSS is invalid.

Since the true DGP is unobserved, a possible approach is to use some model selection methods to choose between CSS and KSS models. However, various model selection methods under different criteria[1] may lead to different selection results. Even under the same criteria, a slight change in data may lead to completely different selection. Furthermore, all the candidate models, rather than only one of them, may reflect the underlying DGP to some extent (Shang 2015). Therefore, model averaging methods that assign a weight to each candidate model according to its ability to explain the data, rather than treating a single model as the "best", are better tools to approximate the underlying mechanism and describe the true DGP. It is worth noting that model selection is a special case of model averaging procedure, when all the zero weight is assigned to all but one candidate models.

There are several weight-determination techniques in the literature. The information criteria-based approach can be utilized in model averaging method (Buckland et al. 1997). However, it is hard to test for effectiveness and quality improvement. Hansen and Racine (2012) propose a Jackknife-based model averaging method, which is asymptotically optimal and approaches the minimum expected square errors when the sample size approaches infinity. Substantially, the Jackknife method assigns weights based on the "leave-one-out" cross-validation criterion.

---

[1]Popular criteria include, but not limited to, the Akaike information criterion (AIC), the Bayesian information criterion (BIC), and the Focused information criterion (FIC).

This chapter first derives the "leave-one-out" cross-validation for CSS and KSS, respectively. The Jackknife estimators of the output $\hat{y}^{\text{CSS}} = \left(\hat{y}_1^{\text{CSS}}, \ldots, \hat{y}_n^{\text{CSS}} \right)$ and $\hat{y}^{\text{KSS}} = \left(\hat{y}_1^{\text{KSS}}, \ldots, \hat{y}_n^{\text{KSS}} \right)$ are predicted, where $\hat{y}_i^{\text{CSS}}$ and $\hat{y}_i^{\text{KSS}}$ are the fitted value of company i's output using the CSS and KSS method, respectively, when the i-th firm is deleted from the dataset. Suppose the weight for CSS is w, the weight for KSS is $1 - w$ accordingly. The Jackknife weight w^* can be achieved by minimizing the cross-validation criteria:

$$w^* = \operatorname*{arg\,min}_{0 \leq w \leq 1} CV_n(w) = \frac{1}{n} \hat{e}(w)' \hat{e}(w), \qquad (8)$$

where $\hat{e}(w) = y - w \hat{y}^{\text{CSS}} - (1 - w) \hat{y}^{\text{KSS}}$.

Then, the model averaging stochastic frontier model this chapter adopted has the form:

$$y = w^* y^{\text{CSS}} + \left(1 - w^* \right) y^{\text{KSS}}, \qquad (9)$$

where y^{CSS} is the CSS estimator follows Eqs. (4) and (6), and y^{KSS} is KSS estimator follows Eqs. (4) and (7). The intercept, coefficients, and efficiency terms are all the Jackknife-weighted average of the CSS and KSS estimators.

3.3   Robustness Checks

This chapter checks the robustness of the efficiency estimates and the model averaging method in the petroleum dataset. x_{it}' in Eq. (4) vector inputs of the oil companies including number of employees, oil reserves, gas reserves, and refining capacity, as well as other repressors including oil price realization and gas price realization, which is denoted as a "four-input model." In the first robustness check, this chapter follows Wolf (2009) to treat total reserves in million barrels of oil equivalent (BOE) as an input, which measures the overall resources held by a company. Replacing the oil and gas reserves with total reserves, the CSS and KSS estimators are re-estimated, followed by the Jackknife model averaging method. The robustness of the efficiency estimates and the model averaging weights can be tested using this "three-input model."

To this end, this chapter uses stochastic frontier models. Although the individual effects of the KSS approach are modeled semi-parametrically, the production frontier is assumed to follow a Cobb-Douglas form. The aforementioned tradeoff between parametric and semi-parametric individual effects in CSS and KSS models also applies to the assumption of the production frontier. If the true input-output relation in the petroleum industry is very different from the Cobb-Douglas form, the efficiency estimated can be inaccurate. Implementing a nonparametric representation of the frontier is another way to estimate efficiency. The most widely used nonparametric approach is DEA, which is the major competing methodology to SFA in efficiency analysis.

DEA is a linear programming method that is powerful and easy, and imposes minimal assumptions on the boundary of the input requirements set, including piece-wise linearity and convexity. The efficiency can be estimated by solving the linear programming problem:

$$D_{it}(y_{it}, x_{it}) = \min_{\theta, \lambda} \theta, \tag{10}$$

s.t. $-y_{it} + Y\lambda \geq 0, \theta x_{it} + X\lambda \geq 0, \lambda \geq 0$,

where λ is a vector of constants. Substantially, this linear program radially contracts the input vector of each company to a projected point $(X\lambda, Y\lambda)$, on the surface of the piece-wise linear isoquant that represents the frontier. The efficiency score of firm i at time t is given by $0 < \theta \leq 1$, which is comparable with those estimated in the SFA models. Therefore, this chapter utilizes this DEA model to check the robustness of the efficiency derived from the weighted average of the CSS and KSS estimators.

3.4 Decomposition of Efficiency

This chapter is interested in the effect of natural gas ratio in portfolio on firm-level efficiency in the petroleum industry. Since the dependent variable, the firm-level efficiency, is in percentage from 0 to 100%, a Tobit regression model is introduced to estimate the efficiency determination equation.

$$Eff_{it} = \alpha + \beta gas_{it} + \rho noc_{it} + \eta gas_{it} noc_{it} + \gamma seg_{it} + \delta reg_{it} + \tau year_t + \varepsilon_{it}. \tag{11}$$

Where Eff_{it} is the firm-level efficiency for firm i at time t, and gas_{it} is the ratio of natural gas in production that measures the share of crude oil and natural gas in portfolio of a company (i.e., output share by product). noc_{it} is a dummy variable of the NOCs. Since different trends of gas_{it} between NOCs and IOCs are observed, this chapter checks the potential heterogeneous effects of gas_{it} on efficiency for NOCs and IOCs by adding an interaction term $gas_{it} noc_{it}$. Moreover, it is necessary to control each company's output share by segment and output share by region, as many energy companies are found to be multi-segment/product firms (Hawdon 2003; Jacobsen et al. 2006; Seeto et al. 2001) or multi-region/national firms (Bertoldi et al. 2006; Bilgin 2007; Conway 2013; Fontaine 2011). seg_{it} is a vector that measures the output share in each segment, respectively. reg_{it} is a vector that measures the output share in each region, respectively. $year_t$ is a vector of year dummy variables to control the time effects.

Endogeneity may also be an issue in the efficiency determination equation due to omitted variable bias and simultaneity bias. On the one hand, this chapter adds some other efficiency determinants into Eq. (11) besides the variables of gas ratio and ownership to check the omitted variable bias. On the other hand, simultaneity bias is another concern as some efficiency determinants may be conversely affected by efficiency. For instance, more efficient companies are more successful and are more likely to step into a new segment or region. As a result, efficiency may affect output share by segment and by region. This chapter replaces all efficiency determinants in Eq. (11) with their lagged values to deal with the causality problem, which can also be treated as a robustness check.

4   Data

The primary data source is the Energy Intelligence's *"Top 100: Global NOC & IOC Rankings"*. The variables required in SFA and DEA, including firm-level revenue (in billion US dollars), number of employees, oil reserves (in million barrels, MMbbl), gas reserves (in billions cubic feet, Bcf), refining capacity (thousand barrels per day, '000 b/d), oil price realization (US dollars per barrel of oil equivalent, $/BOE), and gas realization (US dollars per thousand cubic feet, $/Mcf), are all available in this dataset. This dataset also reports firm-level oil production (in thousand barrels per day, '000 b/d) and gas production (in million cubic feet per day, MMcf/d), which can derive the ratio of natural gas in production. Moreover, another efficiency determinant of interest, the output share by segment, can be calculated, since this dataset provides oil and gas produced in the upstream segment, oil and gas refined in the refining segment, and oil and gas sold in marking segment. Finally, this dataset has firm category information to separate NOCs and IOCs. The last set of efficiency determinants, output share by region, are collected from Rystad Energy's UCube database, where production from Asia-Pacific, Middle East, Africa, America, Europe, and Russia is given for each company-year observation, respectively.

Although Energy Intelligence's *"Top 100: Global NOC & IOC Rankings"* includes one hundred biggest oil companies in the world from 2009 to 2015, this chapter drops firms with missing input or output information. A balanced panel data of 54 companies covering 2009–2015 remains, which is comparable with the sample of 44 petroleum enterprises for 1979–1982 in Al-Obaidan and Scully (1992), the sample of 14 integrated oil companies for the years 1980–1991 in Thompson et al. (1996), the sample of 50 largest oil companies over the period 1987–2006 in Wolf (2009), the sample of 78 oil firms during the period 2002–2004 in Eller et al. (2011), and the sample of 61 oil companies from 2001 to 2009 in Hartley and Medlock III (2013). Among these 54 companies, 16 are NOCs and 38 are IOCs.

Table 1 summarizes firm-level inputs and outputs, oil and gas price realizations, and efficiency determinants in the years 2009 and 2015, respectively. The average annual revenue of these oil companies decreased slightly from 55.73 billion to 55.25 billion US dollars in seven years. Among the four inputs, only the oil reserves increased more than one quarter, while the number of employees, the gas reserves, and the refining capacity all decreased over the period 2009–2015. Due to the price

Table 1 Summary statistics

Variable	Explanation	Unit	2009	2015	Changes (%)
y	Revenue	billion $	55.73	55.25	−0.86
$Labor$	Number of employees	'000	79.81	75.45	−5.46
$OilRsv$	Oil reserves	MMbbl	7505	9472	26.21
$GasRsv$	Gas reserves	Bcf	30401	29951	−1.48
$RefCap$	Refining capacity	'000 b/d	915.2	832.5	−9.04
$OilPr$	Oil price realization	$/BOE	54.24	40.62	−25.11
$GasPr$	Gas price realization	$/Mcf	3.99	3.72	−6.77
gas	Ratio of natural gas in portfolio	%	42.69	40.96	−4.05
$seg1$	Share in upstream segment	%	57.51	64.19	11.62
$seg2$	Share in refining segment	%	20.03	16.70	−16.63
$seg3$	Share in marking segment	%	22.46	19.12	−14.87
$reg1$	Share in Asia-Pacific	%	22.33	20.81	−6.81
$reg2$	Share in Middle East	%	4.86	6.56	34.98
$reg3$	Share in Africa	%	10.35	7.33	−29.18
$reg4$	Share in America	%	41.33	45.82	10.86
$reg5$	Share in Europe	%	8.41	6.39	−24.02
$reg6$	Share in Russia	%	12.72	13.09	2.91

crash since 2014, the average price realization of oil and gas in 2015 was 25.11 and 6.77% lower than the level of 2009, respectively. The ratio of natural gas in oil companies' portfolios on average decreased from 42.69 to 40.96%, indicating a smaller share of natural gas in the total production of the large oil companies. The upstream segment is the largest segment and keeps expanding, while refining and marketing segments are diminishing, which shows the behavior of the large oil companies in favor of the upstream business in recent years. Geographically, more than 40% of the production of these 54 large oil companies is from America, and Asia-Pacific contributes to one-fifth of their total production.

5 Results and Discussion

5.1 Stochastic Frontier and Model Averaging

Following Eller et al. (2011) and Hartley and Medlock III (2013), this chapter assumes that the production technology exhibits constant returns to scale (CRS). The endogeneity of inputs in the production function is tested and the result shows that all the inputs are exogenous. As the first step, a Hausman-Wu test is employed to choose between the CSSW and CSSG, which generates a p-value of 0.5018 in favor of the

Table 2 Estimation results of the stochastic frontier models

	CSSG		KSS		Jackknife average	
	Four-input	Three-input	Four-input	Three-input	Four-input	Three-input
Labor	0.393***	0.344***	0.253***	0.199***	0.292***	0.230***
	(0.013)	(0.012)	(0.028)	(0.027)	(0.025)	(0.025)
OliRsv	0.218***	–	0.144***	–	0.164***	–
	(0.010)	–	(0.039)	–	(0.034)	–
GasRsv	0.300***	–	0.508***	–	0.451***	–
	(0.009)	–	(0.043)	–	(0.037)	–
TotalRsv	–	0.581***	–	0.735***	–	0.702***
	–	(0.010)	–	(0.031)	–	(0.028)
RefCap	0.090***	0.075***	0.095***	0.066***	0.094***	0.068***
	(0.006)	(0.005)	(0.023)	(0.021)	(0.020)	(0.019)
OliPr	0.307***	0.299***	0.059	0.033	0.127***	0.090*
	(0.018)	(0.017)	(0.061)	(0.057)	(0.053)	(0.051)
GasPr	0.092**	0.080*	0.020	-0.005	0.040	0.013
	(0.044)	(0.041)	(0.061)	(0.057)	(0.057)	(0.054)
w^*	–	–	–	–	0.2760	0.2161

Notes Significant at: *10, * *5 and * * * 1%; Standard error in parentheses

CSSG model. In the first robustness check, when oil reserves and gas reserves are aggregated as a single input, the Hausman-Wu test generates a p-value of 0.9695, which again suggests using the CSSG model. Therefore, this chapter uses CSSG and KSS to calculate the firm-level efficiency of oil companies and then estimate the Jackknife model averaging weights accordingly. Table 2 provides the estimation results of the CSSG, KSS, and Jackknife-weighted average stochastic frontier model. The first and third columns in Table 2 present the CSSG and KSS estimator of the "four-input model", respectively. Then, the fifth column reports the Jackknife-weighted average stochastic frontier model accordingly. The second, fourth, and sixth columns in Table 2 provide the estimation results of the "three-input model" as a robustness check, which is comparable with the first, third, and fifth column, respectively.

In Table 2, the Jackknife weight of CSSG is 0.2760 in the "four-input" model, which implies both CSSG and KSS can explain the data-generating process to some extent, but the semi-parametric KSS is more important. The robustness of this conclusion is supported, as the Jackknife weight of CSSG is 0.2161 in the "three-input" model. As a result, the fifth column reports that the coefficients of labor, oil reserves, gas reserves, and refining capacity are 0.292, 0.164, 0.451, and 0.094, respectively, which are all significantly positive. The contributions of labor and reserves are greater than that of the refining capacity. Moreover, the oil price has a significantly positive effect on output, while the effect of natural gas price is insignificant both statistically and economically. The results in the sixth column also confirm the aforementioned findings on inputs and prices.

5.2 Firm-Level Efficiency

The stochastic frontier regressions in the fifth and sixth column of Table 2 can further derive firm-level efficiency of the "four-input" and "three-input" models, which are denoted as Eff_1^{SFA} and Eff_2^{SFA}, respectively. As the second robustness check, this chapter also uses DEA in the "four-input" and "three-input" models to derive firm-level efficiencies, which are denoted as Eff_1^{DEA} and Eff_2^{DEA}, respectively. Table 3 summarizes the distribution of the efficiency scores in the international petroleum industry under the four models. In summary, the efficiencies estimated by the DEA model and the "four-input" model are slightly higher.

In order to check the robustness of the efficiency estimated in the main model (Eff_1^{SFA}), this chapter calculates the correlation of efficiencies for the four models in Table 4. All the correlation coefficients in the table are above 0.7, which implies a strong uphill (positive) linear relationship across the efficiencies derived in the four models. Furthermore, Table 5 reports the estimation results of three Tobit regressions, where Eff_1^{SFA} is the independent variable and the other three groups of efficiencies (Eff_1^{DEA}, Eff_2^{SFA}, and Eff_2^{DEA}) are the dependent variables, one for each regression. The result also verifies the robustness of the efficiency scores under different methods.

Table 3 Technical efficiency statistics

	Four-input model		Three-input model	
	Eff_1^{SFA}	Eff_1^{DEA}	Eff_2^{SFA}	Eff_2^{DEA}
Mean	0.46	0.55	0.45	0.47
Minimum	0.12	0.02	0.10	0.02
25% quantile	0.29	0.28	0.25	0.23
50% quantile	0.42	0.54	0.38	0.42
75% quantile	0.60	0.81	0.63	0.65
Maximum	1.00	1.00	1.00	1.00

Table 4 Correlation of efficiencies across models

	Eff_1^{SFA}	Eff_1^{DEA}	Eff_2^{SFA}	Eff_2^{DEA}
Eff_1^{SFA}	1	0.8156	0.9036	0.7917
Eff_1^{DEA}	0.8156	1	0.7354	0.8940
Eff_2^{SFA}	0.9036	0.7354	1	0.8398
Eff_1^{DEA}	0.7917	0.8940	0.8398	1

Table 5 Robustness of the efficiencies across models

	Eff_1^{DEA}	Eff_2^{SFA}	Eff_2^{DEA}
Eff_1^{SFA}	0.822***	0.914***	0.801***
	(0.059)	(0.045)	(0.050)
Constant term	0.185***	0.037*	0.093***
	(0.029)	(0.022)	(0.025)

To this end, this chapter estimates the production frontier and derives firm-level efficiencies. The robustness of the firm-level efficiencies is also confirmed using different methods (SFA vs. DEA) and input portfolios (aggregate vs. disaggregate reserves). The fact that various approaches yield similar estimations should increase confidence that the efficiencies reflect genuine underlying differences among petroleum enterprises. This chapter uses the robust efficiency estimated in the main model (Eff_1^{SFA}) for efficiency decomposition analysis.

5.3 Efficiency Decomposition

The most important question this chapter seeks to answer is whether or not investing more in natural gas will decrease firm-level efficiency, which reflects the economic impact of producing this clean energy; and, moreover, whether or not this effect is different in NOCs and IOCs, as the former have been increasing share of gas while the latter have reducing share of gas in recent years. Finally, the impacts of the other two sets of efficiency determinants, the output share by segment and by region, can provide valuable information as well. Table 6 reports the estimation results of the efficiency determination equation. Columns (1)–(4) are estimations of the regular Tobit model where different sets of independent variables are utilized to check the robustness of the results. Column (5) presents the results of the full model in Eq. (11) to avoid omitted variable bias. Column (6) replaces the independent variables with their lagged values to deal with the simultaneous bias, which has fairly robust results.

All the six columns in Table 6 report a significantly negative coefficient of natural gas share in portfolio, indicating more investment in this clean energy will lower firms' efficiency. Therefore, the large oil companies reduced the share of clean products in the context of environmental protection, because of economic and commercial concerns. Another robust finding is that NOCs are significantly less efficient than IOCs, holding other factors fixed. However, the magnitude of the difference between NOCs and IOCs is smaller than that found in the literature that uses earlier data.

The follow-up question, whether or not the effect of natural gas share in portfolio is different for NOCs and IOCs, is answered by columns (4)–(6) in Table 6, where insignificant estimates of the interaction term *gas · noc* imply indifferent effect regardless of ownership. In other words, improvement of natural gas share has a negative impact on commercial performance for both NOCs and IOCs. Therefore, IOCs

Table 6 Estimation results of the efficiency determination regressions

	(1)	(2)	(3)	(4)	(5)	(6)
gas	−0.124**	−0.267***	−0.179***	−0.240***	−0.144**	−0.125*
	(0.060)	(0.061)	(0.062)	(0.066)	(0.066)	(0.072)
noc	−	−0.177***	−0.177***	−0.118*	−0.100*	−0.121*
	−	(0.030)	(0.030)	(0.062)	(0.059)	(0.065)
gas · noc	−	−	−	−0.180	−0.233	−0.154
	−	−	−	(0.164)	(0.157)	(0.170)
*seg*1	−	−	−0.329***	−	−0.339***	−0.283***
	−	−	(0.105)	−	(0.105)	(0.106)
*seg*2	−	−	−0.379	−	−0.396*	−0.268
	−	−	(0.240)	−	(0.240)	(0.238)
*reg*1	0.114*	0.281***	0.246***	0.295***	0.262***	0.265***
	(0.059)	(0.062)	(0.061)	(0.064)	(0.061)	(0.065)
*reg*2	0.102	0.064	0.048	0.056	0.036	0.049
	(0.099)	(0.094)	(0.090)	(0.094)	(0.090)	(0.097)
*reg*3	0.358***	0.369***	0.328***	0.377***	0.338***	0.296***
	(0.087)	(0.082)	(0.080)	(0.082)	(0.080)	(0.086)
*reg*4	0.183***	0.253***	0.257***	0.243***	0.244***	0.239***
	(0.049)	(0.048)	(0.046)	(0.049)	(0.047)	(0.050)
*reg*5	0.537***	0.649***	0.570***	0.647***	0.567***	0.563***
	(0.084)	(0.081)	(0.081)	(0.081)	(0.080)	(0.086)
year effects	yes	yes	yes	yes	yes	yes
Intercept	0.355***	0.386***	0.632***	0.376***	0.627***	0.564***
	(0.049)	(0.046)	(0.118)	(0.047)	(0.118)	(0.117)

Notes Significant at: *10, * *5 and * * * 1%; Standard error in parentheses

are reducing share of natural gas, as expected, for economic reasons. However, NOCs are still expanding natural gas share in portfolio in spite of the financial sacrifice.

Such difference in behaviors between NOCs and IOCs indicates a third non-commercial objective of the NOCs, which is the environmental objective. Hartley and Medlock (2008) argue that NOCs have two noneconomic objectives, namely excessive employment and below-market prices, as the result of political pressure. These two actions can be regarded as subsidies to the domestic workforce and consumers in reward for the loss in firm-level efficiency, which is confirmed in Eller et al. (2011) and Hartley and Medlock III (2013). The NOCs' behavior of adding investment in the cleaner natural gas found in this chapter is likely to be a subsidy to domestic residents under political pressure for a better environment. As a comparison, the IOCs have less political pressure on them, and hence reduce share of natural gas for economic purposes. In summary, the different behaviors of IOCs and NOCs are economics-driven and environment-driven, respectively.

Besides the output share by product, Table 6 also predicts the effects of output share by segment and by region on firm-level efficiency. Vertically, the marking segment is more efficient than the upstream and refining segments, hence increasing the share of marking can raise firm-level efficiency. Geographically, companies that have more footprints and activities in Asia-Pacific, Africa, America, and Europe are likely to outperform in efficiency. Although not reported in Table 6, the estimations of the year dummy variables are robust across the five columns. The average efficiency increased in 2010 and 2011, but decreased over the period of 2012–2015. This non-linear and non-monotonic trend verifies the necessity of using CSS and KSS models, rather than the BC model in Hartley and Medlock III (2013). Detailed estimations of the year dummy variables are available on request.

6 Conclusion and Policy Implications

Natural gas is usually compared with coal and renewable energy, as they are the competing sources in electricity generation. However, its main competitor is crude oil from the supply side, since petroleum enterprises can decide the share of natural gas and crude oil in their portfolios. Moreover, oil and gas are competing in the automobile market. This chapter finds large oil and gas companies on average are reducing share of natural gas because producing gas is not as efficient as producing oil in both NOCs and IOCs. As the investment in and expenditure on crude oil are increasing, the gap between oil and gas can be enlarged, which will, in turn, further discourage R&D and the production of natural gas.

The political pressure around environmental concerns can affect the behavior of NOCs, but has achieved limited influence on IOCs to date. On the one hand, governments may adjust the relative tax rate for crude oil and natural gas in favor of the latter. On the other hand, governments can adjust its R&D distribution between crude oil and natural gas to increase the productivity of gas extraction. These actions could be more effective than environmental pressure on IOCs, as this chapter has shown that the commercial objective is the priority for this cohort.

How to make the NOCs more efficient and competitive relative to IOCs is another challenge faced by governments. This chapter shows the efficiency difference between NOCs and IOCs is decreasing as time goes by. Excessive employment is not purely a political burden, but implies massive potential human capital. Training workers' skills and developing their experience can encourage innovation in NOCs, and hence improve their productivity and efficiency, especially in the context of the shale technical revolution.

Moreover, there are tradeoffs among below-market energy prices, excessive employment, and more clean products. When maintaining efficiency at a certain level, governments can adjust the amount of these subsidies. In the context of energy saving and environmental protection, governments may consider cutting the energy price subsidy, while encouraging more production of natural gas. The former action can reduce the total consumption of energy and the volume of emissions, while the latter can increase the share of cleaner energy in portfolio and hence further decrease emissions intensity. As domestic consumers and residents have become more aware of environmental protection and emissions reduction in recent years, such transfer of subsidies is facing fewer obstructions.

In summary, the chapter aims to explore the impact of gas ratio on firm-level efficiency for large petroleum companies during the period 2009–2015. A Jackknife-weighted average of CSS and KSS models helps derive firm-level efficiency more accurately. The derived efficiency is then decomposed to predict the effect of various efficiency determinants with an emphasis on gas ratio and ownership. To our knowledge, this is the first study to analyze the efficiency of the petroleum industry after the financial crisis, and the first to explain the different behaviors on natural gas ratio for NOCs and IOCs.

Using a panel data of 54 large oil and gas companies, the effect of gas ratio on efficiency is found to be significantly negative. Moreover, this impact is indifferent between IOCs and NOCs. These findings imply that the decline in gas ratio for IOCs is economics-driven, and the incline in gas ratio for NOCs is environment-driven. Hence, the environmental objective is the third non-commercial objective of NOCs after the subsidies of below-market energy prices and excessive employment found in the literature. Finally, governments may consider the transfer of subsidies from energy price to clean energy promotion, which leads to energy saving and emissions reduction.

References

Ackerberg D.A., Caves K., and Frazer G. Identification Properties of Recent Production Function Estimators. Econometrica. 2015, 83 (6):2411–2451.

Aigner D., Lovell C.A., and Schmidt P. Formulation and Estimation of Stochastic Frontier Production Function Models. Journal of Econometrics. 1977, 6 (1):21–37.

Al-Obaidan A.M., and Scully G.W. Efficiency Differences between Private and State-Owned Enterprises in the International Petroleum Industry. Applied Economics. 1992, 24 (2):237–246.

Amsler C., Prokhorov A., and Schmidt P. Endogeneity in Stochastic Frontier Models. Journal of Econometrics. 2016, 190 (2):280–288.

Battese G.E., and Coelli T.J. Frontier Production Functions, Technical Efficiency and Panel Data: With Application to Paddy Farmers in India: Springer Netherlands, 1992.

Bertoldi P., Rezessy S., and Vine E. Energy Service Companies in European Countries: Current Status and a Strategy to Foster Their Development. Energy Policy. 2006, 34 (14):1818–1832.

Bilgin M. New Prospects in the Political Economy of Inner-Caspian Hydrocarbons and Western Energy Corridor through Turkey. Energy Policy. 2007, 35 (12):6383–6394.

Buckland S.T., Burnham K.P., and Augustin N.H. Model Selection: An Integral Part of Inference. Biometrics. 1997, 53 (2):603–618.

Conway J.E. The Risk Is in the Relationship (Not the Country): Political Risk Management in the Uranium Industry in Kazakhstan. Energy Policy. 2013, 56:201–209.

Cornwell C., Schmidt P., and Sickles R.C. Production Frontiers with Cross-Sectional and Time-Series Variation in Efficiency Levels. Journal of Econometrics. 1990, 46 (1):185–200.

Eller S.L., Hartley P.R., and Medlock K.B. Empirical Evidence on the Operational Efficiency of National Oil Companies. Empirical Economics. 2011, 40 (3):623–643.

Fontaine G. The Effects of Governance Modes on the Energy Matrix of Andean Countries. Energy Policy. 2011, 39 (5):2888–2898.

Gong B. Multi-Dimensional Interactions in the Oilfield Market: A Jackknife Model Averaging Approach of Spatial Productivity Analysis (Forthcoming). Energy Economics. 2017.

Gong B. The Shale Technical Revolution—Cheer or Fear? Impact Analysis on Efficiency in the Global Oilfield Service Market. Energy Policy. 2018, 112 (1):162–172.

Hansen B.E., and Racine J.S. Jackknife Model Averaging. Journal of Econometrics. 2012, 167 (1):38–46.

Hartley P., and Medlock K.B. A Model of the Operation and Development of a National Oil Company. Energy Economics. 2008, 30 (5):2459–2485.

Hartley P.R., and Medlock III K.B. Changes in the Operational Efficiency of National Oil Companies. The Energy Journal. 2013, 34 (2):27–57.

Hawdon D. Efficiency, Performance and Regulation of the International Gas Industry—a Bootstrap Dea Approach. Energy Policy. 2003, 31 (11):1167–1178.

Hekkert M.P., Hendriks F.H.J.F., Faaij A.P.C., and Neelis M.L. Natural Gas as an Alternative to Crude Oil in Automotive Fuel Chains Well-to-Wheel Analysis and Transition Strategy Development. Energy Policy. 2005, 33 (5):579–594.

Jacobsen H.K., Fristrup P., and Munksgaard J. Integrated Energy Markets and Varying Degrees of Liberalisation: Price Links, Bundled Sales and Chp Production Exemplified by Northern European Experiences. Energy Policy. 2006, 34 (18):3527–3537.

Kneip A., Sickles R.C., and Song W. A New Panel Data Treatment for Heterogeneity in Time Trends. Econometric Theory. 2012, 28 (3):590–628.

Levinsohn J., and Petrin A. Estimating Production Functions Using Inputs to Control for Unobservables. The Review of Economic Studies. 2003, 70 (2):317–341.

Managi S., Opaluch J.J., Jin D., and Grigalunas T.A. Stochastic Frontier Analysis of Total Factor Productivity in the Offshore Oil and Gas Industry. Ecological Economics. 2006, 60 (1):204–215.

Managi S., Opaluch J.J., Jin D., and Grigalunas T.A. Technological Change and Depletion in Offshore Oil and Gas. Journal of Environmental Economics and Management. 2004, 47 (2):388–409.

Meeusen W., and Van den Broeck J. Efficiency Estimation from Cobb-Douglas Production Functions with Composed Error. International Economic Review. 1977, 18 (2):435–444.

Olley G.S., and Pakes A. The Dynamics of Productivity in the Telecommunications Equipment Industry. Econometrica. 1996, 64 (6):1263–1297.

Robinson A.P., Blythe P.T., Bell M.C., Hübner Y., and Hill G.A. Analysis of Electric Vehicle Driver Recharging Demand Profiles and Subsequent Impacts on the Carbon Content of Electric Vehicle Trips. Energy Policy. 2013, 61 (8):337–348.

Schmidt P., and Sickles R.C. Production Frontiers and Panel Data. Journal of Business and Economic Statistics. 1984, 2 (4):367–374.

Seeto D.Q., Woo C.-K., and Horowitz I. Finessing the Unintended Outcomes of Price-Cap Adjustments: An Electric Utility Multi-Product Perspective. Energy Policy. 2001, 29 (13):1111–1118.

Shang C. 2015. "Essays on the Use of Duality, Robust Empirical Methods, Panel Treatments, and Model Averaging with Applications to Housing Price Index Construction and World Productivity Growth." Rice University.

Simsek H.A., and Simsek N. Recent Incentives for Renewable Energy in Turkey. Energy Policy. 2013, 63 (4):521–530.

Thompson R.G., Dharmapala P., Rothenberg L.J., and Thrall R.M. Dea/Ar Efficiency and Profitability of 14 Major Oil Companies in U.S. Exploration and Production. Computers and Operations Research. 1996, 23 (4):357–373.

Wei M., Patadia S., and Kammen D.M. Putting Renewables and Energy Efficiency to Work: How Many Jobs Can the Clean Energy Industry Generate in the Us? Energy Policy. 2010, 38 (2):919–931.

Wolf C. Does Ownership Matter? The Performance and Efficiency of State Oil Vs. Private Oil (1987–2006). Energy Policy. 2009, 37 (7):2642–2652.

Chapter 8
Total-Factor Spillovers, Similarities, and Competitions in the Petroleum Industry

Abstract This chapter investigates multi-dimensional spillovers, similarities, and competitions in the petroleum industry. Spatial techniques are applied first in production function in order to observe the cross-sectional dependence in each of the four dimensions (product-, technology-, segment-, and region-wide). These four single-dimensional spatial models are then aggregated by a model averaging method that assigns weights to different models based on their ability to explain data. Taking all dependences into consideration, this chapter estimates the total-factor spillovers, similarities, and competitions in the spirit of total-factor productivity. Negative spillover effects are observed in all the four dimensions. Moreover, segment-wide competition has negative effect on productivity. Some policy implications concerning human capital, globalization, and development strategies are also discussed.

Keywords Petroleum industry · Spatial econometric model · Multi-dimensional dependence · Spillovers, similarities, and competitions

1 Introduction

In the global petroleum industry, competitions among firms exist in multiple dimensions. The similarities in products generated (oil or gas), technologies employed (conventional or unconventional), segments entered (upstream, refining, or marketing), and regions operated all have a role in determining the levels of competition to some extent between two firms as they compete directly for inputs to outputs in the overlapping business. For example, they are confronted with the same consumers if both produce oil rather than gas, and they face the same endowment constraints in labor and capital inputs if they have footprints in the same regions.

As LeSage (2008) stated, the similarities across firms can measure cross-sectional dependence,[1] which reflects the degree of interactions among firms and helps to

---

[1] Cross-sectional dependence exists when individual units are interdependent. See more detailed introduction of cross-sectional dependence in Sarafidis and Wansbeek (2012).

© Zhejiang University Press 2020
B. Gong, *Shale Energy Revolution*,
https://doi.org/10.1007/978-981-15-4855-0_8

estimate spillover effects[2] when spatial techniques are introduced in the production function. However, the effect of dependence has not been properly addressed in existing studies concerning the petroleum industry. Most researches (e.g., Wolf 2009; Eller et al. 2011; and Hartley and Medlock III 2013) use a classic productivity analysis to estimate the input-output relation, where the production process is independent across firms without the consideration of interactions. On the other hand, cross-sectional dependence is considered in other markets, but the spatial techniques are usually used to control dependence in one dimension at a time.

In regard to the petroleum industry, we need to test the existence of product-, technology-, segment-, and region-wide dependence. The puzzle that particularly needs to be tackled is how to aggregate spillovers, similarities, and competitions if the dependences in multiple dimensions are of importance. In other words, the major issue is how to take multi-dimensional dependences into consideration simultaneously when measuring the overall spillovers, similarities, and competitions in the global oil and gas industry.

Let us briefly turn our attention to productivity analysis. Suppose a deterministic production function in Cobb-Douglas form under constant returns to scale $Y = AL^{\alpha}K^{1-\alpha}$, where Y is output, L is labor, and K is capital. Single-factor productivities, such as labor productivity and capital productivity, can easily be calculated by Y/L and Y/K without considering any other input. On the contrary, many studies (Abbott 2006; Bernstein et al. 2006; Chen and Golley 2014; Du et al. 2013) use total-factor productivity as it considers both inputs jointly. Total-factor productivity in this case is computed by $Y/(L^{\alpha}K^{1-\alpha})$, which is the weighted average of labor and capital productivities when a logarithm is used. It is worth noting that the coefficient α is a weight that is used to combine the two single-factor productivities into the unique total-factor productivity.

Inspired by the idea that converts multiple single-factor productivities to one total-factor productivity, proper weights were needed to combine the results in our four single-dimensional spatial analyses. This chapter uses the model averaging method to assign a set of weights to the four candidates according to their ability to explain the data. Then this set of weights is employed to aggregate the spillovers, similarities, and competitions in different dimensions, called total-factor spillovers, similarities, and competitions in the spirit of total-factor productivity.

For each of the four dimensions (product-, technology-, segment-, and region-wide), data on output by division is used to build a spatial weights matrix that measures the cross-sectional dependence in that dimension. Rows and columns of the matrix reflect single-factor similarities and competitions. The single-factor spillovers are then derived by applying the matrix in a spatial production model. We then assigned weights to the four production models with different matrices based on their Akaike Information Criterion (AIC) and Bayesian Information Criterion (BIC)

---

[2]Spillover effects refer to the impacts that activities in one company can have on other companies. Moreover, this impact can be stronger among companies with greater dependence and interactions. As a result, how to characterize cross-sectional dependence is a precondition to estimate spillover effects in spatial econometrics.

scores. Finally, total-factor spillovers in the petroleum industry are the weighted average of product-, technology-, segment-, and region-wide spillovers. The same rule applies to total-factor similarities and competitions.

This chapter provides three central contributions to existing literature: (1) It combines multiple single-dimensional spatial analyses into a single multi-dimensional analysis to derive overall spillover effects in the spirit of total-factor productivity; (2) it uses spatial weights matrices to measure similarities and competitions among firms, which solves the two frequently asked questions (FAQs) in business, namely, "Who is on my list?" and "Am I on others' lists?" in the eyes of each firm; and (3) to our best knowledge, it is the first study to analyze the spillovers, similarities, and competitions in the petroleum industry.

Using a balanced panel data of 54 major petroleum firms during the period of 2009–2015, this chapter analyzes the cross-sectional dependence in the oil and gas industry from four perspectives. The two aforementioned FAQs for each of the 54 oil and gas companies are answered. The empirical results show that the dependences in all four of the dimensions have relevance, but region-wide dependence carries the most weight, and technology-wide dependence is the least important. The growth in one company discourages growth in other companies as significant negative spillover effects are observed. Moreover, segment-wide competition can reduce output through its negative impact on productivity, in addition to the negative spillover effects. According to these results, this chapter highlights the importance of human capital accumulation in the petroleum industry and the necessity for a dynamic differentiation strategy, particularly for countries with multiple national oil companies.

The remainder of the chapter is structured as follows. Section 2 reviews literature. Section 3 introduces the model. Section 4 gives data descriptions. Section 5 reports the empirical results. Section 6 draws a conclusion.

2 Literature Review

As mentioned by Wolf (2009), Eller et al. (2011), and Hartley and Medlock III (2013), very few studies to date have analyzed the production process of petroleum enterprises. Al-Obaidan and Scully (1992) estimate firm-level efficiency for 44 petroleum enterprises using deterministic and stochastic frontier analysis (SFA). Thompson et al. (1996) introduce a data envelopment analysis (DEA) on 14 major oil companies to estimate the production frontier of the U.S. oilfield market in the 1980s, where the input-output relation is assumed to be non-parametric. Managi et al. (2004) also use a DEA model to analyze a regional market. Different from Thompson et al. (1996), Managi et al. (2004) study the oil and gas industry offshore of the Gulf of Mexico and employ data that are at field level rather than at firm level. Managi et al. (2006) also focus on offshore Gulf of Mexico but instead use an SFA model to estimate changes in total-factor productivity from 1976 to 1995.

The second wave of studies pays more attention to the difference between National Oil Companies (NOCs) and privately-owned International Oil Companies (IOCs).[3] Hartley and Medlock (2008) establish a theoretical model of NOCs and attribute the NOCs' inefficiency, which is found in earlier studies (e.g., Al-Obaidan and Scully 1992), to political pressure that forces them to sell energy at below-market prices and hire more employees than IOCs. Wolf (2009) uses a multivariate production function to study large oil companies over the period of 1987–2006 and finds that NOCs are 20%–30% less efficient than IOCs. Eller et al. (2011) and Hartley and Medlock III (2013) estimate the production process of the global petroleum industry to predict firm-level efficiency, using both SFA and DEA. Contrary to Wolf (2009), they further decompose efficiency using a second-step regression so that the effect of ownership can be more accurately estimated after controlling for other variables.

A few studies have considered the segment-wide and region-wide characteristics of the oil and gas companies. Al-Obaidan and Scully (1992) calculate vertical integration ratio and multi-nationality ratio, which are then treated as controlled variables in the production function. Similarly, Ike and Lee (2014) also include vertical-integration and international operations factors in the second-step equation to estimate their impacts on firm-level efficiency, after the efficiencies of the 38 petroleum enterprises for 2003–2010 are derived from the DEA method. The estimation result shows that a higher degree of vertical integration tends to reduce efficiency but there is no significant difference between local and international firms. Sueyoshi and Goto (2012) point out that international oil companies need to satisfy the international standard, which is more restricted than the national standards and therefore may lead to the difference in efficiency between the two groups. Ohene-Asare et al. (2017) also use the DEA method to evaluate the efficiencies of 50 oil companies for 2001–2010, but further compare local and international companies by some nonparametric statistical significance tests, rather than the regression tests, as in Al-Obaidan and Scully (1992) and Ike and Lee (2014). They find that local oil firms are less efficient than multinational firms.

However, the production process is assumed to be independent across firms in all these studies. None of them considered the cross-sectional dependence or the interactions across firms. Gong (2018d) uses a varying coefficient model to estimate efficiency, where firms are only comparable with firms possessing the same vertical integration index so that companies are not fully independent. However, the interactions across firms are still not considered. Gong (2017) is the only study that considers segment-wide and region-wide dependence using spatial production models, but he focuses on oilfield service companies, rather than petroleum enterprises. Furthermore, the cross-sectional dependences both product-wide and technology-wide are ignored by Gong (2017).

----

[3]State-owned enterprises are very different from private firms and hence studied by many scholars (e.g., Xiao 2016; Zhu 2016; Qiang and Tuohan 2016; Rahman 2018; Moretz 2018). Petroleum industry is ideal to study the differences since many state-owned companies and private companies competed in the global market.

3 Model

3.1 Single-Factor Spillovers, Similarities, and Competitions

As mentioned above, there are four-dimensional interactions among oil and gas companies in the international petroleum industry: product-wide, technology-wide, segment-wide, and region-wide. This subsection establishes a model to measure single-factor spillovers, similarities and competitions among these firms. In other word, the interactions and dependences are analyzed in only one dimension at a time.

In order to capture the potential spillover effects between companies, this chapter introduces spatial econometrics, which is a typical tool that is used to deal with possible interactions in production functions that address cross-sectional dependence explicitly. This chapter starts with a linear production function without cross-sectional interactions:

$$y_{it} = F(X_{it}) = X_{it}\beta + \varepsilon_{it} \tag{1}$$

where y_{it} is the output of firm i at time t in logarithms, X_{it} is a vector of inputs and other regressors in logarithms. Therefore, Eq. (1) follows the classic Cobb-Douglas functional form. β is a vector of the corresponding coefficients of X_{it} to be estimated, and ε_{it} is an i.i.d. error term with zero mean and variance σ_ε^2.

Tobler (1979) claims that although everything is related to everything else, closer things are more related to one another. If the cross-sectional spillover effects exist but are overlooked or consciously ignored by using Eq. (1), we may fail to capture the true input-output relation in the production process. Therefore, many scholars (Artis et al. 2012; Detotto et al. 2014; Eberhardt and Teal 2013) use spatial techniques in productivity analysis to address cross-sectional dependence. This chapter introduces three most widely used spatial models into the petroleum production studies, including the Spatial Autoregressive Model (SAR) (Anselin 2013; Ord 1975), the Spatial Error Model (SEM) (Bivand 1984; Ripley 1981), and the General Spatial Model (GSM) (LeSage and Pace 2009).

Firstly, SAR captures the endogenous interaction effects, that is, the dependence between the response variable y_{it} of each company. In other words, the value of y_{it} in a firm not only depends on its own inputs, but is also affected by the values of y_{it} in other firms. This leads to the spillover effects between companies. Equations (2) and (3) provide the formation of the SAR model.

$$y_{it} = \rho \sum_{j=1}^{N} \omega_{ij} y_{jt} + X_{it}\beta + \varepsilon_{it}, \tag{2}$$

or in matrix notation

$$Y = \rho W Y + X\beta + E, \tag{3}$$

where ω_{ij} is the element of the spatial weights matrix W that measures the distance between firms i and j. This will be further discussed later on in this chapter. ρ is an unknown parameter to be estimated, which is an important index to measure spillover effects.

Secondly, SEM assumes that the dependence comes through the disturbance term ε_{it}, rather than the response variable y_{it}. In the equation, SEM follows the non-spatial production function in Eq. (1), but the disturbance term ε_{it} is assumed to be cross-sectional dependent

$$\varepsilon_{it} = \lambda \sum_{j=1}^{N} \omega_{ij} \varepsilon_{jt} + u_{it}, \tag{4}$$

or in matrix notation

$$E = \lambda W E + U, \tag{5}$$

where λ is a scalar spatial error parameter that measures the existence, sign, and magnitude of the spillover effects, u_{it} is an i.i.d. error term with zero mean and variance σ_u^2, and E is a spatially autocorrelated disturbance vector with constant variance and covariance terms specified by the aforementioned spatial weights matrix W and the unknown parameter λ.

Thirdly, GSM is a general form of SAR and SEM as it allows for endogenous interaction effects and the interaction effects among the error terms to occur simultaneously. In other words, the cross-sectional dependence may come through both the response variable y_{it} as in SAR and the disturbance term ε_{it} as in SEM. The formation of GSM is a combination of SAR in Eq. (2) and SEM in Eq. (4):

$$y_{it} = \rho \sum_{j=1}^{N} \omega_{ij} y_{jt} + X_{it}\beta + \varepsilon_{it}, \quad \varepsilon_{it} = \lambda \sum_{j=1}^{N} \omega_{ij} \varepsilon_{jt} + u_{it}, \tag{6}$$

or in matrix notation, the combination of Eqs. (3) and (5).

$$Y = \rho W Y + X\beta + E, \quad E = \lambda W E + U. \tag{7}$$

With the three candidate models, this chapter applies the widely used fit criteria, Akaike Information Criterion (AIC) and Bayesian Information Criterion (BIC), to select among SAR, SEM and GSM.

We will focus on the spatial weights matrix W, which measures the spatial dependence structure among all of the company pairs, and must be specified prior to the utilization of the aforementioned three spatial models. Inspired by Tobler (1979)'s first law of geography, the spatial weights matrix was most often used to measure the geographic distance in earlier studies of spatial economics. For example, a country may be more affected by its neighboring countries than those that are at a greater geographic distance. As another example, the spillover effects enjoyed by a company as a result of industrial clusters may diminish as it moves away from that area. More recently, the economic distance between two economic units has been introduced. For example, Han et al. (2016) use bilateral trade volume to measure the economic distance among OECD countries. The utilization of economic distance can explain the large dependence between large countries (such as China and the United States) in spite of the great geographic distance.

For competing companies in the same industry, the cross-sectional dependence depends heavily on the extent of competition, or the similarity of business among firms. Take the petroleum industry as an example: if two companies both produce crude oil rather than natural gas, the high similarity between them is likely to cause significant mutual influence as they directly compete with each other from demand of inputs to supply of outputs. In one of the most cited spatial literature, LeSage (2008) states that one might replace geographical distance with measures of similarity for the study of firms, and the context of similarity would be in production processes, resource or product markets where the firms operate, etc.

Besides the ratio in product portfolio between oil and gas, the similarities among petroleum enterprises can also be reflected in the business technology-wide, segment-wide, or region-wide. In the context of the Shale Revolution, new technologies, such as hydraulic fracturing and horizontal drilling, make it possible to produce unconventional oil and gas.[4] Because the technologies used to extract conventional and unconventional resources are significantly different, the competition between two firms that produce the same type of resource must be more severe since they need to compete for the same types of equipment[5] and reservoirs. Therefore, the ratio of products extracted by conventional and unconventional technologies can measure the similarity and competition across firms. Moreover, the petroleum industry can be divided into three segments, including upstream, refining and marketing, while the global market can be divided into sixteen regions in our dataset. On the one hand, companies face direct competition if they have footprints in the same segments, as the outputs target the same buyers. For example, upstream companies compete for exploration and production in the oilfield market. On the other hand, competition exists if two enterprises do business in the same region, as they have to compete for inputs, such as labor and capital, which have endowment constraints within a region. Segment-wide and region-wide information has been used to build spatial weights matrices in Gong (2017). It is worth noting that region-wide similarity can also be regarded as an indicator of geographic distance, as in a typical spatial production function.

Cosine similarity is introduced in this chapter to measure similarities among companies as it is a well-suited method for measuring the homogeneity of two portfolios

---

[4]Unconventional oil and gas is petroleum and gas extracted using techniques other than the conventional ones. According to International Energy Agency (IEA), unconventional oil includes extra-heavy oil, natural bitumen (oil sands), kerogen oil, liquids and gases arising from chemical processing of natural gas (GTL), coal-to-liquids (CTL) and additives, whereas unconventional gas refers mainly to gas extracted from coalbeds (coalbed methane) and from low-permeability sandstone (tight sands) and shale formations (gas shales).

[5]Many of these oil and gas companies rent equipment and services from oilfield service companies (Gong 2016).

(Getmansky et al. 2016) and has been used in many recent studies (e.g., in Hanley and Hoberg 2012; Sias et al. 2015). If we suppose an industry can be divided into N divisions under a single-dimensional segmentation, the business portfolios of firms i and j at time t can be denoted as $R_{it} = \left(r_{it}^1, r_{it}^2, \ldots, r_{it}^N\right)$ and $R_{jt} = \left(r_{jt}^1, r_{jt}^2, \ldots, r_{jt}^N\right)$, respectively, where r_{it}^n is the ratio of output from n-th division over the total output. Then the similarity between firms i and j at time t, defined as the cosine similarity, can be calculated using the formula in Eq. (8):

$$s_{ijt} = \frac{\sum_{n=1}^{N} r_{it}^n r_{jt}^n}{\sqrt{\sum_{n=1}^{N} \left(r_{it}^n\right)^2}\sqrt{\sum_{n=1}^{N} \left(r_{jt}^n\right)^2}}, \tag{8}$$

where s_{ijt} ranges from zero to unity. $s_{ijt} = 1$ demonstrates that firms i and j at time t have the perfectly same portfolio and achieve the highest similarity. $s_{ijt} = 0$ reflects that firms i and j at time t do business in completely different divisions and achieve the lowest similarity. A higher value of s_{ijt} indicates a greater proportion of two companies' business in the overlapping divisions. In other words, s_{ijt} measures the extent of direct competition between two companies. The detailed segmentations of the four dimensions to construct $R_{it} = \left(r_{it}^1, r_{it}^2, \ldots, r_{it}^N\right)$ are given in the data section.

Suppose S_t is an $N \times N$ matrix with s_{ijt} as the element in i-th row and j-th column and zero diagonals; then the i-th row of S_t presents the structure of the industry that firm i faces at time t, and the matrix S_t reflects the interactions of the entire industry at time t. Taking the average of all S_t across time and standardizing by row, this chapter generates a matrix that measures the relative dependence among all of the companies during the period, which is treated as the spatial weights matrix W.

The i-th row of W presents the similarity of each competitor with company i, which can also derive the ranking of all opponents in terms of similarity (such as top five similar companies) in the eyes of company i. In other words, each row shows the similarity and importance of the different opponents in the competitive landscape of a specific firm. In short, the i-th row of W answers the question "Who is on my list?" for company i in terms of similarity.

This chapter also aims to solve the issue of "Am I on others' lists?" In other words, we are interested in the level of competition versus company i in the eyes of all other companies. The aggregated similarity scores of company i on all other firms' lists reflect the overall competitions this company faces, which is the sum of the i-th column of W. Moreover, the average ranking of company i on all other opponents' competitive landscapes can also indicate the intensity of competition confronted by company i.

In summary, each row provides information detailing the similarities, and each column provides information concerning competitions after spatial weights matrix W is established. Given the data, the matching spatial production function F can be selected and estimated. It is worth noting that F is selected from the three spatial models including SAR, SEM, and GSM by AIC standard.

Let W_1, W_2, W_3, and W_4 be the spatial weights matrices that reflect product-, technology-, segment-, and region-wide dependence, respectively. Then F_1, F_2, F_3, and F_4 are the matching spatial production functions that measure the spillovers in each of the four dimensions.

3.2 Total-Factor Spillovers, Similarities, and Competitions

The previous subsection solves single-factor spillovers, similarities, and competitions across firms. In other words, it discusses how to calculate W_i and then uses W_i to derive F_i, one time for each i. This subsection, however, develops a method to take all four of the dimensions into consideration simultaneously to derive total-factor spillovers, similarities, and competitions.

In each of the four dimensions, we have a unique matrix W_i that measures the similarities and competitions between companies on that dimension, and a unique production function F_i, that is selected from SAR, SEM, and GSM and reflects the spillovers between companies on that dimension. $W_1 - W_4$ may all include some useful information concerning cross-sectional dependence, and $F_1 - F_4$ may all capture some of the characteristics of the interaction effects. Therefore, spillovers, similarities, and competitions cannot be fully considered if we only use a general model selection method to choose the "best" single-dimensional analysis among the four.

In order to consider all four of the dimensions in order to capture complete information and describe the true data generating process (DGP), we need to find weights for each dimension that play the same roles as the coefficients of inputs in a Cobb-Douglas production function when estimating total-factor productivity. The model averaging method assigns a weight to every candidate model according to its ability to explain the data when each candidate may specify the true DGP to some extent (Gong, 2018b). As a result, the weighted average estimation fits the data the best. It is worth noting that if the weight of a candidate is one, then the model averaging problem becomes a model selection problem. Thus, the model averaging procedure is a general method of model selection.

Buckland et al. (1997) proposed assigning weights based on an information criterion of the competing models. This chapter uses AIC as the information criterion to assign weights to different candidate models.

$$w_m^* = \exp(-0.5 * AIC_m) / \sum_{m=1}^{4} \exp(-0.5 * AIC_m), \qquad (9)$$

where w_m^* refers to the weight assigned to the m-th model (W_m, F_m). The Akaike Information Criterion (AIC) can be calculated by $AIC_m = 2k - 2\log(L_m)$, where k is the number of unknown parameters, and L_m is the maximized likelihood function for the m-th model. Equation (9) guarantees that the w_m^* sums to unity.

The weights w_m^* measure the ability of the spatial dependence in each dimension to explain the data. For example, a greater w_4^* implies that the geographic dependence across firms can specify the true production process to a greater extent, and therefore it is more important to consider. As a result, the geographic spillovers, similarities, and competitions are more crucial and account for a greater proportion when determining the overall spillovers, similarities, and competitions. On the one hand, the weights w_m^* can be used to derive the aggregated production function $F^* = \sum_{m=1}^{4} w_m^* F_m w_m^* F_m$ when all four dimensions are taken into consideration. Accordingly, the overall spillovers can be estimated. On the other hand, the overall similarities and competitions can be computed through the elements in each row and each column of $W^* = \sum_{m=1}^{4} w_m^* W_m$. Inspired by the total-factor productivity that considers multiple inputs, the overall spillovers, similarities, and competitions in the multi-dimensional analysis are called total-factor spillovers, total-factor similarities, and total-factor competitions, respectively.

3.3   Impact of Competition on Productivity

The previous subsection builds a model to measure the impact of competition on output through spillover effects. On the other hand, competition pressure may affect output directly through productivity. The overall competition that company i faces, as mentioned earlier, is the sum of the i-th column of the spatial weight matrix. Therefore, this chapter generates $comp_{it}^m = \sum_j s_{jit}^m$ where $comp_{it}^m$ is the competition that company i faces at time t in the m-th dimension and s_{jit}^m is the similarity in the m-th dimension between firms j and i at time t, defined as the cosine similarity in Eq. (8). Moreover, the overall competition that company i faces at time t is $comp_{it} = \sum_{m=1}^{4} w_m^* comp_{it}^m$. $comp_{it}$ is included in the production function to check if competition affects output directly.

$$y_{it} = \rho \sum_{j=1}^{N} \omega_{ij}^* y_{jt} + X_{it}\beta + \tau comp_{it} + \varepsilon_{it}, \quad \varepsilon_{it} = \lambda \sum_{j=1}^{N} \omega_{ij}^* \varepsilon_{jt} + u_{it}, \tag{10}$$

where ω_{ij}^* is the element of the spatial weights matrix W^* that measures the overall distance between firms i and j. This chapter further replaces $comp_{it}$ with $comp_{it}^1 - comp_{it}^4$ to identify the potential heterogeneous effects of competition in various dimensions. Moreover, the output shares by product, by technology, by segment and by region are also included in Eq. (10) to control the business portfolio of each company from different perspectives, which can deal with the potential omitted variable bias (Gong 2018c).

4 Data

This chapter follows Eller et al. (2011) and Hartley and Medlock III (2013) in the selection of data, inputs, and outputs. Revenue rather than production is chosen as the output in the production function because it is a typical way to aggregate multiple products to reflect their relative value. Moreover, the revenue figures are easier to achieve and confirm from different sources and can better capture the impact of subsidies for some NOCs (Hartley and Medlock 2008). There are four major inputs for petroleum enterprises: number of employees, oil reserves, gas reserves, and refining capacity. The adoption of physical inputs (reserves and refining capacity) rather than total assets that reflect accounting value helps to avoid distortion by inflation (Wolf 2009). Moreover, the production function also includes three other independent variables: oil price realization, gas price realization, and a dummy variable of NOCs. All these variables are available in the Energy Intelligence's "Top 100: Global NOC & IOC Rankings," which includes one hundred of the biggest oil companies in the world. This chapter drops any firms with missing information. A balanced panel data of 54 companies covering the time period of 2009–2015 remains, which is comparable with the sample of 78 oil firms during the period of 2002–2004 in Eller et al. (2011), and the sample of 61 oil companies from 2001 to 2009 in Hartley and Medlock III (2013), both of which used "Top 100: Global NOC & IOC Rankings" data in earlier years.

In terms of the four dimensional similarities and spillovers, this chapter generates the four spatial weights matrices as follows: (1) product-wide similarity W_1 is calculated based on $R_{it} = \left(r_{it}^1, r_{it}^2\right)$ in Eq. (8), where r_{it}^1 and r_{it}^2 are the output share of oil products (oil_{it}) and gas products (gas_{it}); (2) technology-wide similarity W_2 is calculated based on $R_{it} = \left(r_{it}^1, r_{it}^2\right)$ in Eq. (8), where r_{it}^1 and r_{it}^2 measure the output share of conventional products (con_{it}) and unconventional products ($uncon_{it}$); (3) segment-wide similarity W_3 is calculated based on $R_{it} = \left(r_{it}^1, r_{it}^2, r_{it}^3\right)$ in Eq. (8), where $r_{it}^1 - r_{it}^3$ account for the output share of upstream ($seg1_{it}$), refining ($seg2_{it}$), and marketing ($seg3_{it}$) segments, respectively; and (4) region-wide similarity W_4 is calculated based on $R_{it} = \left(r_{it}^1, r_{it}^2, \ldots, r_{it}^{16}\right)$ in Eq. (8), where $r_{it}^1 - r_{it}^{16}$ indicate the output share in each of the following sixteen regions ($reg1_{it} - reg16_{it}$): Oceania, Australia, East Asia, South East Asia, South Asia, Middle East, North Africa, East Africa, West Africa, South America, North America, Western Europe, Southern Europe, Eastern Europe, Russia, and Central Asia.

On the one hand, the data needed to calculate W_1 and W_3 are collected from Energy Intelligence's "*Top 100: Global NOC & IOC Rankings,*" as it reports firm-level oil production (in thousand barrels per day, '000 b/d) and gas production (in million cubic feet per day, MMcf/d), as well as oil and gas produced in the upstream segment, oil and gas refined in the refining segment, and oil and gas sold in the marking segment. On the other hand, Rystad Energy's UCube database reports firm-level conventional and unconventional productions as well as the output across the aforementioned sixteen regions for each company on an annual basis.

Table 1 Summary statistics

Variable	Notation	Unit	Mean	S.D.	Min	Max
Revenue	y	billion $	76.4	106.5	1.7	482.3
Number of employees	$Labor$	'000	77.5	221.5	1.0	1670
Oil reserves	$OilRsv$	MMbbl	9,102	38,675	0	300,878
Gas reserves	$GasRsv$	'000 Bcf	30.6	93.5	0	678.5
Refining capacity	$RefCap$	'000 b/d	864	1,314	0	6,271
Oil price realization	$OilPr$	$/BOE	71.3	19.8	4.4	111
Gas price realization	$GasPr$	$/Mcf	4.4	1.6	1.2	16.4
Share in oil	oil	–	0.57	0.23	0.00	1.00
Share in conventional	con	–	0.74	0.29	0.00	1.00
Share in refinery	$seg2$	–	0.58	0.32	0.06	1.00
Share in marketing	$seg3$	–	0.23	0.20	0.00	0.70

Table 1 lists summary statistics of the variables in the dataset that cover the 54 largest petroleum enterprises from 2009 to 2015. On average, these companies had 77,500 employees; 9,102 MMbbl (million barrels) oil reserves; 30,600 Bcf (billion cubic feet) gas reserves; and a refining capacity of 0.864 million barrels per day to generate an average revenue of 76.4 billion U.S. dollars during the sample period. Moreover, the average output share of oil products and gas products are 57% and 43%, respectively. The average output share of conventional and unconventional products are 74% and 26%, respectively. Finally, the output share of upstream, refinery, and marketing activities, on average, are 19%, 58% and 23%, respectively.

Table 2 reports the top three most similar companies in each of the four dimensions across firms during the sample period. The first two columns in Table 2 list the 54 petroleum enterprises and their corresponding ID numbers. The next three columns provide the ID numbers of the top three most similar companies for a specific company in terms of product-wide similarity W_1. The top three most similar companies for a specific company in the other three dimensions are then successively included. For each of the 54 companies, Table 2 provides their most important three competitors from different perspectives. The full rankings are reported in the supplementary file.

5   Results

5.1   Production Function and Spatial Dependences

We follow Eller et al. (2011) and Hartley and Medlock III (2013) to introduce constant returns to scale (CRS) restriction to the production function of the petroleum industry.

Table 2 Top three similar companies in the four dimensions

Firm name	ID	Product similarity			Technology similarity			Segment similarity			Region similarity		
		1st	2nd	3rd	1st	2nd	3rd	1st	2nd	3rd	1st	2nd	3rd
Anadarko	1	30	37	28	30	4	14	2	4	13	6	7	13
Apache	2	18	49	33	20	27	42	1	4	13	1	50	11
Bashneft	3	51	50	43	28	41	31	22	6	19	31	51	19
BHP Billiton	4	37	42	27	1	14	6	1	2	13	1	6	7
BP	5	11	10	47	52	44	36	52	44	39	18	32	44
Cenovus	6	40	23	2	1	26	4	3	22	19	7	13	15
Chesapeake	7	19	15	41	40	22	13	40	48	15	6	13	15
Chevron	8	10	21	26	18	9	38	25	18	21	20	29	5
CNOOC(*)	9	38	35	24	8	18	35	49	36	24	12	44	18
CNPC(*)	10	8	21	5	33	39	46	35	50	38	32	52	23
CNR	11	26	5	10	21	30	1	17	23	15	6	7	13
ConocoPhillips	12	52	49	34	35	20	2	26	27	46	50	11	20
Devon Energy	13	1	28	30	22	48	50	1	2	4	6	7	15
Ecopetrol(*)	14	24	38	25	1	4	21	43	16	25	35	38	46
EnCana	15	19	31	7	17	11	30	23	40	48	6	7	13
Eni	16	49	33	52	51	53	43	14	43	25	45	2	44
EOG	17	13	1	30	40	50	15	11	23	15	6	7	13
ExxonMobil	18	52	49	16	8	9	38	41	8	21	30	44	5
Gazprom(*)	19	31	15	48	28	31	41	24	3	36	3	31	51
Hess	20	32	46	21	2	12	27	29	38	10	12	29	30
Husky Energy	21	8	10	26	30	1	11	8	25	18	6	7	13
Imperial	22	25	50	14	13	50	40	3	37	42	6	7	13
Inpex	23	47	11	5	25	16	34	15	40	7	27	39	37
Kazmunaigas(*)	24	38	14	35	3	19	41	36	19	14	47	8	10
Lukoil	25	14	22	24	34	47	23	8	14	21	19	51	3
Marathon Oil	26	11	21	8	6	29	1	27	12	1	30	20	18
Mitsui	27	54	39	42	42	32	2	26	12	1	23	32	44
Mol	28	30	1	37	31	41	19	45	46	37	33	52	44
Murphy Oil	29	10	8	5	26	6	12	20	52	37	20	12	8
Noble Energy	30	28	1	37	1	21	11	1	2	4	11	1	6
Novatek	31	19	15	48	28	41	19	1	2	4	3	51	19
Occidental	32	20	46	21	45	36	44	15	48	23	5	18	10
OMV	33	16	18	44	39	47	34	42	37	22	53	28	25
ONGC	34	49	16	47	47	25	23	43	14	9	33	25	43
PDVSA(*)	35	38	24	45	9	12	8	10	50	19	14	38	46
PEMEX(*)	36	9	46	35	44	45	52	24	19	9	6	7	13
Pertamina(*)	37	1	30	42	24	3	19	42	52	22	41	39	23
Petrobras(*)	38	24	35	14	18	9	8	50	39	35	14	35	46

(continued)

Table 2 (continued)

Firm name	ID	Product similarity			Technology similarity			Segment similarity			Region similarity		
		1st	2nd	3rd	1st	2nd	3rd	1st	2nd	3rd	1st	2nd	3rd
PETRONAS(*)	39	28	30	27	33	34	47	38	50	52	37	41	23
Pioneer	40	6	23	2	17	50	22	7	15	48	6	7	13
PTT(*)	41	53	7	39	28	31	19	18	46	45	37	39	23
Repsol	42	37	39	44	32	27	45	33	37	22	46	38	14
Rosneft(*)	43	25	14	24	53	51	37	14	34	16	3	31	51
Shell	44	33	18	16	36	52	45	52	37	5	18	52	5
Sinopec(*)	45	35	46	38	36	44	32	28	46	22	16	5	26
SK Energy	46	32	45	35	39	33	23	28	45	41	38	14	35
Socar(*)	47	34	49	5	34	25	23	10	3	35	24	8	10
Southwestern	48	31	19	15	13	22	50	40	7	15	6	7	13
Statoil(*)	49	16	34	18	36	44	52	9	36	34	44	18	12
Suncor	50	22	25	3	22	40	17	38	35	10	11	6	7
Tatneft	51	3	50	43	16	53	43	35	47	10	3	31	19
Total	52	16	18	49	5	44	36	5	44	37	44	18	32
Wintershall	53	41	54	39	43	16	51	1	2	4	43	19	3
Woodside	54	27	39	53	5	52	44	1	2	4	4	27	44

The potential endogeneity of inputs in the production function is tested using the control function method proposed in Amsler et al. (2016) and Gong (2018a). The result indicates that all four inputs are exogenous. This chapter tests the cross-sectional dependence to see if it is necessary to use spatial techniques in the production function. Pesaran's CD test (Pesaran 2004) and the Breusch-Pagan LM test (Breusch and Pagan 1980) are utilized on the data, and both find the existence of spatial dependency, thereby recommending the use of spatial models. In a second step, the Moran's I index is significantly different from zero when each of four spatial weights matrices is employed, which further confirms the existence of spatial autocorrelation in all the four dimensions. In a third step, this chapter adopts the Hausman test for spatial panel data models (Millo and Piras 2012) to choose between a fixed effects model and random effects model when using each of the four spatial weights matrices. The Hausman test gives a p-value of 0.98, 0.30, 0.87, and 0.58, when $W_1 - W_4$ are respectively selected to control cross-sectional dependence. Therefore, the random effects model is preferred for all four of the single-dimensional spatial analyses.

The next thing to consider is the selection of the "best" model among SAR, SEM, and GSM when each spatial weights matrix is employed. Controlling the dependency by $W_1 - W_4$, the AIC values in GSM (401.49, 401.08, 402.55, and 403.31) are all smaller than the corresponding ones in SAR (404.44, 404.58, 405.59, and 406.44) and in SEM (402.88, 402.75, 403.30, and 403.32), which implies that GSM is preferred in all four of the single-dimensional studies. The BIC values also confirm that GSM (452.64, 452.23, 453.70, and 454.46) outperforms SAR (455.59, 455.74, 456.75, and 457.59) and SEM (454.03, 453.91, 454.45, and 454.48) in all four models. Table 3 reports the estimation results when $W_1 - W_4$ are respectively used as the spatial

Table 3 Estimation results

Determinants	Product dependence	Technology dependence	Segment dependence	Region dependence
log($Labor$)	0.680***	0.678***	0.684***	0.690***
	(0.036)	(0.036)	(0.036)	(0.035)
log($OilRsv$)	0.122***	0.129***	0.126***	0.111***
	(0.036)	(0.034)	(0.036)	(0.035)
log($GasRsv$)	0.111***	0.107***	0.111***	0.115***
	(0.035)	(0.034)	(0.035)	(0.035)
log($RefCap$)	0.087***	0.087***	0.079***	0.084***
	(0.016)	(0.017)	(0.016)	(0.015)
log($OilPr$)	0.127	0.149	0.142	0.132
	(0.098)	(0.098)	(0.098)	(0.097)
log($GasPr$)	−0.0003	0.021	0.006	0.019
	(0.083)	(0.081)	(0.082)	(0.079)
NOC	−0.860***	−0.916***	−0.919***	−0.843***
	(0.231)	(0.232)	(0.229)	(0.229)
Year dummies	Controlled	Controlled	Controlled	Controlled
Intercept	3.006***	2.646***	1.905***	0.737*
	(0.412)	(0.410)	(0.413)	(0.407)
ρ	−0.389***	−0.342***	−0.204***	−0.358*
	(0.036)	(0.028)	(0.025)	(0.212)
λ	6.357***	6.449***	6.230***	6.122***
	(1.393)	(1.427)	(1.353)	(1.355)
AIC	401.49	401.08	402.55	403.31
Weight w_m^*	0.167	0.136	0.283	0.414

Notes Significant at: * 10, ** 5 and *** 1 percent; Standard error in parentheses

weights matrices in GSM. The results are consistent across the four specifications, suggesting that our model is robust with respect to the controlled variables and the direct effects of the inputs.

Of the four input variables, the coefficients of the number of employees are the most significant both statistically and economically, indicating the importance and contribution of labor to oil and gas production. The difference in magnitude of the labor elasticity is small, ranging from 0.67 to 0.69, across specifications. The coefficients for the other three inputs, including oil reserves, gas reserves, and refining capacity, are all around 0.1 and highly significant statistically in all four of the spatial models. The effects of oil and gas realization on revenue are insignificant when time effect is controlled. Finally, the production realized by NOCs is much less than the production of IOCs when input quantities and energy prices are fixed, indicating the low efficiency of the former cohort even after the price subsidy is considered.

The model averaging weights obtained using AIC are also reported in Table 3, which are, respectively, 0.167, 0.136, 0.283, and 0.414 for the four specifications controlling different dimensional dependencies. Therefore, it is necessary to control the dependence in all four of the dimensions as each of them can explain the data to some extent as expected. Furthermore, the region-wide dependence is the most important, followed by the segment-wide dependence and then the product-wide dependence, whereas the technology-wide dependence weights the least. These weights are utilized to aggregate single-factor spillovers, similarities and competitions into total-factor spillovers, similarities and competitions in the petroleum industry.

5.2 Spillovers

Besides the direct effects of the inputs on output that are reported in Table 3, LeSage and Pace (2009) suggest reporting the average of the indirect effects for each input, which is a measure of the potential spillover effects. We calculate the average effects for the four spatial production models and then combine them to derive the aggregated direct, indirect, and total effects of the inputs, which can be seen in Table 4. The direct effects are calculated by averaging the diagonal elements of $(I - \rho W_m)^{-1}\beta$ in Eq. (7), and the indirect effects are computed by averaging the row sums of the off-diagonal elements of the same matrix. The latter measures the average level of the total-factor spillover effects. As a result, the total effects are the summation of the direct and indirect effects. For all four of these inputs, significantly negative indirect effects are observed, which implies that negative spillover effects exist between these petroleum enterprises in the sample period. In other words, the expansion of one company, on average, has a negative effect on the growth of their competitors.

Compared with the average level in Table 4, the total-factor spillover effects for each petroleum enterprise are of greater interest. We follow LeSage and Pace (2009) to compute the spillover effects from other firms to a specific firm and the spillover effects of a specific firm to all other firms for each petroleum enterprise in the sample. The spillover effects from increasing one unit of factor inputs on all other firms are very robust across companies at the average levels, which have already been reported in Table 4 (−0.086 for labor, −0.016 for oil reserves, −0.014 for gas

Table 4 Direct, indirect, and total effects of inputs

Variables	Direct effects		Indirect effects		Total effects	
	Estimate	S.E.	Estimate	S.E.	Estimate	S.E.
log($Labor$)	0.685***	(0.034)	−0.086**	(0.044)	0.599***	(0.056)
log($OilRsv$)	0.120***	(0.037)	−0.016***	(0.005)	0.104***	(0.037)
log($GasRsv$)	0.112***	(0.035)	−0.014***	(0.004)	0.098***	(0.036)
log($RefCap$)	0.083***	(0.016)	−0.010***	(0.003)	0.073***	(0.016)

Notes Significant at: * 10, ** 5 and *** 1 percent; Standard error in parentheses

reserves, and −0.01 for refining capacity). The spillover effects from increasing one unit of factor inputs in a specific company to all other companies, however, vary across companies, and these variations are reported in Table 5. The labor spillover effects of a company on other companies range from −0.094 to −0.062. The spillover effects of a company's oil and gas reserves on the cohort fall in the intervals (−0.018, −0.011) and (−0.016, −0.01), respectively. The spillover effects of one's refining capacity on all its competitors are between −0.02 and −0.012 across firms. To summarize, the spillover effects of a specific company on other companies have greater variation than those from all other companies to a specific company.

Table 5 The aggregated spillover effects to all other companies

Company Name	Indirect effects			
	Labor	Oil reserves	Gas reserves	Refining capacity
Anadarko	−0.088	−0.016	−0.014	−0.018
Apache	−0.089	−0.017	−0.014	−0.018
Bashneft	−0.086	−0.016	−0.014	−0.018
BHP Billiton	−0.088	−0.016	−0.014	−0.018
BP	−0.084	−0.016	−0.014	−0.017
Cenovus	−0.094	−0.017	−0.015	−0.019
Chesapeake	−0.072	−0.013	−0.012	−0.015
Chevron	−0.090	−0.017	−0.014	−0.018
CNOOC(*)	−0.084	−0.015	−0.013	−0.017
CNPC(*)	−0.091	−0.017	−0.015	−0.019
CNR	−0.089	−0.016	−0.014	−0.018
ConocoPhillips	−0.091	−0.017	−0.015	−0.019
Devon Energy	−0.077	−0.014	−0.012	−0.015
Ecopetrol(*)	−0.088	−0.016	−0.014	−0.018
EnCana	−0.077	−0.014	−0.012	−0.016
Eni	−0.091	−0.017	−0.015	−0.018
EOG	−0.082	−0.015	−0.013	−0.017
ExxonMobil	−0.092	−0.017	−0.015	−0.019
Gazprom(*)	−0.082	−0.015	−0.013	−0.017
Hess	−0.087	−0.016	−0.014	−0.018
Husky Energy	−0.092	−0.017	−0.015	−0.019
Imperial	−0.080	−0.015	−0.013	−0.016

(continued)

Table 5 (continued)

Company Name	Indirect effects			
	Labor	Oil reserves	Gas reserves	Refining capacity
Inpex	−0.088	−0.016	−0.014	−0.018
Kazmunaigas(*)	−0.087	−0.016	−0.014	−0.018
Lukoil	−0.085	−0.016	−0.014	−0.017
Marathon Oil	−0.090	−0.017	−0.014	−0.018
Mitsui	−0.087	−0.016	−0.014	−0.018
Mol	−0.092	−0.017	−0.015	−0.019
Murphy Oil	−0.088	−0.016	−0.014	−0.018
Noble Energy	−0.088	−0.016	−0.014	−0.018
Novatek	−0.077	−0.014	−0.012	−0.016
Occidental	−0.087	−0.016	−0.014	−0.018
OMV	−0.089	−0.016	−0.014	−0.018
ONGC	−0.084	−0.016	−0.014	−0.017
PDVSA(*)	−0.092	−0.017	−0.015	−0.019
PEMEX(*)	−0.087	−0.016	−0.014	−0.018
Pertamina(*)	−0.090	−0.017	−0.015	−0.018
Petrobras(*)	−0.089	−0.017	−0.014	−0.018
PETRONAS(*)	−0.088	−0.016	−0.014	−0.018
Pioneer	−0.082	−0.015	−0.013	−0.016
PTT(*)	−0.087	−0.016	−0.014	−0.018
Repsol	−0.091	−0.017	−0.015	−0.018
Rosneft(*)	−0.082	−0.015	−0.013	−0.017
Shell	−0.087	−0.016	−0.014	−0.018
Sinopec(*)	−0.090	−0.017	−0.015	−0.018
SK Energy	−0.090	−0.017	−0.014	−0.018
Socar(*)	−0.092	−0.017	−0.015	−0.019
Southwestern	−0.062	−0.011	−0.010	−0.013
Statoil(*)	−0.085	−0.016	−0.014	−0.017
Suncor	−0.078	−0.014	−0.013	−0.016
Tatneft	−0.075	−0.014	−0.012	−0.015
Total	−0.090	−0.017	−0.014	−0.018
Wintershall	−0.082	−0.015	−0.013	−0.017
Woodside	−0.087	−0.016	−0.014	−0.018

5.3 *Similarities*

In addition to the total-factor spillovers, this chapter also aims to estimate total-factor similarities among companies when the dependencies of all four dimensions are considered. Using the weights estimated in Table 3, the spatial weights matrix W^* can be computed; this reflects the total-factor similarities among all 54 of the petroleum enterprises. The off-diagonal elements of the $54*54$ spatial weights matrix W^* present the dependence of each pair of companies. More specifically, the element in i-th row and j-th column measures the relative similarity of company j among all of the competitors to company i as the matrix is standardized by row. Companies with more similarities have a greater proportion of their business that directly competes with each other, and therefore they face higher levels of competition. The i-th row of W^* measures the levels of competition versus each competitor for company i. In other words, it reports the importance and ranking of each competitor on company i's competitive landscape. Table 6 presents the top three most similar competitors each company faces in terms of overall dependence in the four dimensions. The full rankings for each of the four dimensions are listed in Appendix 1.

Table 6 Top three similar companies in total-factor similarity (who is on my list)

Company name	Total-factor similarity		
	1st	2nd	3rd
Anadarko	CNR	Devon Energy	Pioneer
Apache	Anadarko	CNR	ConocoPhillips
Bashneft	Lukoil	Rosneft(*)	Tatneft
BHP Billiton	Anadarko	CNR	Devon Energy
BP	ExxonMobil	Shell	Sinopec(*)
Cenovus	Husky Energy	PEMEX(*)	Imperial
Chesapeake	Southwestern	EnCana	Devon Energy
Chevron	Hess	Murphy Oil	ExxonMobil
CNOOC(*)	ConocoPhillips	Shell	ExxonMobil
CNPC(*)	Occidental	Total	Inpex
CNR	Pioneer	Anadarko	EOG
ConocoPhillips	Hess	Anadarko	CNR
Devon Energy	Pioneer	Chesapeake	EOG
Ecopetrol(*)	PDVSA(*)	Petrobras(*)	SK Energy
EnCana	Chesapeake	Southwestern	EOG
Eni	Sinopec(*)	Apache	Shell
EOG	Pioneer	Devon Energy	CNR

(continued)

Table 6 (continued)

Company name	Total-factor similarity		
	1st	2nd	3rd
ExxonMobil	Shell	BP	ConocoPhillips
Gazprom(*)	Novatek	Bashneft	Rosneft(*)
Hess	Murphy Oil	ConocoPhillips	Chevron
Husky Energy	Cenovus	Imperial	PEMEX(*)
Imperial	Suncor	Husky Energy	Cenovus
Inpex	Mitsui	Pertamina(*)	PETRONAS(*)
Kazmunaigas(*)	Socar(*)	Chevron	CNPC(*)
Lukoil	Rosneft(*)	Bashneft	Tatneft
Marathon Oil	Noble Energy	Hess	ExxonMobil
Mitsui	Inpex	Occidental	Shell
Mol	OMV	Shell	Total
Murphy Oil	Hess	ConocoPhillips	Chevron
Noble Energy	Anadarko	CNR	Devon Energy
Novatek	Gazprom(*)	Bashneft	Rosneft(*)
Occidental	ExxonMobil	BP	CNPC(*)
OMV	Wintershall	Mol	Bashneft
ONGC	OMV	Rosneft(*)	Lukoil
PDVSA(*)	Petrobras(*)	Ecopetrol(*)	SK Energy
PEMEX(*)	Cenovus	Husky Energy	Suncor
Pertamina(*)	PTT(*)	PETRONAS(*)	Inpex
Petrobras(*)	PDVSA(*)	Ecopetrol(*)	SK Energy
PETRONAS(*)	Pertamina(*)	PTT(*)	Inpex
Pioneer	Devon Energy	EOG	CNR
PTT(*)	Pertamina(*)	PETRONAS(*)	Inpex
Repsol	SK Energy	Petrobras(*)	PDVSA(*)
Rosneft(*)	Lukoil	Bashneft	Tatneft
Shell	Total	ExxonMobil	BP
Sinopec(*)	Eni	BP	Marathon Oil
SK Energy	Petrobras(*)	PDVSA(*)	Ecopetrol(*)
Socar(*)	Kazmunaigas(*)	Chevron	CNPC(*)
Southwestern	Chesapeake	EnCana	Devon Energy
Statoil(*)	Shell	ExxonMobil	Total
Suncor	Imperial	Husky Energy	Cenovus
Tatneft	Bashneft	Rosneft(*)	Lukoil
Total	Shell	ExxonMobil	BP
Wintershall	Novatek	Gazprom(*)	Bashneft
Woodside	BHP Billiton	Mitsui	Shell

An implication is that NOCs may compete more with IOCs, and different NOCs in a country may not directly compete with each other. For example, the top three similar companies for the three Chinese NOCs are all IOCs: (1) Eni, BP and Marathon Oil are the most similar companies to Sinopec; (2) ConocoPhillips, Shell and Exxon-Mobil have the closest portfolio to CNOOC; and (3) Occidental, Total, and Inpex are the top three most similar firms to CNPC. Moreover, these three Chinese NOCs have a differentiation strategy for development and allocate resources and activities differently. In 2015, Sinopec generated 9% of its revenue in upstream activities, 55% in refinery, and 36% in marketing. At the same time, CNPC generated 31% of its revenue in upstream activities, 45% in refinery, and 24% in marketing, whereas CNOOC generated 69% of its revenue in upstream activities, 15% in refinery, and 16% in marketing. It is clear that Sinopec focused more on the downstream activities, CNOOC concentrated more on the upstream activities, and CNPC was more balanced. As a result, these three NOCs faced less competition with each other.

5.4 Competitions

After answering the question of "Who is on my list?" we are also interested in the question "Am I on others' lists?" In other words, this chapter explores the levels of competition versus a specific company, i, in the eyes of all other companies. For each company, we accumulate its levels of competition (similarity values) on all other companies' lists. Moreover, the average ranking of a specific company on all other companies' competitive landscapes is also calculated. Table 7 reports the aggregated similarity and average ranking of each company from the perspectives of all of its competitors. A greater value of similarity and a higher ranking (smaller in numbers) of a company imply that it faces more intensive competition in the petroleum industry. The average levels of competition for various cohorts are also presented in Table 7.

Table 7 Overall levels of competition faced (Am I on others' lists)

Company name	Aggregated similarity	Company name	Average ranking
Shell	1.310	Shell	13.2
Chevron	1.306	ExxonMobil	13.6
BP	1.295	BP	15.4
ExxonMobil	1.236	ConocoPhillips	15.7
Sinopec(*)	1.228	Sinopec(*)	15.8
ConocoPhillips	1.200	Chevron	16.1
Repsol	1.189	Hess	18.3
Mitsui	1.171	Total	19.0

(continued)

Table 7 (continued)

Company name	Aggregated similarity	Company name	Average ranking
Hess	1.151	Cenovus	19.2
OMV	1.130	Repsol	19.6
Murphy Oil	1.115	Husky Energy	20.4
BHP Billiton	1.098	PEMEX(*)	21.0
Wintershall	1.096	Mitsui	21.3
Cenovus	1.083	Apache	22.1
Husky Energy	1.077	Murphy Oil	22.2
Total	1.074	Noble Energy	22.5
Noble Energy	1.069	Occidental	22.8
Apache	1.055	Anadarko	22.9
Anadarko	1.054	Eni	23.5
CNR	1.051	CNR	23.5
EOG	1.049	Marathon Oil	24.0
Occidental	1.049	EOG	24.6
PEMEX(*)	1.039	CNPC(*)	24.8
Inpex	1.024	BHP Billiton	25.4
Lukoil	1.016	Inpex	25.8
Marathon Oil	1.015	SK Energy	26.3
SK Energy	1.014	Suncor	26.3
Suncor	1.008	Imperial	26.9
Imperial	1.008	OMV	27.8
Pioneer	0.998	Wintershall	27.9
Bashneft	0.995	Pioneer	28.0
CNPC(*)	0.976	EnCana	29.1
EnCana	0.974	PETRONAS(*)	29.5
Gazprom(*)	0.970	Devon Energy	29.8
Devon Energy	0.968	Statoil(*)	30.1
Rosneft(*)	0.956	PDVSA(*)	31.0
Chesapeake	0.946	Chesapeake	31.5
Eni	0.935	CNOOC(*)	31.8
Novatek	0.927	Petrobras(*)	32.4
PETRONAS(*)	0.913	Pertamina(*)	32.6
Tatneft	0.901	Mol	33.0
Southwestern	0.892	Bashneft	33.8
PDVSA(*)	0.883	Southwestern	34.1

(continued)

Table 7 (continued)

Company name	Aggregated similarity	Company name	Average ranking
Petrobras(*)	0.872	Lukoil	34.2
Ecopetrol(*)	0.857	Ecopetrol(*)	34.4
Pertamina(*)	0.850	PTT(*)	34.4
PTT(*)	0.822	Socar(*)	34.7
Socar(*)	0.819	Gazprom(*)	36.6
Kazmunaigas(*)	0.798	Kazmunaigas(*)	36.6
Statoil(*)	0.790	Rosneft(*)	37.4
Mol	0.729	Novatek	37.5
CNOOC(*)	0.722	ONGC	37.5
ONGC	0.662	Woodside	39.1
Woodside	0.632	Tatneft	41.1
Small-size	**0.974**	**Small-size**	**29.1**
Mid-size	**0.980**	**Mid-size**	**27.3**
Large-size	**1.046**	**Large-size**	**24.6**
NOCs	**0.885**	**NOCs**	**31.3**
IOCs	**1.049**	**IOCs**	**25.2**

On the one hand, the six companies that faced the most intensive competitions are all petroleum giants including BP, Chevron, ConocoPhillips, ExxonMobil, Shell, and Sinopec; in terms of both aggregated similarity and average ranking, this implies the potential positive correlation between firm size and levels of competition faced. On the other hand, the national-owned companies (with the sign (*) in Table 7) are mainly allocated to the second half of the list, which indicates the possible lower levels of competition for NOCs. In order to verify the two hypotheses, we divide all firms according to their firm size and ownership respectively.

In terms of firm size, the 54 petroleum enterprises are divided into three groups based on their average revenue during the sample period, including 18 smaller firms (3–17 billion U.S. dollars), 18 mid-sized firms (17–70 billion U.S. dollars), and 18 larger firms (70–400 billion U.S. dollars). It is worth noting that the group of firms that generate smaller revenue is relatively small compared to the large-sized and mid-sized groups as all of them are still ranked among the top 100 petroleum enterprises with average annual revenue over 3 billion U.S. dollars. In Table 7, the large firm group achieved the greatest average similarity score (1.046) and the highest average ranking (24.6), followed by the group of mid-sized firms that obtained an average similarity score of 0.98 and an average ranking of 27.3, whereas the small firm cohort, on average, owned both the lowest similarity score (0.974) and ranking (29.1). Therefore, larger firms are, on average, ranked higher in their opponents' competitive landscapes and therefore faced more intensive competitions in the petroleum industry.

In terms of ownership, the 54 petroleum enterprises are classified into two categories: 16 National Oil Companies (NOCs) and 38 privately-owned International

Oil Companies (IOCs). Table 7 shows that the average similarity of the IOCs (1.049) is greater than that of the NOCs (0.885), and the average ranking of the IOCs (25.2) is higher than that of the NOCs (31.3); both confirm that the IOCs, on average, faced much more severe competitions than the NOCs. Many studies (Al-Obaidan and Scully 1992; Eller et al. 2011; Hartley and Medlock III 2013; Wolf 2009) find that IOCs are much more efficient than NOCs when it comes to production. Hartley and Medlock (2008) attribute lower efficiency in NOCs to their liability of some non-commercial objectives under political pressures, such as domestic consumer surplus and employment. According to our findings, the intensive competitions that IOCs faced may be a determinant that forces IOCs to improve productivity and become more competitive. On the contrary, lack of competitions and competitors may be another reason for the loss in efficiency for NOCs, in addition to non-commercial objectives. This hypothesis is tested in Table 8, which answers whether more competition leads to productivity growth when other things are equal. The first two columns in Table 8 test the overall effect of competition on productivity, whereas the next two columns test the effects of product-wide, technology-wide, segment-wide, and region-wide competition on productivity, respectively.

Table 8 Impact of competition intensity on productivity

Determinants	(1)	(2)	(3)	(4)
$comp_{it}$	−0.808*	−0.759*	–	–
	(0.478)	(0.440)	–	–
$comp_{it}^1$	–	–	0.248	−0.592
	–	–	(0.495)	(0.539)
$comp_{it}^2$	–	–	−0.053	−0.524
	–	–	(0.367)	(0.390)
$comp_{it}^3$	–	–	−0.921***	−0.855***
	–	–	(0.250)	(0.274)
$comp_{it}^4$	–	–	0.174	0.135
	–	–	(0.255)	(0.231)
oil_{it}	–	0.358	–	0.560*
	–	(0.302)	–	(0.324)
con_{it}	–	0.673**	–	0.789**
	–	(0.278)	–	(0.322)
$seg2_{it}$	–	0.017	–	0.164
	–	(0.163)	–	(0.170)
$seg3_{it}$	–	−0.034	–	0.224
	–	(0.246)	–	(0.264)
log($Labor$)	0.692***	0.712***	0.667***	0.672***
	(0.035)	(0.034)	(0.037)	(0.037)
log($OilRsv$)	0.121***	0.100***	0.120***	0.117***
	(0.035)	(0.038)	(0.035)	(0.039)

(continued)

Table 8 (continued)

Determinants	(1)	(2)	(3)	(4)
log($Gas Rsv$)	0.106***	0.126***	0.126***	0.148***
	(0.035)	(0.039)	(0.034)	(0.040)
log($Ref Cap$)	0.081***	0.062***	0.087***	0.063***
	(0.016)	(0.017)	(0.016)	(0.015)
log($Oil Pr$)	0.132	0.097	0.121	0.098
	(0.096)	(0.094)	(0.096)	(0.093)
log($Gas Pr$)	0.013	0.001	−0.004	−0.001
	(0.079)	(0.078)	(0.079)	(0.077)
NOC	−1.000***	−1.114***	−0.765***	−0.902***
	(0.250)	(0.197)	(0.248)	(0.205)
Year dummies	Controlled	Controlled	Controlled	Controlled
Region dummies	–	Controlled	–	Controlled
Intercept	1.918***	−2.177	1.389*	−2.948
	(0.642)	(2.538)	(0.811)	(2.342)

Notes Significant at: * 10, ** 5 and *** 1 percent; Standard error in parentheses. In this table, $comp_{it}$ is the overall competition that company i faces at time t, $comp_{it}^1 - comp_{it}^4$ are the product-wide, technology-wide, segment-wide and region-wide competition that company i faces at time t, respectively. oil_{it} is the output share of crude oil, con_{it} is the output share of conventional products, $seg2_{it}$ is the output share of refining and $seg3_{it}$ is the output share of marketing

The result of the first column in Table 8 implies that more severe overall competition experienced by a firm can reduce productivity and therefore lead to a lower level of output. Moreover, this estimation is robust when more controlled variables are included in Column 2. Therefore, the competition decreases output level through two channels, including the negative spillovers and productivity reduction. However, it is worth noting that the effect of overall competition is only at the 10% level of significance. Therefore, it is necessary to decompose the overall competition to find which dimension of competition can more significantly affect productivity. Column 3 in Table 8 replaces the overall level of competition with the competition levels in each of the four dimensions. Segment-wide competition intensity, $comp_{it}^3$, is the only one that generates a statistically and economically significant coefficient. Such a result shows that segment-wide competition is the major driver of productivity reduction, whereas competition in the other three dimensions has no significant effect on productivity. This conclusion is verified in the fourth column when controlled variables are included. Furthermore, oil production is more productive than gas production, whereas unconventional technologies are still not as productive as conventional ones.

6 Conclusion and Policy Implications

Dependence among petroleum enterprises exists in multiple dimensions. The utilization of spatial techniques on production function can estimate spillovers, similarities, and competitions in each dimension. Inspired by the idea of total-factor productivity, this chapter introduces a model averaging method that can be used to derive total-factor spillovers, similarities, and competitions in the oil and gas industry when all four dimensions are considered simultaneously. A balanced panel data of 54 major petroleum firms covering the years 2009–2015 are utilized in this multi-dimensional analysis.

We find that the dependences in all four dimensions matter, but region-wide dependence is the most important, and technology-wide dependence carries the least weight. Significant negative spillover effects can be observed, indicating that growth in one company discourages growth in other companies. For each firm, we provide the list of its top three similar opponents and calculate the overall levels of competition it faces, which solves the two frequently asked business questions: "Who is on my list?" and "Am I on others' lists?" Furthermore, IOCs and larger companies are confronted with more severe competitions that NOCs and smaller companies. Finally, segment-wide competition can decrease output level through two channels, including negative spillovers and productivity reduction, whereas the competition in the other three dimensions decreases output level only through negative spillover effects. Besides the solutions to business issues, this chapter also provides some policy implications and promising directions for future studies.

Firstly, the globalization of oil companies may cause severe competitions, as the contribution of geographical dependence to total-factor competitions is the highest among the four dimensions. Some countries, such as China, are lack of domestic resources. In order to meet domestic demand, these countries can either buy oil and gas from foreign countries and companies, or establish resource-seeking multinationals. For energy security reasons, these countries may prefer the latter option. However, the empirical finding of this chapter implies that NOCs may be unable and unwilling to enter the international market and become multinationals, since doing so will suffer from more competition and severer negative spillover effects. Therefore, how to motivate NOCs to go abroad is a big challenge for those governments and an important research question for future studies.

Secondly, a dynamic differentiation strategy for development should be encouraged to avoid intense competition, which reduces output through both negative spillovers and productivity reduction. For central governments who own multiple NOCs, a differentiation strategy for these NOCs is necessary. Such differentiation strategies have been clearly found in China, where Sinopec, CNOOC, and CNPC have very different business portfolios. Future studies can investigate how to design an optimal differentiation strategy.

Thirdly, many present-day conglomerates generate multiple products in different segments globally. Therefore, the interactions and competitions among firms are multi-dimensional in many industries. This chapter provides an approach to calculate overall levels of competition and estimate the overall spillover effects in those markets where multi-dimensional dependences exist. Future studies can apply this model to study other industries. Moreover, competitions also exist among cities or provinces in the same country (Hale 2016; Yang and Yan 2018) and across various countries (Huang et al. 2017), which can be studied using this model as well.

Appendix 1: Full Ranking in Different Dimentional Similarity

Tables 9, 10, 11, 12 and 13 report the full ranking in terms of the product-wide similarity for each of the 54 companies. Tables 14, 15, 16, 17 and 18 report the full ranking in terms of the technology-wide similarity for each of the 54 companies. Tables 19, 20, 21, 22 and 23 report the full ranking in terms of the segment-wide similarity for each of the 54 companies. Tables 24, 25, 26, 27 and 28 report the full ranking in terms of the region-wide similarity for each of the 54 companies. Tables 29, 30, 31, 32 and 33 report the full ranking in terms of the total-factor similarity for each of the 54 companies.

Table 9 Company ranking in product-wide similarity (1st to 11th)

Firm name	ID	1st	2nd	3rd	4th	5th	6th	7th	8th	9th	10th	11th
Anadarko	1	30	37	28	13	39	44	42	2	17	33	4
Apache	2	18	49	33	16	44	40	47	23	12	52	34
Bashneft	3	51	50	43	22	25	14	24	38	9	35	36
BHP Billiton	4	37	42	27	44	18	33	28	1	52	16	39
BP	5	11	10	47	8	26	23	34	12	21	49	29
Cenovus	6	40	23	2	11	47	26	5	49	34	16	12
Chesapeake	7	19	15	41	31	53	48	39	28	54	30	13
Chevron	8	10	21	26	11	5	20	32	29	46	47	45
CNOOC(*)	9	38	35	24	14	36	25	45	46	22	32	43
CNPC(*)	10	8	21	5	26	11	20	29	32	47	46	23
CNR	11	26	5	10	8	21	23	47	29	34	20	12
ConocoPhillips	12	52	49	34	16	18	47	33	5	44	2	23
Devon Energy	13	1	28	30	17	37	39	2	44	42	4	18
Ecopetrol(*)	14	24	38	25	9	35	22	43	45	36	46	50
EnCana	15	19	31	7	48	41	53	39	54	28	27	13
Eni	16	49	33	52	34	18	12	44	47	2	5	23
EOG	17	13	1	30	40	28	2	37	6	44	39	33
ExxonMobil	18	52	49	16	33	12	44	34	2	47	23	5
Gazprom(*)	19	31	15	48	7	41	53	54	39	27	28	30
Hess	20	32	46	21	8	36	45	26	35	10	9	38

(continued)

Table 9 (continued)

Firm name	ID	1st	2nd	3rd	4th	5th	6th	7th	8th	9th	10th	11th
Husky Energy	21	8	10	26	20	32	11	46	5	29	45	36
Imperial	22	25	50	14	9	38	24	43	35	3	36	51
Inpex	23	47	11	5	6	40	26	2	49	34	12	16
Kazmunaigas(*)	24	38	14	35	9	25	45	43	46	36	22	32
Lukoil	25	14	22	24	38	43	9	35	50	36	45	3
Marathon Oil	26	11	21	8	10	5	20	32	23	29	47	46
Mitsui	27	54	39	42	4	28	37	53	30	1	41	44
Mol	28	30	1	37	39	13	42	27	4	44	41	53
Murphy Oil	29	10	8	5	21	11	26	12	32	20	47	34
Noble Energy	30	28	1	37	39	42	13	44	27	4	33	17
Novatek	31	19	15	48	7	41	53	54	39	27	28	30
Occidental	32	20	46	21	36	45	35	8	9	10	26	38
OMV	33	16	18	44	52	49	34	12	47	2	23	37
ONGC	34	49	16	47	52	12	33	18	5	44	23	2
PDVSA(*)	35	38	24	45	9	46	14	36	25	32	43	20
PEMEX(*)	36	9	46	35	38	32	45	24	20	14	25	22
Pertamina(*)	37	1	30	42	28	44	39	4	33	18	13	27
Petrobras(*)	38	24	35	14	9	25	45	36	46	43	22	32
PETRONAS(*)	39	28	30	27	42	37	54	1	53	41	13	4
Pioneer	40	6	23	2	47	49	11	16	18	5	33	34
PTT(*)	41	53	7	39	19	31	28	54	30	15	27	1
Repsol	42	37	39	44	30	27	28	4	1	33	54	18
Rosneft(*)	43	25	14	24	38	22	35	9	3	51	50	45
Shell	44	33	18	16	52	49	37	34	2	12	42	47
Sinopec(*)	45	35	46	38	24	9	32	36	14	20	25	43
SK Energy	46	32	45	35	20	36	9	38	24	21	14	8
Socar(*)	47	34	49	5	16	12	23	52	18	33	11	2
Southwestern	48	31	19	15	7	41	53	54	39	27	28	30
Statoil(*)	49	16	34	18	52	12	47	33	44	2	5	23
Suncor	50	22	25	3	51	14	43	9	38	24	35	36
Tatneft	51	3	50	43	22	25	14	24	38	9	35	36
Total	52	16	18	49	12	34	33	44	47	2	5	23
Wintershall	53	41	54	39	27	7	28	31	19	30	15	42
Woodside	54	27	39	53	42	41	28	37	30	4	1	44

Table 10 Company ranking in product-wide similarity (12th to 22nd)

Firm name	ID	12th	13th	14th	15th	16th	17th	18th	19th	20th	21st	22nd
Anadarko	1	18	16	27	49	52	40	34	12	47	41	54
Apache	2	6	1	37	5	11	13	30	4	42	26	28
Bashneft	3	45	46	32	20	21	8	26	10	29	11	5
BHP Billiton	4	30	49	12	2	34	13	54	47	23	5	53
BP	5	16	52	18	33	20	32	2	6	40	44	46
Cenovus	6	33	18	10	8	21	52	44	29	20	32	17
Chesapeake	7	27	1	37	42	17	4	44	2	33	18	16
Chevron	8	23	36	34	12	35	9	49	38	24	52	16
CNOOC(*)	9	20	50	21	3	51	8	26	10	29	11	5
CNPC(*)	10	34	12	45	49	36	52	35	16	9	18	38
CNR	11	32	49	6	16	52	46	40	33	18	2	36
ConocoPhillips	12	29	11	10	8	26	21	40	4	6	37	42
Devon Energy	13	33	27	40	41	16	49	53	52	12	6	54
Ecopetrol(*)	14	32	20	3	51	21	8	26	10	11	29	5
EnCana	15	30	1	37	42	17	4	44	2	33	18	16
Eni	16	11	37	40	10	42	4	29	8	26	6	1
EOG	17	18	23	49	16	42	47	52	34	4	41	12
ExxonMobil	18	37	4	40	42	11	1	29	10	6	30	26
Gazprom(*)	19	13	1	42	37	17	4	44	33	2	18	16
Hess	20	24	11	14	5	29	25	22	43	23	47	50
Husky Energy	21	35	9	23	38	47	24	34	14	12	49	25
Imperial	22	45	46	32	20	21	8	26	10	11	29	5
Inpex	23	10	18	33	52	8	21	29	44	20	32	46
Kazmunaigas(*)	24	20	50	3	51	21	8	10	26	29	11	5
Lukoil	25	51	46	32	20	21	8	26	10	29	11	5
Marathon Oil	26	6	36	34	12	45	49	35	40	9	16	52
Mitsui	27	13	33	18	52	16	49	2	12	34	7	47
Mol	28	54	33	17	2	18	16	52	49	34	12	7
Murphy Oil	29	23	49	52	46	45	16	18	36	33	35	2
Noble Energy	30	2	41	18	16	53	54	49	52	34	12	40
Novatek	31	13	1	42	37	4	17	44	33	2	18	16
Occidental	32	24	14	11	29	25	5	22	43	50	23	47
OMV	33	5	42	4	11	40	1	30	6	10	29	26
ONGC	34	11	10	8	26	29	40	21	6	37	42	4
PDVSA(*)	35	22	21	50	8	10	3	26	51	29	11	5
PEMEX(*)	36	21	43	50	8	26	10	11	29	3	51	5
Pertamina(*)	37	2	16	52	49	34	12	54	47	17	40	23
Petrobras(*)	38	20	50	3	51	21	8	10	26	29	11	5
PETRONAS(*)	39	44	33	18	7	2	16	52	17	49	34	12
Pioneer	40	12	26	44	52	17	10	1	8	21	29	37

(continued)

Table 10 (continued)

Firm name	ID	12th	13th	14th	15th	16th	17th	18th	19th	20th	21st	22nd
PTT(*)	41	13	37	42	48	4	17	44	33	2	18	16
Repsol	42	16	52	49	2	34	13	12	47	53	41	23
Rosneft(*)	43	36	46	32	20	21	8	10	26	29	11	5
Shell	44	1	4	30	23	5	28	40	39	13	11	27
Sinopec(*)	45	21	22	8	10	26	50	29	11	3	51	5
SK Energy	46	25	10	26	43	22	11	29	50	5	3	51
Socar(*)	47	44	10	26	8	40	6	29	21	20	37	32
Southwestern	48	13	1	42	37	17	4	44	33	2	18	16
Statoil(*)	49	11	40	10	29	37	8	26	6	4	42	21
Suncor	50	45	46	32	20	21	8	26	10	11	29	5
Tatneft	51	45	46	32	20	21	8	26	10	29	11	5
Total	52	11	37	10	29	4	42	8	40	26	1	21
Wintershall	53	37	1	13	4	48	44	17	33	18	2	16
Woodside	54	13	7	31	19	33	18	52	16	15	49	2

Table 11 Company ranking in product-wide similarity (23rd to 33rd)

Firm name	ID	23rd	24th	25th	26th	27th	28th	29th	30th	31st	32nd	33rd
Anadarko	1	23	53	6	5	11	7	26	29	10	8	21
Apache	2	10	17	29	8	21	39	20	27	32	46	36
Bashneft	3	23	6	47	12	34	49	40	52	16	18	2
BHP Billiton	4	40	29	11	41	17	10	6	8	26	21	7
BP	5	45	36	35	9	38	24	14	37	4	42	25
Cenovus	6	1	46	37	36	13	30	45	9	35	28	42
Chesapeake	7	52	49	40	34	12	47	23	6	5	11	29
Chevron	8	6	14	18	33	40	25	2	22	43	44	50
CNOOC(*)	9	23	47	6	12	34	49	40	52	16	18	33
CNPC(*)	10	6	33	24	2	14	40	44	25	22	43	50
CNR	11	45	35	44	9	38	24	14	25	22	43	37
ConocoPhillips	12	20	1	32	30	46	28	45	13	36	27	39
Devon Energy	13	47	34	23	7	5	11	15	29	26	19	31
Ecopetrol(*)	14	23	47	6	34	12	49	40	52	16	18	33
EnCana	15	52	49	40	34	12	47	23	6	5	11	29
Eni	16	21	30	28	13	20	39	32	27	17	46	45
EOG	17	27	5	11	53	7	26	54	10	29	8	21
ExxonMobil	18	8	28	21	13	39	27	17	20	32	46	54
Gazprom(*)	19	52	49	34	12	40	47	23	6	5	11	29

(continued)

Table 11 (continued)

Firm name	ID	23rd	24th	25th	26th	27th	28th	29th	30th	31st	32nd	33rd
Hess	20	12	34	6	49	16	52	3	51	40	18	33
Husky Energy	21	6	16	52	22	43	18	40	33	2	50	44
Imperial	22	23	6	47	12	34	40	49	52	16	18	2
Inpex	23	37	1	36	45	4	42	35	30	17	9	13
Kazmunaigas(*)	24	23	47	12	34	6	49	52	16	40	18	33
Lukoil	25	23	47	6	12	34	49	40	52	16	18	33
Marathon Oil	26	38	24	2	18	33	14	25	22	44	43	50
Mitsui	27	31	17	19	15	23	40	5	29	11	6	48
Mol	28	40	47	23	6	5	19	31	15	11	29	10
Murphy Oil	29	9	6	38	40	24	44	14	25	22	43	4
Noble Energy	30	47	23	7	6	5	11	19	29	10	26	31
Novatek	31	52	49	34	12	40	47	23	6	5	11	29
Occidental	32	12	34	6	3	51	49	52	16	40	18	33
OMV	33	28	8	21	13	39	27	17	20	32	54	46
ONGC	34	1	20	32	30	46	28	45	13	36	39	35
PDVSA(*)	35	23	47	12	34	6	49	52	16	40	18	33
PEMEX(*)	36	23	47	6	12	34	49	40	52	16	18	2
Pertamina(*)	37	53	41	5	6	11	29	10	26	8	7	21
Petrobras(*)	38	23	47	6	12	34	49	52	16	40	18	33
PETRONAS(*)	39	19	47	31	15	40	23	5	6	11	48	29
Pioneer	40	13	30	20	32	28	42	4	46	36	39	45
PTT(*)	41	52	49	34	12	40	47	23	6	5	11	29
Repsol	42	5	40	17	11	6	29	10	8	26	7	21
Rosneft(*)	43	23	47	34	12	6	49	52	16	40	18	33
Shell	44	6	10	29	26	8	17	21	54	20	32	53
Sinopec(*)	45	23	47	12	34	49	6	52	16	18	40	33
SK Energy	46	23	47	34	12	6	49	52	16	40	18	33
Socar(*)	47	1	42	4	46	30	45	36	28	13	35	17
Southwestern	48	52	49	34	12	40	47	23	6	5	11	29
Statoil(*)	49	1	30	20	28	32	13	39	46	17	27	45
Suncor	50	23	6	47	12	34	40	49	52	16	18	2
Tatneft	51	23	6	47	12	34	40	49	52	16	18	2
Total	52	6	30	28	20	32	13	39	27	46	17	45
Wintershall	53	52	49	34	12	47	40	23	6	5	11	29
Woodside	54	34	12	48	17	47	23	40	5	6	11	29

Table 12 Company ranking in product-wide similarity (34th to 44th)

Firm name	ID	34th	35th	36th	37th	38th	39th	40th	41st	42nd	43rd	44th
Anadarko	1	15	19	31	20	32	46	36	45	48	35	9
Apache	2	54	45	35	9	41	53	38	24	14	25	22
Bashneft	3	33	44	4	37	42	1	17	30	13	28	27
BHP Billiton	4	20	32	46	45	19	31	36	15	35	9	38
BP	5	1	22	43	30	28	13	50	17	39	27	3
Cenovus	6	4	38	24	14	22	25	39	50	43	27	3
Chesapeake	7	10	26	8	21	20	32	46	45	36	35	9
Chevron	8	3	51	4	37	42	1	30	17	13	28	39
CNOOC(*)	9	2	44	4	37	42	1	17	30	13	28	39
CNPC(*)	10	4	37	42	3	51	1	30	28	13	17	39
CNR	11	4	1	42	50	30	17	13	28	3	51	39
ConocoPhillips	12	35	17	9	38	24	14	54	25	22	43	53
Devon Energy	13	10	8	21	20	32	48	46	36	45	35	9
Ecopetrol(*)	14	2	44	4	37	42	1	17	30	13	28	39
EnCana	15	10	26	8	21	20	32	46	45	36	35	9
Eni	16	36	54	35	9	38	24	14	53	41	25	22
EOG	17	15	19	20	32	31	46	36	45	35	9	48
ExxonMobil	18	45	36	35	9	53	38	24	41	14	25	22
Gazprom(*)	19	10	26	8	21	20	32	46	45	36	35	9
Hess	20	2	44	4	37	42	1	30	17	13	28	39
Husky Energy	21	3	51	4	37	42	1	30	17	13	28	39
Imperial	22	33	44	4	37	1	42	17	30	13	28	39
Inpex	23	38	28	24	14	25	22	39	43	27	50	54
Kazmunaigas(*)	24	2	44	4	37	42	1	17	30	13	28	27
Lukoil	25	2	44	4	37	42	1	17	30	13	28	39
Marathon Oil	26	37	3	51	4	1	42	30	17	13	28	39
Mitsui	27	10	8	26	21	20	32	46	45	36	35	9
Mol	28	26	8	21	48	20	32	46	36	45	35	9
Murphy Oil	29	37	50	42	1	3	51	30	13	28	17	27
Noble Energy	30	15	8	21	20	32	48	46	36	45	35	9
Novatek	31	10	26	8	21	20	32	46	45	36	35	9
Occidental	32	2	44	4	37	42	1	30	17	13	28	39
OMV	33	45	36	35	53	9	41	38	24	14	25	22
ONGC	34	27	17	9	38	24	14	54	25	22	43	53
PDVSA(*)	35	2	44	4	37	42	1	17	30	13	28	39
PEMEX(*)	36	33	44	4	37	1	42	17	30	13	28	39
Pertamina(*)	37	20	32	19	31	15	46	45	36	35	9	48
Petrobras(*)	38	2	44	4	37	42	1	17	30	13	28	39
PETRONAS(*)	39	10	26	8	21	20	32	46	45	36	35	9
Pioneer	40	9	35	38	24	14	27	22	25	43	50	54

(continued)

Table 12 (continued)

Firm name	ID	34th	35th	36th	37th	38th	39th	40th	41st	42nd	43rd	44th
PTT(*)	41	10	26	8	21	20	32	46	45	36	35	9
Repsol	42	19	31	20	32	15	46	45	36	35	48	9
Rosneft(*)	43	2	44	4	37	42	1	17	30	13	28	27
Shell	44	41	46	45	36	35	9	38	24	7	14	25
Sinopec(*)	45	2	44	4	37	42	1	30	17	13	28	27
SK Energy	46	2	44	4	37	42	1	30	17	13	28	39
Socar(*)	47	9	38	24	39	14	27	25	22	43	54	50
Southwestern	48	10	26	8	21	20	32	46	45	36	35	9
Statoil(*)	49	36	35	9	54	38	24	14	25	22	53	43
Suncor	50	33	44	4	37	1	17	42	30	13	28	39
Tatneft	51	33	44	4	37	42	1	17	30	13	28	27
Total	52	36	54	35	9	38	24	14	53	25	41	22
Wintershall	53	10	26	8	21	20	32	46	45	36	35	9
Woodside	54	10	8	26	21	20	32	46	45	36	35	9

Table 13 Company ranking in product-wide similarity (45th to 53rd)

Firm name	ID	45th	46th	47th	48th	49th	50th	51st	52nd	53rd
Anadarko	1	38	24	14	25	22	43	50	3	51
Apache	2	43	7	50	3	51	15	19	31	48
Bashneft	3	39	54	53	41	7	19	15	31	48
BHP Billiton	4	24	14	25	48	22	43	50	3	51
BP	5	51	54	53	41	7	19	31	15	48
Cenovus	6	51	54	41	53	7	15	19	31	48
Chesapeake	7	38	24	14	25	22	43	50	3	51
Chevron	8	27	54	53	41	7	19	31	15	48
CNOOC(*)	9	27	54	53	41	7	19	15	31	48
CNPC(*)	10	27	54	53	41	7	19	31	15	48
CNR	11	27	54	53	41	7	19	31	15	48
ConocoPhillips	12	50	41	3	51	7	19	31	15	48
Devon Energy	13	38	24	14	25	22	43	50	3	51
Ecopetrol(*)	14	27	54	53	41	7	19	15	31	48
EnCana	15	38	24	14	25	22	43	50	3	51
Eni	16	43	50	7	3	51	19	31	15	48
EOG	17	38	24	14	22	25	43	50	3	51
ExxonMobil	18	43	50	7	3	51	19	31	15	48
Gazprom(*)	19	38	24	14	25	22	43	50	3	51

(continued)

Table 13 (continued)

Firm name	ID	45th	46th	47th	48th	49th	50th	51st	52nd	53rd
Hess	20	27	54	53	41	7	19	15	31	48
Husky Energy	21	27	54	53	41	7	19	31	15	48
Imperial	22	27	54	53	41	7	19	15	31	48
Inpex	23	3	51	53	41	7	19	15	31	48
Kazmunaigas(*)	24	39	54	53	41	7	19	15	31	48
Lukoil	25	27	54	53	41	7	19	15	31	48
Marathon Oil	26	27	54	53	41	7	19	15	31	48
Mitsui	27	38	24	14	25	43	22	50	3	51
Mol	28	38	24	14	25	22	43	50	3	51
Murphy Oil	29	39	54	53	41	7	19	31	15	48
Noble Energy	30	38	24	14	25	22	43	50	3	51
Novatek	31	38	24	14	25	22	43	50	3	51
Occidental	32	27	54	53	41	7	19	15	31	48
OMV	33	43	7	50	3	51	19	31	15	48
ONGC	34	50	41	3	51	7	19	31	15	48
PDVSA(*)	35	27	54	53	41	7	19	15	31	48
PEMEX(*)	36	27	54	53	41	7	19	15	31	48
Pertamina(*)	37	38	24	14	25	22	43	50	3	51
Petrobras(*)	38	27	54	53	41	7	19	15	31	48
PETRONAS(*)	39	38	24	14	25	22	43	50	3	51
Pioneer	40	41	53	3	51	7	15	19	31	48
PTT(*)	41	38	24	14	25	22	43	50	3	51
Repsol	42	38	24	14	25	43	22	50	3	51
Rosneft(*)	43	39	54	53	41	7	19	31	15	48
Shell	44	22	43	19	31	15	50	3	51	48
Sinopec(*)	45	39	54	53	41	7	19	31	15	48
SK Energy	46	27	54	53	41	7	19	31	15	48
Socar(*)	47	53	41	3	51	7	19	31	15	48
Southwestern	48	38	24	14	25	22	43	50	3	51
Statoil(*)	49	41	50	3	51	7	19	31	15	48
Suncor	50	27	54	53	41	7	19	15	31	48
Tatneft	51	39	54	53	41	7	19	15	31	48
Total	52	43	50	3	7	51	19	31	15	48
Wintershall	53	38	24	14	25	22	43	50	3	51
Woodside	54	38	24	14	25	43	22	50	3	51

Table 14 Company ranking in technology-wide similarity (1st to 11th)

Firm name	ID	1st	2nd	3rd	4th	5th	6th	7th	8th	9th	10th	11th
Anadarko	1	30	4	14	21	6	11	26	29	15	12	35
Apache	2	20	27	42	32	18	8	12	45	36	9	49
Bashneft	3	28	41	31	19	24	37	43	53	51	16	25
BHP Billiton	4	1	14	6	30	21	11	26	29	15	12	35
BP	5	52	44	36	10	45	54	49	33	39	32	46
Cenovus	6	1	26	4	14	30	29	21	11	12	35	20
Chesapeake	7	40	22	13	50	17	48	15	11	30	21	1
Chevron	8	18	9	38	35	42	32	27	45	20	2	12
CNOOC(*)	9	8	18	35	38	42	12	32	45	20	27	2
CNPC(*)	10	33	39	46	5	47	34	23	25	52	16	53
CNR	11	21	30	1	14	15	4	6	17	26	50	40
ConocoPhillips	12	35	20	2	9	8	18	27	42	29	38	32
Devon Energy	13	22	48	50	40	7	17	15	11	21	30	1
Ecopetrol(*)	14	1	4	21	30	6	11	26	29	15	12	35
EnCana	15	17	11	30	40	21	50	1	14	22	4	7
Eni	16	51	53	43	25	23	34	37	47	24	3	19
EOG	17	40	50	15	22	13	7	11	48	30	21	1
ExxonMobil	18	8	9	38	42	35	32	27	45	2	20	36
Gazprom(*)	19	28	31	41	3	24	37	43	53	51	16	25
Hess	20	2	12	27	8	18	35	42	9	32	45	36
Husky Energy	21	30	1	11	14	4	6	26	15	29	17	12
Imperial	22	13	50	40	48	17	7	15	11	21	30	1
Inpex	23	25	16	34	47	53	51	43	33	37	39	24
Kazmunaigas(*)	24	3	19	41	28	31	37	43	53	51	16	25
Lukoil	25	34	47	23	16	53	43	51	37	33	39	24
Marathon Oil	26	6	29	1	4	30	14	21	12	11	20	35
Mitsui	27	42	32	2	45	36	49	44	52	18	20	5
Mol	28	31	41	19	3	24	37	43	53	51	16	25
Murphy Oil	29	26	6	12	20	35	4	1	2	14	9	8
Noble Energy	30	1	21	11	14	4	6	15	26	29	17	12
Novatek	31	28	41	19	3	24	37	43	53	51	16	25
Occidental	32	45	36	44	42	52	27	49	5	10	54	18
OMV	33	39	47	34	25	23	16	46	53	51	43	10
ONGC	34	47	25	23	33	16	53	43	51	39	37	24
PDVSA(*)	35	9	12	8	18	20	38	2	42	27	32	45
PEMEX(*)	36	44	45	52	32	5	49	10	42	54	27	39
Pertamina(*)	37	24	3	19	41	28	31	43	53	51	16	25
Petrobras(*)	38	18	9	8	45	42	32	44	54	36	52	5
PETRONAS(*)	39	33	34	47	23	25	46	16	51	53	43	10
Pioneer	40	17	50	22	13	7	15	48	11	30	21	1

(continued)

Table 14 (continued)

Firm name	ID	1st	2nd	3rd	4th	5th	6th	7th	8th	9th	10th	11th
PTT(*)	41	28	31	19	3	24	37	43	53	51	16	25
Repsol	42	32	27	45	36	44	49	18	52	2	8	5
Rosneft(*)	43	53	51	37	16	25	24	3	19	41	28	31
Shell	44	36	52	45	5	32	49	10	42	54	39	33
Sinopec(*)	45	36	44	32	52	5	42	49	27	10	54	39
SK Energy	46	39	33	23	34	47	25	16	51	10	53	43
Socar(*)	47	34	25	23	33	16	53	43	51	39	37	24
Southwestern	48	13	22	50	40	7	17	15	11	21	30	1
Statoil(*)	49	36	44	52	10	32	5	45	39	46	33	27
Suncor	50	22	40	17	13	7	48	15	11	21	30	1
Tatneft	51	16	53	43	37	25	23	24	3	19	41	28
Total	52	5	44	36	45	10	49	32	54	33	39	46
Wintershall	53	43	16	51	37	25	23	24	3	34	19	41
Woodside	54	5	52	44	36	10	45	33	32	39	46	47

Table 15 Company ranking in technology-wide similarity (12th to 22nd)

Firm name	ID	12th	13th	14th	15th	16th	17th	18th	19th	20th	21st	22nd
Anadarko	1	20	17	9	8	18	2	38	50	42	27	40
Apache	2	44	35	52	38	5	10	54	39	46	33	47
Bashneft	3	23	34	47	33	39	46	10	5	49	52	44
BHP Billiton	4	20	9	8	18	2	17	38	42	27	32	45
BP	5	47	34	23	25	16	53	51	43	37	42	24
Cenovus	6	15	9	8	2	18	38	27	42	32	45	36
Chesapeake	7	14	4	6	26	29	12	35	9	20	8	18
Chevron	8	36	44	52	5	54	49	10	39	33	46	47
CNOOC(*)	9	36	44	52	54	5	49	10	39	33	46	47
CNPC(*)	10	51	43	49	37	44	36	24	3	19	41	28
CNR	11	29	22	7	12	35	13	9	20	8	18	38
ConocoPhillips	12	45	36	44	49	52	5	54	10	39	46	6
Devon Energy	13	14	4	6	26	29	12	35	9	20	8	18
Ecopetrol(*)	14	9	20	8	18	17	38	2	42	27	32	50
EnCana	15	6	13	26	48	29	12	35	9	20	8	18
Eni	16	41	28	31	33	39	46	10	5	49	52	44
EOG	17	14	4	6	26	29	12	35	9	20	8	18
ExxonMobil	18	44	12	52	5	54	49	10	39	33	46	47
Gazprom(*)	19	23	34	47	33	39	46	10	5	49	52	44

(continued)

Table 15 (continued)

Firm name	ID	12th	13th	14th	15th	16th	17th	18th	19th	20th	21st	22nd
Hess	20	38	44	49	52	5	54	29	10	46	39	33
Husky Energy	21	35	50	40	9	20	8	18	2	38	22	42
Imperial	22	14	4	6	26	29	12	35	9	20	8	18
Inpex	23	3	19	41	28	31	46	10	5	49	52	44
Kazmunaigas(*)	24	23	34	47	33	39	46	10	5	49	52	44
Lukoil	25	3	19	41	28	31	46	10	5	52	49	44
Marathon Oil	26	2	9	8	18	15	27	42	38	32	45	36
Mitsui	27	8	10	9	38	54	39	46	33	47	34	23
Mol	28	23	34	47	33	39	46	10	5	49	52	44
Murphy Oil	29	18	27	30	42	21	38	32	45	36	44	49
Noble Energy	30	35	50	40	20	9	8	18	2	22	38	7
Novatek	31	23	34	47	33	39	46	10	5	49	52	44
Occidental	32	39	8	46	2	33	38	47	34	23	25	16
OMV	33	37	24	3	19	41	28	31	5	52	49	44
ONGC	34	3	19	41	28	31	46	10	5	52	49	44
PDVSA(*)	35	36	44	52	5	54	49	29	10	39	33	46
PEMEX(*)	36	33	46	47	34	23	25	16	51	53	43	37
Pertamina(*)	37	23	34	47	33	39	46	10	5	49	52	44
Petrobras(*)	38	35	27	49	10	2	20	33	12	39	46	47
PETRONAS(*)	39	37	24	3	19	41	28	31	5	49	52	44
Pioneer	40	14	4	6	26	29	12	35	9	20	8	18
PTT(*)	41	23	34	47	33	39	46	10	5	49	52	44
Repsol	42	54	38	10	9	20	46	39	33	47	34	23
Rosneft(*)	43	23	34	47	33	39	46	10	5	49	52	44
Shell	44	46	27	47	34	23	25	16	51	53	43	37
Sinopec(*)	45	33	46	18	38	47	34	8	23	25	16	51
SK Energy	46	37	24	3	19	41	28	31	5	49	52	44
Socar(*)	47	3	41	19	28	31	46	10	5	52	49	44
Southwestern	48	14	4	6	26	29	12	35	9	20	8	18
Statoil(*)	49	42	47	34	23	25	16	51	53	43	54	37
Suncor	50	14	4	6	26	29	12	35	9	20	8	18
Tatneft	51	31	34	47	39	33	46	10	5	49	52	44
Total	52	47	34	42	23	25	16	53	51	43	37	27
Wintershall	53	28	31	47	33	39	46	10	5	49	52	44
Woodside	54	34	49	23	25	16	53	42	43	51	37	24

Table 16 Company ranking in technology-wide similarity (23rd to 33rd)

Firm name	ID	23rd	24th	25th	26th	27th	28th	29th	30th	31st	32nd	33rd
Anadarko	1	32	45	36	44	52	54	49	5	22	10	7
Apache	2	34	23	25	16	51	53	43	37	24	3	19
Bashneft	3	54	36	45	32	42	27	38	18	2	8	9
BHP Billiton	4	36	44	50	40	52	54	49	5	10	46	39
BP	5	3	19	41	28	31	27	38	18	8	9	2
Cenovus	6	44	17	52	49	5	54	10	39	46	33	47
Chesapeake	7	38	2	42	27	32	45	36	44	54	52	5
Chevron	8	34	23	25	16	53	51	43	37	24	3	19
CNOOC(*)	9	34	23	25	16	53	51	43	37	24	3	19
CNPC(*)	10	31	54	45	32	42	27	38	18	8	2	9
CNR	11	2	48	42	27	32	45	36	44	52	54	5
ConocoPhillips	12	33	47	34	23	25	16	26	51	53	43	37
Devon Energy	13	38	2	42	27	32	45	36	44	54	52	5
Ecopetrol(*)	14	45	36	40	44	52	54	5	49	10	22	39
EnCana	15	2	38	42	27	32	45	36	44	52	54	5
Eni	16	36	54	45	32	42	27	38	18	2	8	9
EOG	17	38	2	42	27	32	45	36	44	52	54	5
ExxonMobil	18	34	23	25	16	53	51	43	37	24	3	19
Gazprom(*)	19	54	36	45	32	42	27	38	18	2	8	9
Hess	20	47	34	23	25	16	51	53	43	37	24	3
Husky Energy	21	27	32	45	7	13	36	44	52	54	5	49
Imperial	22	38	2	42	27	32	45	36	44	54	52	5
Inpex	23	54	36	45	32	42	27	38	18	2	8	9
Kazmunaigas(*)	24	54	36	45	32	42	27	38	18	2	8	9
Lukoil	25	54	36	45	32	42	27	38	18	2	8	9
Marathon Oil	26	44	49	52	5	54	10	17	39	46	33	47
Mitsui	27	25	16	35	51	12	53	43	37	24	3	19
Mol	28	54	36	45	32	42	27	38	18	2	8	9
Murphy Oil	29	52	11	5	54	10	46	39	33	47	34	23
Noble Energy	30	42	27	13	32	45	36	44	52	54	49	5
Novatek	31	54	36	45	32	42	27	38	18	2	8	9
Occidental	32	51	53	9	43	37	24	3	19	41	28	31
OMV	33	36	54	45	32	42	27	38	18	8	2	9
ONGC	34	54	36	45	32	42	27	38	18	8	2	9
PDVSA(*)	35	47	34	23	25	16	53	51	43	37	24	3
PEMEX(*)	36	18	38	24	3	19	41	28	31	8	2	9
Pertamina(*)	37	54	36	45	32	42	27	38	18	2	8	9
Petrobras(*)	38	34	23	25	16	53	51	43	37	24	3	41
PETRONAS(*)	39	36	54	45	32	42	27	38	18	2	8	9
Pioneer	40	38	2	42	27	32	45	36	44	52	54	5

(continued)

Table 16 (continued)

Firm name	ID	23rd	24th	25th	26th	27th	28th	29th	30th	31st	32nd	33rd
PTT(*)	41	54	36	45	32	42	27	38	18	2	8	9
Repsol	42	25	35	16	51	53	43	37	24	3	19	41
Rosneft(*)	43	54	36	45	32	42	27	38	18	2	8	9
Shell	44	24	38	3	19	41	28	31	18	8	2	9
Sinopec(*)	45	53	43	37	2	9	24	3	19	41	28	31
SK Energy	46	36	54	45	32	42	27	38	18	2	8	9
Socar(*)	47	54	36	45	32	42	27	38	18	8	2	9
Southwestern	48	38	2	42	27	32	45	36	44	54	52	5
Statoil(*)	49	24	3	19	41	28	31	2	18	38	8	9
Suncor	50	38	2	42	27	32	45	36	44	54	52	5
Tatneft	51	36	54	45	32	42	27	38	18	2	8	9
Total	52	24	3	19	41	28	31	38	18	8	2	9
Wintershall	53	54	36	45	32	42	27	38	18	2	8	9
Woodside	54	3	19	41	28	31	38	27	18	8	9	2

Table 17 Company ranking in technology-wide similarity (34th to 44th)

Firm name	ID	34th	35th	36th	37th	38th	39th	40th	41st	42nd	43rd	44th
Anadarko	1	39	46	33	47	34	13	23	25	16	51	53
Apache	2	41	28	31	29	6	26	4	14	1	21	30
Bashneft	3	20	35	12	29	6	26	14	4	1	21	30
BHP Billiton	4	33	22	47	34	23	25	16	51	53	43	37
BP	5	20	35	12	29	6	26	14	4	1	21	30
Cenovus	6	34	23	25	16	51	53	43	37	50	24	3
Chesapeake	7	49	10	39	33	46	47	34	23	25	16	53
Chevron	8	41	28	31	29	6	26	14	4	1	21	30
CNOOC(*)	9	41	28	31	29	6	14	26	4	1	21	30
CNPC(*)	10	20	35	12	29	6	26	14	4	1	21	30
CNR	11	49	10	39	33	46	47	34	23	25	16	53
ConocoPhillips	12	24	3	19	41	28	31	4	14	1	21	30
Devon Energy	13	49	10	33	39	46	47	34	23	25	16	53
Ecopetrol(*)	14	33	46	47	34	23	25	16	53	51	43	7
EnCana	15	49	10	39	33	46	47	34	23	25	16	53
Eni	16	20	35	12	29	6	26	14	4	1	21	30
EOG	17	49	10	39	33	46	47	34	23	25	16	53
ExxonMobil	18	41	28	31	29	6	26	14	4	1	21	30
Gazprom(*)	19	20	35	12	29	6	26	14	4	1	21	30

(continued)

Table 17 (continued)

Firm name	ID	34th	35th	36th	37th	38th	39th	40th	41st	42nd	43rd	44th
Hess	20	19	41	28	31	6	26	4	14	1	21	30
Husky Energy	21	10	39	33	46	47	34	23	25	16	48	53
Imperial	22	49	10	33	39	46	47	34	23	25	16	53
Inpex	23	20	35	12	29	6	26	14	4	1	21	30
Kazmunaigas(*)	24	20	35	12	29	6	26	14	4	1	21	30
Lukoil	25	20	35	12	29	6	26	14	4	1	21	30
Marathon Oil	26	34	23	25	16	51	53	43	37	24	3	19
Mitsui	27	41	28	31	29	6	26	4	14	1	21	30
Mol	28	20	35	12	29	6	26	14	4	1	21	30
Murphy Oil	29	25	16	51	53	43	37	24	3	19	41	28
Noble Energy	30	10	39	46	33	48	47	34	23	25	16	51
Novatek	31	20	35	12	29	6	26	14	4	1	21	30
Occidental	32	20	35	12	29	6	26	14	4	1	21	30
OMV	33	20	35	12	29	6	26	14	4	1	21	30
ONGC	34	20	35	12	29	6	26	14	4	1	21	30
PDVSA(*)	35	19	41	28	31	6	14	26	4	1	21	30
PEMEX(*)	36	20	35	12	29	6	26	14	4	1	21	30
Pertamina(*)	37	20	35	12	29	6	26	14	4	1	21	30
Petrobras(*)	38	19	28	31	29	6	14	4	26	1	21	30
PETRONAS(*)	39	20	35	12	29	6	26	14	4	1	21	30
Pioneer	40	49	10	39	33	46	47	34	23	25	16	53
PTT(*)	41	20	35	12	29	6	26	14	4	1	21	30
Repsol	42	28	31	12	29	6	26	14	4	1	21	30
Rosneft(*)	43	20	35	12	29	6	26	14	4	1	21	30
Shell	44	20	35	12	29	6	26	14	4	1	21	30
Sinopec(*)	45	20	35	12	29	6	26	14	4	1	21	30
SK Energy	46	20	35	12	29	6	26	14	4	1	21	30
Socar(*)	47	20	35	12	29	6	26	14	4	1	21	30
Southwestern	48	49	10	33	39	46	47	34	23	25	16	53
Statoil(*)	49	20	35	12	29	6	26	14	4	1	21	30
Suncor	50	49	10	33	39	46	47	34	23	25	16	53
Tatneft	51	20	35	12	29	6	26	14	4	1	21	30
Total	52	20	35	12	29	6	26	14	4	1	21	30
Wintershall	53	20	35	12	29	6	26	14	4	1	21	30
Woodside	54	20	35	12	29	6	26	14	4	1	21	30

Table 18 Company ranking in technology-wide similarity (45th to 53rd)

Firm name	ID	45th	46th	47th	48th	49th	50th	51st	52nd	53rd
Anadarko	1	43	37	24	3	19	41	28	31	48
Apache	2	11	15	17	50	40	22	7	13	48
Bashneft	3	11	15	17	50	40	22	7	13	48
BHP Billiton	4	7	24	3	19	41	28	31	13	48
BP	5	11	15	17	50	40	22	7	13	48
Cenovus	6	40	19	41	28	31	22	7	13	48
Chesapeake	7	51	43	37	24	3	19	41	28	31
Chevron	8	11	15	17	50	40	22	7	13	48
CNOOC(*)	9	11	15	17	50	40	22	7	13	48
CNPC(*)	10	11	15	17	50	40	22	7	13	48
CNR	11	51	43	37	24	3	19	41	28	31
ConocoPhillips	12	11	15	17	50	40	22	7	13	48
Devon Energy	13	51	43	37	24	3	19	41	28	31
Ecopetrol(*)	14	37	24	3	19	41	28	31	13	48
EnCana	15	51	43	37	24	3	19	41	28	31
Eni	16	11	15	17	50	40	22	7	13	48
EOG	17	51	43	37	24	3	19	41	28	31
ExxonMobil	18	11	15	17	50	40	22	7	13	48
Gazprom(*)	19	11	15	17	50	40	22	7	13	48
Hess	20	11	15	17	50	40	22	7	13	48
Husky Energy	21	51	43	37	24	3	19	41	28	31
Imperial	22	51	43	37	24	3	19	41	28	31
Inpex	23	11	15	17	50	40	22	7	13	48
Kazmunaigas(*)	24	11	15	17	50	40	22	7	13	48
Lukoil	25	11	15	17	50	40	22	7	13	48
Marathon Oil	26	41	28	31	40	50	22	7	13	48
Mitsui	27	11	15	17	50	40	22	7	13	48
Mol	28	11	15	17	50	40	22	7	13	48
Murphy Oil	29	31	15	17	50	40	22	7	13	48
Noble Energy	30	53	43	37	24	3	19	41	28	31
Novatek	31	11	15	17	50	40	22	7	13	31
Occidental	32	11	15	17	50	40	22	7	13	48
OMV	33	11	15	17	50	40	22	7	13	48
ONGC	34	11	15	17	50	40	22	7	13	48
PDVSA(*)	35	11	15	17	50	40	22	7	13	48
PEMEX(*)	36	11	15	17	50	40	22	7	13	48
Pertamina(*)	37	11	15	17	50	40	22	7	13	48
Petrobras(*)	38	11	15	17	50	40	22	7	13	48
PETRONAS(*)	39	11	15	17	50	40	22	7	13	48
Pioneer	40	51	43	37	24	3	19	41	28	31

(continued)

Table 18 (continued)

Firm name	ID	45th	46th	47th	48th	49th	50th	51st	52nd	53rd
PTT(*)	41	11	15	17	50	40	22	7	13	48
Repsol	42	11	15	17	50	40	22	7	13	48
Rosneft(*)	43	11	15	17	50	40	22	7	13	48
Shell	44	11	15	17	50	40	22	7	13	48
Sinopec(*)	45	11	15	17	50	40	22	7	13	48
SK Energy	46	11	15	17	50	40	22	7	13	48
Socar(*)	47	11	15	17	50	40	22	7	13	48
Southwestern	48	51	43	37	24	3	19	41	28	31
Statoil(*)	49	11	15	17	50	40	22	7	13	48
Suncor	50	51	43	37	24	3	19	41	28	31
Tatneft	51	11	15	17	50	40	22	7	13	48
Total	52	11	15	17	50	40	22	7	13	48
Wintershall	53	11	15	17	50	40	22	7	13	48
Woodside	54	11	15	17	50	40	22	7	13	48

Table 19 Company ranking in segment-wide similarity (1st to 11th)

Firm name	ID	1st	2nd	3rd	4th	5th	6th	7th	8th	9th	10th	11th
Anadarko	1	2	4	13	30	31	53	54	7	11	40	48
Apache	2	1	4	13	30	31	53	54	7	11	40	48
Bashneft	3	22	6	19	35	45	21	10	38	50	42	24
BHP Billiton	4	1	2	13	30	31	53	54	7	11	40	48
BP	5	52	44	39	37	22	38	33	42	8	19	50
Cenovus	6	3	22	19	21	35	38	10	24	50	39	45
Chesapeake	7	40	48	15	23	32	11	17	1	2	4	13
Chevron	8	25	18	21	44	16	39	14	41	22	52	19
CNOOC(*)	9	49	36	24	34	43	14	35	19	16	50	39
CNPC(*)	10	35	50	38	47	3	19	6	22	42	39	33
CNR	11	17	23	15	40	7	48	32	1	2	4	13
ConocoPhillips	12	26	27	46	45	28	18	1	2	4	13	30
Devon Energy	13	1	2	4	30	31	53	54	7	11	40	48
Ecopetrol(*)	14	43	16	25	24	34	21	36	8	19	35	9
EnCana	15	23	40	48	7	32	11	17	1	2	4	13
Eni	16	14	43	25	24	21	8	19	36	35	34	3
EOG	17	11	23	15	40	7	32	48	1	2	4	13
ExxonMobil	18	41	8	21	46	44	28	25	22	45	37	3
Gazprom(*)	19	24	3	36	35	6	22	39	38	50	21	16

(continued)

Table 19 (continued)

Firm name	ID	1st	2nd	3rd	4th	5th	6th	7th	8th	9th	10th	11th
Hess	20	29	38	10	39	22	3	50	35	42	19	52
Husky Energy	21	8	25	18	16	14	6	3	19	24	41	22
Imperial	22	3	37	42	6	52	33	19	28	38	45	39
Inpex	23	15	40	7	32	48	11	17	1	2	4	13
Kazmunaigas(*)	24	36	19	14	16	43	35	9	21	25	3	6
Lukoil	25	8	14	21	16	18	39	43	24	19	44	36
Marathon Oil	26	27	12	1	2	4	13	30	31	53	54	46
Mitsui	27	26	12	1	2	4	13	30	31	53	54	7
Mol	28	45	46	37	22	18	41	42	44	3	52	33
Murphy Oil	29	20	52	37	39	44	38	22	5	42	33	28
Noble Energy	30	1	2	4	13	31	53	54	7	11	40	48
Novatek	31	1	2	4	13	30	53	54	7	11	40	48
Occidental	32	15	48	23	40	7	11	17	1	2	4	13
OMV	33	42	37	22	38	52	50	3	44	39	46	5
ONGC	34	43	14	9	16	24	49	36	25	21	35	19
PDVSA(*)	35	10	50	19	38	3	36	24	39	6	22	16
PEMEX(*)	36	24	19	9	35	14	43	16	39	49	50	6
Pertamina(*)	37	42	52	22	44	28	33	46	45	5	18	3
Petrobras(*)	38	50	39	35	10	22	33	19	3	42	6	52
PETRONAS(*)	39	38	50	52	5	19	22	35	25	8	44	36
Pioneer	40	7	15	48	23	32	11	17	1	2	4	13
PTT(*)	41	18	46	45	28	21	8	22	44	37	3	42
Repsol	42	33	37	22	46	28	52	3	38	45	18	44
Rosneft(*)	43	14	34	16	24	36	25	9	21	49	19	35
Shell	44	52	37	5	18	8	22	39	28	33	42	41
Sinopec(*)	45	28	46	22	3	41	18	37	42	6	52	19
SK Energy	46	28	45	41	42	37	18	22	3	33	44	52
Socar(*)	47	10	3	35	50	6	22	42	38	19	33	17
Southwestern	48	40	7	15	32	23	11	17	1	2	4	13
Statoil(*)	49	9	36	34	43	24	35	14	16	19	50	10
Suncor	50	38	35	10	39	19	3	22	33	6	36	42
Tatneft	51	35	47	10	50	3	9	6	49	24	19	38
Total	52	5	44	37	22	39	33	42	38	28	3	18
Wintershall	53	1	2	4	13	30	31	54	7	11	40	48
Woodside	54	1	2	4	13	30	31	53	7	11	40	48

Table 20 Company ranking in segment-wide similarity (12th to 22nd)

Firm name	ID	12th	13th	14th	15th	16th	17th	18th	19th	20th	21st	22nd
Anadarko	1	15	23	17	32	27	26	12	45	46	28	41
Apache	2	15	23	17	32	27	26	12	45	46	28	41
Bashneft	3	28	18	39	37	46	33	52	47	8	41	36
BHP Billiton	4	15	23	17	32	27	26	12	45	46	28	41
BP	5	29	25	3	6	18	28	36	35	24	45	41
Cenovus	6	42	36	52	33	37	18	8	47	28	25	41
Chesapeake	7	30	31	53	54	27	45	26	46	12	28	3
Chevron	8	3	38	24	37	6	5	43	35	28	50	36
CNOOC(*)	9	38	10	25	6	3	51	21	8	22	5	52
CNPC(*)	10	24	36	21	16	14	25	20	8	37	43	49
CNR	11	30	31	53	54	27	26	45	46	47	12	28
ConocoPhillips	12	31	53	54	21	7	11	40	3	41	22	20
Devon Energy	13	15	23	17	32	27	26	12	45	46	28	41
Ecopetrol(*)	14	39	49	50	3	6	18	38	10	22	41	44
EnCana	15	30	31	53	54	45	27	26	46	28	12	47
Eni	16	18	39	50	10	6	9	38	22	49	41	44
EOG	17	30	31	53	54	27	26	45	47	46	12	28
ExxonMobil	18	42	52	33	6	19	39	16	38	14	5	12
Gazprom(*)	19	10	25	14	8	52	43	45	18	9	37	5
Hess	20	37	6	28	12	33	45	46	44	18	8	36
Husky Energy	21	43	35	45	39	36	38	10	50	44	46	28
Imperial	22	18	44	46	35	50	10	8	41	5	21	25
Inpex	23	30	31	53	54	45	27	26	46	28	12	47
Kazmunaigas(*)	24	39	34	49	50	8	22	38	10	52	18	45
Lukoil	25	3	22	38	35	50	41	52	6	5	34	10
Marathon Oil	26	7	45	11	40	28	48	15	23	17	32	18
Mitsui	27	11	40	48	15	23	17	45	46	32	28	18
Mol	28	6	8	19	21	12	5	26	29	39	38	25
Murphy Oil	29	3	18	8	19	46	50	45	6	25	35	10
Noble Energy	30	15	23	17	32	27	26	12	45	46	28	41
Novatek	31	15	23	17	32	27	26	12	45	46	28	41
Occidental	32	30	31	53	54	45	27	26	28	46	47	12
OMV	33	6	18	28	10	41	45	35	8	19	47	29
ONGC	34	8	50	39	10	6	3	38	51	18	22	47
PDVSA(*)	35	14	47	21	25	43	9	49	42	8	33	52
PEMEX(*)	36	3	25	38	34	21	10	22	8	52	5	44
Pertamina(*)	37	41	39	38	6	8	29	19	50	21	25	35
Petrobras(*)	38	5	37	8	36	25	24	44	29	21	47	18
PETRONAS(*)	39	3	24	6	33	37	10	42	21	14	18	16
Pioneer	40	30	31	53	54	45	27	26	46	28	12	3

(continued)

Table 20 (continued)

Firm name	ID	12th	13th	14th	15th	16th	17th	18th	19th	20th	21st	22nd
PTT(*)	41	25	33	52	6	19	39	16	38	5	12	35
Repsol	42	6	50	41	10	39	5	35	47	19	8	29
Rosneft(*)	43	8	39	50	10	3	6	38	18	22	41	52
Shell	44	25	46	45	3	38	29	19	21	6	50	35
Sinopec(*)	45	21	44	33	12	7	8	40	48	15	26	23
SK Energy	46	12	6	21	8	26	19	11	27	29	17	38
Socar(*)	47	45	46	11	51	21	24	23	37	15	28	39
Southwestern	48	30	31	53	54	45	27	26	46	28	12	3
Statoil(*)	49	39	38	25	6	3	51	21	47	8	22	20
Suncor	50	24	47	25	52	8	16	14	21	5	9	37
Tatneft	51	36	14	43	22	16	34	21	39	33	25	42
Total	52	8	19	6	45	29	25	50	46	41	35	21
Wintershall	53	15	23	17	32	27	26	12	45	46	28	41
Woodside	54	15	23	17	32	27	26	12	45	46	28	41

Table 21 Company ranking in segment-wide similarity (23rd to 33rd)

Firm name	ID	23rd	24th	25th	26th	27th	28th	29th	30th	31st	32nd	33rd
Anadarko	1	3	47	18	21	22	6	42	10	19	37	16
Apache	2	3	47	18	21	22	6	42	10	19	37	16
Bashneft	3	25	16	44	14	5	29	20	43	12	9	51
BHP Billiton	4	3	47	18	21	22	6	42	10	19	37	16
BP	5	21	46	10	20	16	14	9	43	47	49	12
Cenovus	6	46	44	16	14	5	43	29	20	9	49	51
Chesapeake	7	47	41	22	6	42	19	18	21	10	37	35
Chevron	8	42	45	33	46	29	10	34	12	20	9	47
CNOOC(*)	9	47	20	44	29	18	33	42	37	45	28	41
CNPC(*)	10	45	52	18	9	46	28	29	51	5	41	44
CNR	11	3	42	22	6	10	41	37	19	18	21	35
ConocoPhillips	12	48	15	23	17	42	8	16	32	37	19	29
Devon Energy	13	3	47	18	21	22	6	42	10	19	37	16
Ecopetrol(*)	14	52	45	5	47	20	33	42	51	28	29	37
EnCana	15	3	22	6	42	41	10	19	37	18	21	35
Eni	16	45	52	12	28	47	42	46	27	20	37	5
EOG	17	3	42	10	22	6	41	37	35	19	18	33
ExxonMobil	18	35	24	29	50	10	36	26	43	27	20	47
Gazprom(*)	19	44	42	28	33	47	49	41	46	29	34	20
Hess	20	21	24	5	16	25	41	47	14	27	26	49

(continued)

Table 21 (continued)

Firm name	ID	23rd	24th	25th	26th	27th	28th	29th	30th	31st	32nd	33rd
Husky Energy	21	52	42	37	33	34	12	47	5	29	27	20
Imperial	22	24	47	36	29	16	14	20	12	43	26	27
Inpex	23	3	22	6	42	41	10	19	37	18	21	35
Kazmunaigas(*)	24	5	44	47	41	28	37	42	20	33	51	29
Lukoil	25	37	33	42	28	45	9	46	29	49	20	12
Marathon Oil	26	41	3	42	22	21	37	16	20	8	19	47
Mitsui	27	21	3	16	41	22	10	42	19	47	20	6
Mol	28	27	7	40	48	15	23	35	10	32	20	11
Murphy Oil	29	21	41	36	12	24	16	14	26	47	43	9
Noble Energy	30	3	47	18	21	22	6	42	10	19	37	16
Novatek	31	3	47	18	21	22	6	42	10	19	37	16
Occidental	32	3	22	6	42	41	19	10	37	35	18	21
OMV	33	21	25	20	24	36	16	14	12	51	17	43
ONGC	34	41	52	44	5	20	45	27	33	42	12	29
PDVSA(*)	35	18	37	5	45	34	20	51	44	28	46	29
PEMEX(*)	36	18	45	47	20	37	42	28	33	29	41	51
Pertamina(*)	37	10	20	47	24	36	12	16	26	14	27	23
Petrobras(*)	38	20	16	14	9	28	46	45	41	43	49	51
PETRONAS(*)	39	29	9	43	28	20	41	45	49	46	47	34
Pioneer	40	47	22	6	41	42	19	10	37	18	21	35
PTT(*)	41	14	24	50	29	10	26	47	27	1	2	4
Repsol	42	21	25	20	12	24	16	36	26	17	27	11
Rosneft(*)	43	44	51	47	20	45	5	12	27	42	29	33
Shell	44	24	36	16	14	20	10	12	43	47	26	9
Sinopec(*)	45	32	11	27	1	2	4	13	30	31	53	54
SK Energy	46	1	2	4	13	30	31	53	54	7	23	40
Socar(*)	47	36	16	32	40	41	18	7	48	52	20	27
Southwestern	48	47	22	6	41	42	19	37	10	18	21	35
Statoil(*)	49	5	52	29	18	33	42	44	37	45	27	12
Suncor	50	49	43	18	44	20	29	45	51	46	28	41
Tatneft	51	8	45	41	17	52	18	37	11	20	46	23
Total	52	36	24	10	20	16	14	47	43	12	9	49
Wintershall	53	3	47	18	21	22	6	42	10	19	37	16
Woodside	54	3	47	18	21	22	6	42	10	19	37	16

Table 22 Company ranking in segment-wide similarity (34th to 44th)

Firm name	ID	34th	35th	36th	37th	38th	39th	40th	41st	42nd	43rd	44th
Anadarko	1	35	8	24	20	33	14	25	44	43	29	50
Apache	2	35	8	24	20	33	14	25	44	43	29	50
Bashneft	3	11	23	15	17	40	7	48	27	32	49	26
BHP Billiton	4	35	8	24	20	33	14	25	44	43	29	50
BP	5	34	51	26	27	32	15	23	48	40	7	11
Cenovus	6	12	34	23	11	15	17	40	32	7	48	27
Chesapeake	7	20	24	33	16	52	36	29	8	38	44	50
Chevron	8	27	49	26	51	1	2	4	13	30	31	53
CNOOC(*)	9	46	12	27	26	23	15	32	11	40	48	17
CNPC(*)	10	34	12	27	17	11	23	26	15	40	32	7
CNR	11	33	20	24	50	38	16	29	51	52	36	8
ConocoPhillips	12	10	6	25	44	35	52	47	14	24	33	38
Devon Energy	13	35	8	24	20	33	14	25	44	43	29	50
Ecopetrol(*)	14	46	12	27	26	1	2	4	13	30	31	53
EnCana	15	20	33	24	52	16	38	36	29	50	44	51
Eni	16	33	29	26	51	1	2	4	13	30	31	53
EOG	17	21	20	50	38	51	24	16	29	52	8	36
ExxonMobil	18	1	2	4	13	30	31	53	54	7	34	11
Gazprom(*)	19	12	51	27	26	15	23	40	48	7	32	11
Hess	20	43	9	17	11	23	15	40	32	7	48	34
Husky Energy	21	9	49	26	1	2	4	13	30	31	53	54
Imperial	22	9	11	23	17	15	40	7	32	48	49	51
Inpex	23	20	33	24	52	38	50	16	29	36	51	44
Kazmunaigas(*)	24	46	12	27	26	7	40	48	15	23	32	11
Lukoil	25	47	27	26	51	1	2	4	13	30	31	53
Marathon Oil	26	10	6	35	29	44	25	33	52	24	14	38
Mitsui	27	35	8	37	24	25	14	43	36	38	29	44
Mol	28	50	24	1	2	4	13	30	31	53	54	47
Murphy Oil	29	49	27	11	17	23	15	40	32	7	48	51
Noble Energy	30	35	8	24	20	33	14	25	44	43	29	50
Novatek	31	35	8	24	20	33	14	25	44	43	29	50
Occidental	32	20	33	24	52	36	38	29	50	16	44	51
OMV	33	11	26	9	23	27	15	40	32	7	48	49
ONGC	34	28	37	46	26	1	2	4	13	30	31	53
PDVSA(*)	35	41	27	12	26	17	11	23	15	40	32	7
PEMEX(*)	36	46	12	27	26	48	32	15	40	23	7	11
Pertamina(*)	37	11	15	17	40	32	7	48	43	1	2	4
Petrobras(*)	38	34	12	27	26	17	11	23	15	32	40	7
PETRONAS(*)	39	12	51	27	26	11	23	17	15	40	32	7
Pioneer	40	20	33	24	16	52	36	29	38	50	44	8

(continued)

Table 22 (continued)

Firm name	ID	34th	35th	36th	37th	38th	39th	40th	41st	42nd	43rd	44th
PTT(*)	41	13	30	31	53	54	20	36	7	43	11	40
Repsol	42	14	23	15	40	32	7	48	1	2	4	13
Rosneft(*)	43	28	37	46	26	1	2	4	13	30	31	53
Shell	44	27	34	49	7	40	15	48	23	11	32	17
Sinopec(*)	45	17	35	25	10	38	39	47	24	29	5	16
SK Energy	46	15	10	25	47	48	39	35	32	5	50	20
Socar(*)	47	14	1	2	4	13	30	31	53	54	8	25
Southwestern	48	20	24	33	52	16	36	29	38	44	50	8
Statoil(*)	49	28	41	46	26	11	17	23	15	40	32	7
Suncor	50	34	12	27	17	26	11	23	15	32	40	7
Tatneft	51	5	15	29	32	40	28	7	44	48	1	2
Total	52	26	27	34	32	15	51	23	48	40	7	11
Wintershall	53	35	8	24	20	33	14	25	44	43	29	50
Woodside	54	35	8	24	20	33	14	25	44	43	29	50

Table 23 Company ranking in segment-wide similarity (45th to 53rd)

Firm name	ID	45th	46th	47th	48th	49th	50th	51st	52nd	53rd
Anadarko	1	38	52	36	51	39	34	5	49	9
Apache	2	38	52	36	51	39	34	5	49	9
Bashneft	3	1	2	4	13	30	31	53	54	34
BHP Billiton	4	38	52	36	51	39	34	5	49	9
BP	5	17	1	2	4	13	30	31	53	54
Cenovus	6	1	2	4	13	30	31	53	54	26
Chesapeake	7	51	14	25	39	43	5	49	9	34
Chevron	8	54	7	11	40	48	15	23	17	32
CNOOC(*)	9	7	1	2	4	13	30	31	53	54
CNPC(*)	10	48	1	2	4	13	30	31	53	54
CNR	11	44	39	14	25	43	5	49	9	34
ConocoPhillips	12	39	50	43	36	5	34	49	9	51
Devon Energy	13	38	52	36	51	39	34	5	49	9
Ecopetrol(*)	14	54	7	11	40	48	15	23	17	32
EnCana	15	8	39	14	25	43	5	49	9	34
Eni	16	54	7	11	40	48	15	23	17	32
EOG	17	44	39	14	25	43	5	49	9	34
ExxonMobil	18	40	48	15	23	17	32	9	49	51
Gazprom(*)	19	17	1	2	4	13	30	31	53	54
Hess	20	1	2	4	13	30	31	53	54	51

(continued)

Table 23 (continued)

Firm name	ID	45th	46th	47th	48th	49th	50th	51st	52nd	53rd
Husky Energy	21	51	7	11	40	48	15	23	17	32
Imperial	22	1	2	4	13	30	31	53	54	34
Inpex	23	8	39	14	25	43	5	49	9	34
Kazmunaigas(*)	24	1	2	4	13	30	31	53	54	17
Lukoil	25	54	7	11	40	48	15	23	17	32
Marathon Oil	26	50	39	43	36	5	34	49	9	51
Mitsui	27	50	33	52	39	34	49	5	9	51
Mol	28	17	16	36	14	43	9	51	34	49
Murphy Oil	29	34	1	2	4	13	30	31	53	54
Noble Energy	30	38	52	36	51	39	34	5	49	9
Novatek	31	38	52	36	51	39	34	5	49	9
Occidental	32	8	39	14	25	5	43	49	9	34
OMV	33	1	2	4	13	30	31	53	54	34
ONGC	34	54	7	11	40	48	15	23	17	32
PDVSA(*)	35	48	1	2	4	13	30	31	53	54
PEMEX(*)	36	17	1	2	4	13	30	31	53	54
Pertamina(*)	37	13	30	31	53	54	9	51	49	34
Petrobras(*)	38	48	1	2	4	13	30	31	53	54
PETRONAS(*)	39	48	1	2	4	13	30	31	53	54
Pioneer	40	51	14	25	39	43	5	49	9	34
PTT(*)	41	48	15	23	17	32	34	51	9	49
Repsol	42	30	31	53	54	43	51	9	49	34
Rosneft(*)	43	54	7	11	40	48	15	23	17	32
Shell	44	1	2	4	13	30	31	53	54	51
Sinopec(*)	45	50	20	36	14	43	51	9	34	49
SK Energy	46	16	24	14	36	43	51	9	34	49
Socar(*)	47	49	12	43	9	26	5	44	29	34
Southwestern	48	51	14	25	39	43	5	49	9	34
Statoil(*)	49	48	1	2	4	13	30	31	53	54
Suncor	50	48	1	2	4	13	30	31	53	54
Tatneft	51	4	13	30	31	53	54	12	27	26
Total	52	17	1	2	4	13	30	31	53	54
Wintershall	53	38	52	36	51	39	34	5	49	9
Woodside	54	38	52	36	51	39	34	5	49	9

Table 24   Company ranking in region-wide similarity (1st to 11th)

Firm name	ID	1st	2nd	3rd	4th	5th	6th	7th	8th	9th	10th	11th
Anadarko	1	6	7	13	15	22	36	40	48	11	50	21
Apache	2	1	50	11	6	7	13	15	22	36	40	48
Bashneft	3	31	51	19	43	25	53	33	27	45	34	44
BHP Billiton	4	1	6	7	13	15	22	36	40	48	11	50
BP	5	18	32	44	45	30	8	17	1	12	52	2
Cenovus	6	7	13	15	22	36	40	48	11	21	50	1
Chesapeake	7	6	13	15	22	36	40	48	11	21	50	1
Chevron	8	20	29	5	18	12	30	44	26	39	17	11
CNOOC(*)	9	12	44	18	52	5	8	20	23	21	26	45
CNPC(*)	10	32	52	23	5	27	44	45	46	18	16	24
CNR	11	6	7	13	15	22	36	40	48	21	50	1
ConocoPhillips	12	50	11	20	21	6	7	13	15	22	36	40
Devon Energy	13	6	7	15	22	36	40	48	11	21	50	1
Ecopetrol(*)	14	35	38	46	42	45	5	53	44	10	17	32
EnCana	15	6	7	13	22	36	40	48	11	21	50	1
Eni	16	45	2	44	5	26	52	10	18	20	8	49
EOG	17	6	7	13	15	22	36	40	48	11	21	50
ExxonMobil	18	30	44	5	12	20	32	52	26	50	11	1
Gazprom(*)	19	3	31	51	43	25	53	33	27	45	34	44
Hess	20	12	29	30	26	8	18	50	11	1	6	7
Husky Energy	21	6	7	13	15	22	36	40	48	11	50	1
Imperial	22	6	7	13	15	36	40	48	11	21	50	1
Inpex	23	27	39	37	41	52	10	44	8	32	29	5
Kazmunaigas(*)	24	47	8	10	5	23	45	16	18	25	44	39
Lukoil	25	19	51	3	31	43	53	33	27	45	44	34
Marathon Oil	26	30	20	18	45	1	11	50	6	7	13	15
Mitsui	27	23	32	44	52	10	18	5	39	37	29	8
Mol	28	33	52	44	10	34	27	32	18	23	49	53
Murphy Oil	29	20	12	8	6	7	13	15	22	36	40	48
Noble Energy	30	11	1	6	7	13	15	22	36	40	48	21
Novatek	31	3	51	19	43	25	53	33	27	45	34	44
Occidental	32	5	18	10	52	27	44	30	17	50	6	7
OMV	33	53	28	25	19	51	3	31	43	49	44	45
ONGC	34	33	25	43	19	51	3	31	53	28	5	16
PDVSA(*)	35	14	38	46	42	45	5	53	44	10	17	32
PEMEX(*)	36	6	7	13	15	22	40	48	11	21	50	1
Pertamina(*)	37	41	39	23	29	8	27	20	44	52	12	42
Petrobras(*)	38	14	35	46	42	45	5	53	44	10	17	52
PETRONAS(*)	39	37	41	23	29	8	27	20	44	52	12	42
Pioneer	40	6	7	13	15	22	36	48	11	21	50	1

(continued)

Table 24 (continued)

Firm name	ID	1st	2nd	3rd	4th	5th	6th	7th	8th	9th	10th	11th
PTT(*)	41	37	39	23	29	8	27	20	44	12	52	42
Repsol	42	46	38	14	35	5	45	44	8	12	17	20
Rosneft(*)	43	3	31	51	19	25	53	33	27	45	34	44
Shell	44	18	52	5	12	20	27	8	32	45	49	23
Sinopec(*)	45	16	5	26	44	52	2	18	42	8	20	30
SK Energy	46	38	14	35	42	5	45	10	44	52	32	23
Socar(*)	47	24	8	10	5	23	45	16	18	25	44	39
Southwestern	48	6	7	13	15	22	36	40	11	21	50	1
Statoil(*)	49	44	18	12	52	53	33	20	26	45	16	2
Suncor	50	11	6	7	13	15	22	36	40	48	21	1
Tatneft	51	3	31	19	43	25	53	33	27	45	34	44
Total	52	44	18	32	23	5	27	10	45	8	20	26
Wintershall	53	43	19	3	31	51	25	33	49	44	42	45
Woodside	54	4	27	44	33	5	8	12	18	9	6	7

Table 25 Company ranking in region-wide similarity (12th to 22nd)

Firm name	ID	12th	13th	14th	15th	16th	17th	18th	19th	20th	21st	22nd
Anadarko	1	17	30	12	2	4	20	29	18	26	5	8
Apache	2	21	12	17	30	4	20	5	26	18	29	45
Bashneft	3	28	42	18	23	52	49	5	1	2	3	4
BHP Billiton	4	21	17	30	12	2	29	20	18	5	26	54
BP	5	50	11	20	6	7	13	15	22	36	40	48
Cenovus	6	17	30	12	4	2	29	20	18	26	5	32
Chesapeake	7	17	30	12	4	2	29	20	18	26	5	32
Chevron	8	23	1	50	45	6	7	13	15	22	36	40
CNOOC(*)	9	30	49	32	17	27	42	29	10	50	11	4
CNPC(*)	10	47	8	42	38	35	14	39	9	2	30	28
CNR	11	17	30	12	4	2	20	29	18	26	5	8
ConocoPhillips	12	48	1	17	29	18	30	2	4	44	8	5
Devon Energy	13	17	30	12	4	2	29	20	18	26	5	32
Ecopetrol(*)	14	8	52	9	4	16	34	23	49	12	43	18
EnCana	15	17	30	12	4	2	29	20	18	26	5	32
Eni	16	42	33	30	53	12	32	1	23	39	27	50
EOG	17	1	30	12	4	2	29	20	18	5	26	32
ExxonMobil	18	6	7	13	15	22	36	40	48	21	17	8
Gazprom(*)	19	28	42	18	23	52	49	16	5	2	39	10
Hess	20	13	15	22	36	40	48	21	17	2	44	5

(continued)

Table 25 (continued)

Firm name	ID	12th	13th	14th	15th	16th	17th	18th	19th	20th	21st	22nd
Husky Energy	21	17	30	12	4	2	29	20	18	26	5	32
Imperial	22	17	30	12	4	2	29	20	18	26	5	32
Inpex	23	18	20	46	12	42	24	47	45	16	9	30
Kazmunaigas(*)	24	49	33	34	19	52	1	2	3	4	6	7
Lukoil	25	24	47	28	10	23	18	5	8	42	52	32
Marathon Oil	26	22	36	40	48	21	2	17	12	8	5	4
Mitsui	27	41	12	4	20	54	30	46	33	25	45	43
Mol	28	5	25	19	51	3	31	43	12	45	16	46
Murphy Oil	29	11	21	50	1	17	30	4	39	2	18	41
Noble Energy	30	50	17	18	20	26	12	4	5	2	29	8
Novatek	31	28	42	18	23	52	49	5	1	2	4	6
Occidental	32	13	15	22	36	40	48	11	21	1	12	23
OMV	33	16	27	52	2	18	34	12	42	5	54	20
ONGC	34	44	27	42	45	46	39	37	35	14	38	41
PDVSA(*)	35	52	8	9	16	34	23	4	49	12	43	18
PEMEX(*)	36	17	30	12	4	2	29	20	18	26	5	32
Pertamina(*)	37	46	16	5	18	10	9	45	34	2	32	26
Petrobras(*)	38	8	32	9	16	4	34	23	49	12	26	18
PETRONAS(*)	39	16	5	46	18	10	45	2	26	9	32	24
Pioneer	40	17	30	12	4	2	29	20	18	26	5	32
PTT(*)	41	46	18	5	9	16	10	34	54	4	43	33
Repsol	42	2	29	53	50	1	11	52	6	7	13	15
Rosneft(*)	43	28	42	18	23	52	46	14	38	35	49	5
Shell	44	2	26	42	30	29	16	10	50	11	17	1
Sinopec(*)	45	46	10	1	12	17	32	53	38	14	50	35
SK Energy	46	53	27	8	17	18	39	37	41	29	12	16
Socar(*)	47	49	33	34	19	52	1	2	3	4	6	7
Southwestern	48	17	30	12	4	2	29	20	18	26	5	32
Statoil(*)	49	42	5	8	50	30	11	9	1	17	6	7
Suncor	50	17	30	12	2	4	20	29	18	26	5	32
Tatneft	51	28	42	18	23	52	49	5	10	32	46	16
Total	52	16	49	30	12	46	42	39	29	37	41	2
Wintershall	53	35	14	38	46	16	52	27	5	2	12	18
Woodside	54	13	15	22	36	40	48	21	11	50	1	17

Table 26 Company ranking in region-wide similarity (23rd to 33rd)

Firm name	ID	23rd	24th	25th	26th	27th	28th	29th	30th	31st	32nd	33rd
Anadarko	1	32	44	45	42	27	16	52	9	49	39	46
Apache	2	16	44	8	32	42	49	52	33	27	53	9
Bashneft	3	6	7	8	9	10	11	12	13	14	15	16
BHP Billiton	4	8	32	44	27	45	42	52	16	9	49	33
BP	5	21	26	42	4	10	29	46	16	27	23	38
Cenovus	6	8	44	45	42	27	52	9	49	16	39	46
Chesapeake	7	8	44	45	42	27	52	9	49	16	39	46
Chevron	8	48	21	52	37	41	4	27	2	42	32	24
CNOOC(*)	9	1	6	7	13	15	22	36	40	48	2	46
CNPC(*)	10	33	53	12	37	25	26	20	41	49	17	1
CNR	11	32	44	45	42	27	52	49	9	16	39	46
ConocoPhillips	12	26	32	49	42	52	27	45	39	23	37	41
Devon Energy	13	8	44	45	42	27	52	9	49	16	39	46
Ecopetrol(*)	14	6	7	13	15	22	36	40	48	11	21	50
EnCana	15	8	44	45	42	27	52	9	49	16	39	46
Eni	16	4	24	47	11	46	29	17	37	6	7	13
EOG	17	8	42	44	45	27	52	46	38	14	35	9
ExxonMobil	18	2	4	29	45	27	49	10	23	16	42	9
Gazprom(*)	19	26	37	20	41	8	12	1	29	32	24	47
Hess	20	4	45	52	39	42	32	37	41	27	16	49
Husky Energy	21	8	44	45	42	27	52	9	49	16	39	46
Imperial	22	8	44	45	42	27	52	9	49	16	39	46
Inpex	23	28	33	26	25	4	38	34	14	35	54	17
Kazmunaigas(*)	24	9	11	12	13	14	15	17	20	21	22	24
Lukoil	25	16	39	49	46	2	30	9	12	37	26	1
Marathon Oil	26	44	29	52	16	32	49	42	27	9	33	53
Mitsui	27	19	51	3	31	50	11	42	6	7	13	15
Mol	28	9	20	30	2	42	8	26	39	50	37	11
Murphy Oil	29	37	5	44	26	27	23	32	42	52	45	9
Noble Energy	30	32	45	44	52	42	27	16	49	9	23	10
Novatek	31	7	8	9	10	11	12	13	14	15	16	17
Occidental	32	4	2	29	20	8	45	26	46	42	16	9
OMV	33	10	26	4	9	8	23	32	50	39	24	47
ONGC	34	23	8	10	29	52	24	47	20	12	18	32
PDVSA(*)	35	39	19	1	2	3	6	7	11	13	15	20
PEMEX(*)	36	8	44	45	42	27	52	9	49	16	39	46
Pertamina(*)	37	33	53	1	30	43	49	28	4	50	25	19
Petrobras(*)	38	30	20	43	11	1	6	7	13	15	22	36
PETRONAS(*)	39	47	1	30	50	4	11	6	7	13	15	22
Pioneer	40	8	44	45	42	27	52	9	49	16	39	46

(continued)

Table 26 (continued)

Firm name	ID	23rd	24th	25th	26th	27th	28th	29th	30th	31st	32nd	33rd
PTT(*)	41	45	19	2	1	53	49	25	50	26	32	3
Repsol	42	22	36	40	48	21	4	18	26	16	32	30
Rosneft(*)	43	41	37	39	8	29	20	12	10	17	32	9
Shell	44	4	53	21	6	7	13	15	22	36	40	48
Sinopec(*)	45	11	4	6	7	13	15	22	36	40	48	21
SK Energy	46	20	9	30	4	50	26	1	2	11	6	7
Socar(*)	47	9	11	12	13	14	15	17	20	21	22	26
Southwestern	48	8	44	45	42	27	52	9	49	16	39	46
Statoil(*)	49	13	15	22	36	40	48	21	4	29	28	27
Suncor	50	8	44	45	42	27	52	49	16	9	39	33
Tatneft	51	30	12	8	9	50	39	37	1	2	4	6
Total	52	50	53	11	33	9	1	17	6	7	13	15
Wintershall	53	34	20	10	26	28	9	8	17	50	32	39
Woodside	54	45	23	30	2	29	20	41	26	32	16	42

Table 27 Company ranking in region-wide similarity (34th to 44th)

Firm name	ID	34th	35th	36th	37th	38th	39th	40th	41st	42nd	43rd	44th
Anadarko	1	54	10	33	23	53	38	37	14	34	25	43
Apache	2	10	39	46	37	54	23	28	38	14	34	25
Bashneft	3	17	20	21	22	24	26	29	30	32	35	36
BHP Billiton	4	46	39	38	14	23	35	53	10	41	37	34
BP	5	14	35	24	47	49	53	9	39	33	54	37
Cenovus	6	54	23	38	14	43	53	37	3	6	10	19
Chesapeake	7	54	23	38	14	43	53	37	3	7	10	19
Chevron	8	47	16	46	10	49	9	38	14	35	54	53
CNOOC(*)	9	16	53	39	38	14	35	37	33	41	54	28
CNPC(*)	10	34	29	4	50	21	43	19	11	51	3	6
CNR	11	54	23	53	33	38	14	28	43	10	37	19
ConocoPhillips	12	9	16	53	33	46	10	54	28	38	14	35
Devon Energy	13	54	23	38	14	43	53	37	3	10	13	19
Ecopetrol(*)	14	1	30	2	29	20	26	27	39	54	19	37
EnCana	15	54	23	38	14	43	53	37	3	10	15	19
Eni	16	15	22	36	40	48	21	9	34	41	28	38
EOG	17	49	16	53	39	54	10	23	34	43	33	28
ExxonMobil	18	33	46	53	39	24	47	37	28	41	54	25
Gazprom(*)	19	4	46	50	9	30	35	14	38	11	17	6
Hess	20	23	9	33	53	46	10	54	28	34	38	14

(continued)

Table 27 (continued)

Firm name	ID	34th	35th	36th	37th	38th	39th	40th	41st	42nd	43rd	44th
Husky Energy	21	54	23	38	14	10	43	53	37	3	19	21
Imperial	22	54	23	38	14	43	53	37	3	10	19	22
Inpex	23	21	50	49	11	1	6	7	13	15	22	36
Kazmunaigas(*)	24	26	27	28	29	30	31	32	35	36	37	38
Lukoil	25	20	4	50	41	6	7	11	13	14	15	17
Marathon Oil	26	39	23	46	10	54	37	38	28	14	34	25
Mitsui	27	22	36	40	48	21	1	17	53	26	2	16
Mol	28	4	17	1	6	7	13	14	15	21	22	24
Murphy Oil	29	46	16	49	10	54	34	38	14	43	19	53
Noble Energy	30	46	39	54	28	38	33	14	37	25	53	34
Novatek	31	20	21	22	24	26	29	30	31	32	35	36
Occidental	32	38	14	35	28	49	39	33	53	25	37	54
OMV	33	1	46	11	37	30	41	17	6	7	13	14
ONGC	34	17	9	2	49	4	26	1	30	50	6	7
PDVSA(*)	35	21	22	24	25	26	27	28	29	30	31	33
PEMEX(*)	36	54	23	38	14	43	53	37	3	10	19	24
Pertamina(*)	37	11	38	6	7	13	15	22	36	40	48	17
Petrobras(*)	38	40	48	21	50	29	2	27	39	54	37	19
PETRONAS(*)	39	36	40	48	21	17	33	34	49	53	25	28
Pioneer	40	54	23	38	14	43	53	37	3	10	19	24
PTT(*)	41	6	7	11	13	14	15	17	21	22	24	28
Repsol	42	39	37	41	49	27	10	23	33	9	34	43
Rosneft(*)	43	4	16	6	7	13	15	22	36	40	48	11
Shell	44	33	46	39	37	41	9	38	14	35	25	54
Sinopec(*)	45	49	33	29	27	23	24	47	25	9	43	19
SK Energy	46	13	15	22	36	40	48	21	34	49	28	33
Socar(*)	47	27	28	29	30	31	32	35	36	37	38	40
Southwestern	48	54	23	38	14	43	53	37	3	10	19	24
Statoil(*)	49	32	24	47	46	10	38	14	35	39	23	25
Suncor	50	53	46	54	23	10	28	38	14	37	43	34
Tatneft	51	7	11	13	14	15	17	20	21	22	24	26
Total	52	22	36	40	48	21	4	38	14	35	28	25
Wintershall	53	4	1	23	11	37	30	41	6	7	13	15
Woodside	54	52	39	49	46	14	38	43	53	37	3	10

Table 28 Company ranking in region-wide similarity (45th to 53rd)

Firm name	ID	45th	46th	47th	48th	49th	50th	51st	52nd	53rd
Anadarko	1	19	41	1	3	24	28	31	35	47
Apache	2	19	43	41	2	3	24	31	35	47
Bashneft	3	37	38	39	40	41	46	47	48	50
BHP Billiton	4	43	28	25	19	3	4	24	31	47
BP	5	28	41	34	25	43	19	51	3	31
Cenovus	6	24	25	28	31	33	34	35	41	47
Chesapeake	7	24	25	28	31	33	34	35	41	47
Chevron	8	33	25	34	28	43	19	51	3	8
CNOOC(*)	9	34	25	43	19	51	3	9	24	31
CNPC(*)	10	7	10	13	15	22	31	36	40	48
CNR	11	3	11	24	25	31	34	35	41	47
ConocoPhillips	12	34	25	43	19	51	3	12	24	31
Devon Energy	13	24	25	28	31	33	34	35	41	47
Ecopetrol(*)	14	3	14	24	25	28	31	33	41	47
EnCana	15	24	25	28	31	33	34	35	41	47
Eni	16	14	35	25	54	19	43	51	3	16
EOG	17	37	19	3	17	24	25	31	41	47
ExxonMobil	18	43	19	51	3	31	38	34	14	35
Gazprom(*)	19	7	13	15	19	21	22	36	40	48
Hess	20	43	19	25	3	20	24	31	35	47
Husky Energy	21	24	25	28	31	33	34	35	41	47
Imperial	22	24	25	28	31	33	34	35	41	47
Inpex	23	40	48	2	53	43	19	51	3	31
Kazmunaigas(*)	24	40	41	42	43	46	48	50	51	53
Lukoil	25	21	22	25	29	35	36	38	40	48
Marathon Oil	26	19	43	41	3	24	26	31	35	47
Mitsui	27	9	28	49	34	38	14	24	27	35
Mol	28	28	29	35	36	38	40	41	47	48
Murphy Oil	29	3	24	25	28	29	31	33	35	47
Noble Energy	30	43	19	51	3	24	30	31	35	41
Novatek	31	37	38	39	40	41	46	47	48	50
Occidental	32	34	43	19	51	41	3	24	31	32
OMV	33	15	21	22	29	33	35	36	38	40
ONGC	34	11	13	15	21	22	34	36	40	48
PDVSA(*)	35	35	36	37	40	41	47	48	50	51
PEMEX(*)	36	25	28	31	33	34	35	36	41	47
Pertamina(*)	37	21	51	14	54	3	24	31	35	37
Petrobras(*)	38	3	24	25	28	31	33	38	41	47
PETRONAS(*)	39	54	43	19	38	14	35	51	3	31
Pioneer	40	25	28	31	33	34	35	40	41	47

(continued)

Table 28 (continued)

Firm name	ID	45th	46th	47th	48th	49th	50th	51st	52nd	53rd
PTT(*)	41	30	31	35	36	38	40	41	47	48
Repsol	42	25	19	3	31	51	28	54	24	42
Rosneft(*)	43	21	50	1	30	2	26	54	24	43
Shell	44	28	43	19	51	3	31	24	47	34
Sinopec(*)	45	51	3	31	39	28	34	37	54	41
SK Energy	46	43	25	54	19	51	3	24	31	46
Socar(*)	47	41	42	43	46	47	48	50	51	53
Southwestern	48	25	28	31	33	34	35	41	47	48
Statoil(*)	49	43	19	51	3	31	37	54	34	41
Suncor	50	25	19	41	51	3	24	31	35	47
Tatneft	51	29	35	36	38	40	41	47	48	51
Total	52	34	43	19	51	3	31	54	24	47
Wintershall	53	22	36	40	48	21	29	54	24	47
Woodside	54	19	24	25	28	31	34	35	47	51

Table 29 Company ranking in total-factor similarity (1st to 11th)

Firm name	ID	1st	2nd	3rd	4th	5th	6th	7th	8th	9th	10th	11th
Anadarko	1	11	13	40	15	17	30	7	48	6	21	2
Apache	2	1	11	12	30	40	13	17	15	4	7	6
Bashneft	3	25	43	51	19	31	53	33	27	45	34	44
BHP Billiton	4	1	11	13	40	15	17	30	7	48	21	6
BP	5	18	44	45	52	8	36	42	6	20	32	21
Cenovus	6	21	36	22	50	11	1	40	17	15	13	7
Chesapeake	7	48	15	13	40	17	1	11	30	22	6	4
Chevron	8	20	29	18	5	44	12	39	21	52	45	36
CNOOC(*)	9	12	44	18	52	8	49	5	20	21	36	10
CNPC(*)	10	32	52	23	5	27	44	45	46	18	16	47
CNR	11	40	1	17	13	15	7	30	6	21	22	48
ConocoPhillips	12	20	1	11	21	18	29	6	2	30	36	40
Devon Energy	13	40	7	17	48	15	11	1	30	22	21	6
Ecopetrol(*)	14	35	38	46	42	45	5	53	10	44	8	52
EnCana	15	7	48	17	13	1	40	11	30	6	4	21
Eni	16	45	2	44	5	52	26	10	18	8	20	49
EOG	17	40	13	11	7	15	1	48	30	6	22	21
ExxonMobil	18	44	5	12	52	30	20	8	21	6	26	36
Gazprom(*)	19	31	3	43	25	51	53	33	27	34	44	45
Hess	20	29	12	8	26	18	36	6	21	50	30	11

(continued)

Table 29 (continued)

Firm name	ID	1st	2nd	3rd	4th	5th	6th	7th	8th	9th	10th	11th
Husky Energy	21	6	22	36	50	11	1	40	13	17	30	15
Imperial	22	50	21	6	40	11	17	13	7	1	36	15
Inpex	23	27	37	39	41	52	10	32	44	8	29	18
Kazmunaigas(*)	24	47	8	10	5	23	45	16	18	25	44	39
Lukoil	25	43	3	51	19	31	53	33	27	45	44	34
Marathon Oil	26	30	20	18	45	1	11	12	2	40	21	17
Mitsui	27	23	32	44	52	18	10	41	39	37	12	8
Mol	28	33	44	52	10	27	32	18	34	23	53	5
Murphy Oil	29	20	12	8	6	21	36	22	50	11	1	18
Noble Energy	30	1	11	13	15	40	17	7	48	26	6	21
Novatek	31	19	3	43	25	51	53	33	27	45	44	34
Occidental	32	18	5	10	27	30	52	11	23	1	44	40
OMV	33	53	28	3	25	19	43	51	31	44	49	45
ONGC	34	33	43	25	19	3	51	31	53	28	16	5
PDVSA(*)	35	38	14	46	42	45	5	53	10	44	8	52
PEMEX(*)	36	6	21	50	22	11	1	12	40	20	17	29
Pertamina(*)	37	41	39	23	29	8	27	20	44	52	42	12
Petrobras(*)	38	35	14	46	42	45	5	53	10	44	8	52
PETRONAS(*)	39	37	41	23	8	29	27	20	44	52	42	12
Pioneer	40	13	17	11	7	15	1	48	22	30	6	21
PTT(*)	41	37	39	23	29	8	27	20	44	52	42	12
Repsol	42	46	38	35	14	5	45	44	8	12	20	29
Rosneft(*)	43	25	3	51	19	31	53	33	27	34	45	44
Shell	44	52	18	5	8	12	45	20	42	27	49	29
Sinopec(*)	45	16	5	26	44	52	18	42	2	8	20	30
SK Energy	46	38	35	14	42	5	45	10	44	52	32	23
Socar(*)	47	24	8	10	5	23	45	16	18	25	44	39
Southwestern	48	7	15	13	17	40	1	11	30	22	4	6
Statoil(*)	49	44	18	52	12	33	53	20	16	26	45	2
Suncor	50	22	21	6	11	36	40	17	13	1	7	15
Tatneft	51	3	43	25	19	31	53	33	27	45	34	44
Total	52	44	18	5	10	45	23	32	27	8	20	16
Wintershall	53	31	19	3	33	25	43	51	42	44	45	49
Woodside	54	4	27	44	33	8	5	12	18	1	23	30

Table 30 Company ranking in total-factor similarity (12th to 22nd)

Firm name	ID	12th	13th	14th	15th	16th	17th	18th	19th	20th	21st	22nd
Anadarko	1	4	12	22	36	50	26	18	20	29	32	5
Apache	2	21	48	36	26	22	50	18	45	20	16	32
Bashneft	3	28	18	42	24	38	35	46	36	10	52	8
BHP Billiton	4	2	12	22	36	50	26	54	18	29	20	32
BP	5	12	50	10	22	29	46	16	30	26	2	11
Cenovus	6	30	12	48	4	29	20	2	18	5	26	8
Chesapeake	7	21	50	12	2	36	26	29	18	20	32	5
Chevron	8	26	6	37	30	41	22	50	42	23	1	11
CNOOC(*)	9	45	50	23	6	29	26	42	16	22	32	27
CNPC(*)	10	24	8	42	35	38	14	39	9	33	2	28
CNR	11	4	50	12	36	2	26	20	29	18	32	5
ConocoPhillips	12	17	13	15	4	22	50	7	44	26	8	48
Devon Energy	13	4	50	12	2	36	26	29	18	20	32	8
Ecopetrol(*)	14	17	32	9	16	34	49	21	43	36	12	25
EnCana	15	22	12	2	50	36	18	29	26	20	32	5
Eni	16	42	33	12	30	53	39	32	23	27	1	24
EOG	17	4	50	12	2	36	26	29	20	18	32	5
ExxonMobil	18	32	1	11	22	50	45	29	2	40	4	17
Gazprom(*)	19	28	42	18	39	41	52	37	16	49	47	10
Hess	20	22	44	5	1	40	2	17	45	15	13	52
Husky Energy	21	12	7	48	4	29	18	20	2	26	5	8
Imperial	22	48	30	12	4	29	20	18	2	26	5	8
Inpex	23	5	46	20	12	47	45	42	24	16	30	9
Kazmunaigas(*)	24	49	33	34	36	43	35	3	9	38	14	21
Lukoil	25	24	47	8	10	18	5	28	16	52	42	36
Marathon Oil	26	13	6	4	8	22	15	7	50	36	48	5
Mitsui	27	4	54	29	5	20	30	31	46	1	53	45
Mol	28	49	25	19	31	3	45	12	43	16	46	51
Murphy Oil	29	40	39	17	37	15	30	13	5	7	44	4
Noble Energy	30	4	12	2	18	22	36	50	20	32	29	8
Novatek	31	28	54	2	42	23	1	30	4	41	15	18
Occidental	32	17	12	6	15	2	36	13	21	4	7	22
OMV	33	16	27	52	18	42	2	12	5	34	10	20
ONGC	34	44	27	14	39	35	42	45	8	38	46	41
PDVSA(*)	35	32	17	9	16	49	34	43	23	36	24	3
PEMEX(*)	36	30	15	13	18	7	5	2	4	48	8	26
Pertamina(*)	37	46	5	18	16	10	45	9	33	28	2	19
Petrobras(*)	38	32	17	9	16	49	34	36	20	18	3	12
PETRONAS(*)	39	5	16	18	10	46	45	9	24	47	2	33
Pioneer	40	50	4	12	36	2	26	29	20	18	32	5

(continued)

Table 30   (continued)

Firm name	ID	12th	13th	14th	15th	16th	17th	18th	19th	20th	21st	22nd
PTT(*)	41	46	18	5	16	10	54	28	9	34	33	19
Repsol	42	2	53	17	52	18	6	39	37	21	1	16
Rosneft(*)	43	14	24	35	36	28	16	9	18	49	8	38
Shell	44	32	16	10	23	26	33	2	39	6	21	36
Sinopec(*)	45	46	10	32	12	38	35	1	6	14	21	36
SK Energy	46	53	8	27	18	37	41	39	17	29	12	20
Socar(*)	47	49	33	34	35	42	38	3	46	6	37	32
Southwestern	48	21	50	12	2	26	36	29	18	20	32	5
Statoil(*)	49	8	5	42	9	50	36	6	21	30	11	29
Suncor	50	12	30	48	29	20	4	18	2	26	5	8
Tatneft	51	35	9	24	10	47	38	36	49	28	42	14
Total	52	26	49	12	46	39	42	37	30	29	41	33
Wintershall	53	46	35	27	38	14	2	16	12	52	18	5
Woodside	54	2	11	15	13	17	45	7	40	48	6	21

Table 31   Company ranking in total-factor similarity (23rd to 33rd)

Firm name	ID	23rd	24th	25th	26th	27th	28th	29th	30th	31st	32nd	33rd
Anadarko	1	8	45	44	42	27	16	54	53	52	23	31
Apache	2	5	29	44	42	8	53	27	52	49	33	54
Bashneft	3	47	5	20	6	23	16	9	21	14	32	29
BHP Billiton	4	27	5	8	44	45	42	53	23	16	52	46
BP	5	1	38	17	35	40	4	27	15	14	13	7
Cenovus	6	32	44	45	42	52	27	9	16	49	39	46
Chesapeake	7	8	44	42	45	27	54	52	53	31	23	28
Chevron	8	24	27	4	17	16	40	2	13	47	15	7
CNOOC(*)	9	30	35	14	38	11	39	46	2	17	4	1
CNPC(*)	10	12	37	30	53	25	20	49	26	41	34	29
CNR	11	8	45	44	42	27	52	23	54	46	53	16
ConocoPhillips	12	5	32	27	42	45	52	49	23	39	37	41
Devon Energy	13	5	45	44	42	27	54	52	23	53	14	31
Ecopetrol(*)	14	6	50	24	18	22	4	3	20	29	23	26
EnCana	15	8	44	42	27	45	54	31	53	52	23	28
Eni	16	47	36	21	46	50	9	6	37	4	29	34
EOG	17	8	42	45	44	27	46	35	14	52	53	23
ExxonMobil	18	13	15	27	7	48	10	16	49	42	23	33
Gazprom(*)	19	5	6	8	54	36	23	12	24	35	29	2
Hess	20	4	7	39	48	42	37	32	16	27	49	41

(continued)

Table 31 (continued)

Firm name	ID	23rd	24th	25th	26th	27th	28th	29th	30th	31st	32nd	33rd
Husky Energy	21	32	44	45	42	52	27	9	16	49	14	46
Imperial	22	32	44	45	42	52	14	9	27	35	38	16
Inpex	23	28	54	26	2	4	11	53	1	33	17	31
Kazmunaigas(*)	24	52	6	51	20	46	29	37	42	28	19	12
Lukoil	25	38	35	14	46	39	23	9	21	49	6	20
Marathon Oil	26	29	44	16	52	32	42	27	49	53	46	23
Mitsui	27	42	2	19	33	26	11	15	25	21	6	17
Mol	28	42	8	2	20	30	39	37	9	26	41	54
Murphy Oil	29	41	48	2	26	42	27	23	52	32	45	46
Noble Energy	30	5	45	44	27	52	42	16	23	54	53	31
Novatek	31	12	7	32	17	13	11	48	37	47	26	40
Occidental	32	48	45	50	20	46	26	29	8	42	16	35
OMV	33	54	8	26	39	47	37	4	46	9	23	32
ONGC	34	10	24	37	23	52	47	9	49	29	18	20
PDVSA(*)	35	12	25	6	47	21	18	20	33	4	50	51
PEMEX(*)	36	32	44	45	42	52	9	49	16	27	24	35
Pertamina(*)	37	34	38	6	47	32	3	25	35	26	53	36
Petrobras(*)	38	6	43	25	29	24	33	21	23	50	47	39
PETRONAS(*)	39	36	6	21	34	26	49	19	28	50	25	38
Pioneer	40	8	45	44	42	27	52	23	54	46	53	14
PTT(*)	41	53	31	45	4	2	47	6	21	1	30	25
Repsol	42	36	41	11	4	50	26	32	22	30	10	15
Rosneft(*)	43	42	10	21	52	46	39	20	5	6	47	12
Shell	44	46	37	30	50	22	41	1	4	53	11	17
Sinopec(*)	45	53	11	4	17	22	50	33	40	29	49	27
SK Energy	46	16	9	30	4	28	26	2	6	21	33	36
Socar(*)	47	28	36	52	51	2	19	20	41	12	27	21
Southwestern	48	8	42	44	27	45	54	31	53	52	23	28
Statoil(*)	49	24	22	10	1	35	28	47	38	39	14	4
Suncor	50	32	44	45	42	52	9	49	14	16	35	38
Tatneft	51	18	6	16	8	21	50	46	23	52	20	32
Total	52	6	36	2	9	21	38	50	28	35	22	53
Wintershall	53	28	26	10	32	4	54	1	20	34	23	17
Woodside	54	9	32	41	26	36	20	53	29	22	31	42

Table 32 Company ranking in total-factor similarity (34th to 44th)

Firm name	ID	34th	35th	36th	37th	38th	39th	40th	41st	42nd	43rd	44th
Anadarko	1	46	28	41	47	10	49	37	33	39	9	19
Apache	2	23	10	46	31	28	47	39	41	37	3	9
Bashneft	3	37	49	12	39	22	26	50	2	11	41	4
BHP Billiton	4	31	33	28	41	47	49	10	35	9	14	37
BP	5	23	24	48	39	47	33	49	37	9	28	25
Cenovus	6	35	38	10	14	33	3	47	24	37	28	25
Chesapeake	7	16	41	14	46	19	49	47	39	37	9	35
Chevron	8	32	46	10	48	49	38	9	14	35	25	33
CNOOC(*)	9	40	33	37	15	13	7	24	34	43	41	48
CNPC(*)	10	3	36	6	43	21	50	51	19	1	4	17
CNR	11	49	47	9	31	28	35	10	3	33	14	38
ConocoPhillips	12	16	53	46	9	33	10	54	28	35	38	14
Devon Energy	13	16	46	28	9	35	41	47	49	10	37	39
Ecopetrol(*)	14	39	51	47	33	11	37	1	19	2	28	27
EnCana	15	41	19	16	39	47	37	46	49	33	10	9
Eni	16	11	22	35	41	38	14	25	28	17	43	40
EOG	17	54	38	31	16	47	10	9	28	49	41	37
ExxonMobil	18	46	39	28	37	9	41	53	24	47	25	3
Gazprom(*)	19	38	21	15	46	20	1	30	9	4	14	32
Hess	20	23	9	46	33	10	38	35	3	24	28	25
Husky Energy	21	35	39	25	38	24	10	3	43	33	34	47
Imperial	22	46	49	3	10	25	39	33	24	47	37	43
Inpex	23	40	35	15	6	3	25	38	13	21	7	36
Kazmunaigas(*)	24	32	50	41	22	27	26	2	11	54	4	53
Lukoil	25	37	29	12	32	41	50	22	26	2	54	11
Marathon Oil	26	33	9	54	10	28	39	37	35	3	14	47
Mitsui	27	13	3	40	7	43	16	36	48	28	22	50
Mol	28	47	6	29	4	38	11	1	21	35	24	36
Murphy Oil	29	9	16	38	49	10	33	35	3	28	25	14
Noble Energy	30	46	10	28	49	41	47	9	37	39	33	19
Novatek	31	46	16	39	52	10	6	8	21	20	49	29
Occidental	32	28	38	53	54	9	14	47	33	3	31	37
OMV	33	24	38	50	41	6	35	29	36	21	1	11
ONGC	34	36	12	21	6	32	2	50	26	54	22	4
PDVSA(*)	35	39	29	22	37	28	26	19	11	27	41	2
PEMEX(*)	36	43	39	38	25	3	14	10	34	46	47	51
Pertamina(*)	37	24	21	54	49	1	43	31	30	4	14	22
Petrobras(*)	38	37	22	51	4	28	26	19	41	11	27	2
PETRONAS(*)	39	32	1	35	22	30	4	43	3	11	14	53
Pioneer	40	16	9	31	35	47	28	49	10	3	38	37

(continued)

Table 32 (continued)

Firm name	ID	34th	35th	36th	37th	38th	39th	40th	41st	42nd	43rd	44th
PTT(*)	41	3	38	24	35	26	36	32	43	15	49	11
Repsol	42	40	27	7	13	33	23	49	48	9	28	19
Rosneft(*)	43	29	50	37	23	41	26	22	32	2	54	11
Shell	44	40	15	38	13	7	35	28	9	25	14	48
Sinopec(*)	45	13	23	15	7	3	24	25	47	48	43	9
SK Energy	46	11	1	3	22	25	47	50	40	24	34	43
Socar(*)	47	54	9	43	11	53	4	26	1	29	14	31
Southwestern	48	19	41	14	16	39	49	37	47	9	46	35
Statoil(*)	49	27	34	17	43	40	15	32	19	25	13	7
Suncor	50	27	10	33	3	46	39	25	24	43	47	51
Tatneft	51	5	39	29	22	37	11	2	12	41	26	4
Total	52	11	1	14	17	4	40	15	25	7	13	3
Wintershall	53	30	8	11	41	15	37	47	13	7	39	40
Woodside	54	16	50	28	46	47	52	39	37	19	10	3

Table 33 Company ranking in total-factor similarity (45th to 53rd)

Firm name	ID	45th	46th	47th	48th	49th	50th	51st	52nd	53rd
Anadarko	1	35	3	14	38	24	25	34	43	51
Apache	2	35	19	24	25	38	14	43	34	51
Bashneft	3	54	1	30	40	17	13	15	7	48
BHP Billiton	4	39	3	38	19	24	25	43	34	51
BP	5	41	3	34	19	53	43	54	51	31
Cenovus	6	23	19	41	43	34	54	51	53	31
Chesapeake	7	33	10	38	3	24	34	25	43	51
Chevron	8	43	34	3	28	54	19	53	51	31
CNOOC(*)	9	25	3	53	51	47	28	19	54	31
CNPC(*)	10	11	22	54	31	40	15	13	7	48
CNR	11	37	41	39	24	51	19	25	43	34
ConocoPhillips	12	3	47	31	25	24	19	43	34	51
Devon Energy	13	38	33	19	3	24	25	34	43	51
Ecopetrol(*)	14	30	41	40	13	54	15	7	31	48
EnCana	15	35	14	38	3	24	34	25	43	51
Eni	16	15	13	19	3	7	54	48	51	31
EOG	17	33	39	3	19	24	51	25	34	43
ExxonMobil	18	54	38	19	35	43	14	34	31	51
Gazprom(*)	19	26	7	17	48	11	13	40	22	50
Hess	20	47	14	53	43	34	19	51	54	31

(continued)

214   8   Total-Factor Spillovers, Similarities, and Competitions …

Table 33 (continued)

Firm name	ID	45th	46th	47th	48th	49th	50th	51st	52nd	53rd
Husky Energy	21	37	28	41	23	54	19	51	53	31
Imperial	22	23	28	51	54	41	34	19	53	31
Inpex	23	19	14	49	34	48	51	22	43	50
Kazmunaigas(*)	24	1	30	31	40	17	13	15	7	48
Lukoil	25	4	1	30	40	17	13	15	7	48
Marathon Oil	26	31	38	41	25	24	43	19	34	51
Mitsui	27	51	9	49	34	47	35	24	38	14
Mol	28	15	50	17	14	40	22	7	13	48
Murphy Oil	29	24	47	19	43	34	54	51	53	31
Noble Energy	30	35	14	3	38	24	25	34	43	51
Novatek	31	35	24	5	36	38	14	9	22	50
Occidental	32	49	24	39	25	41	51	43	19	34
OMV	33	14	22	30	17	40	15	13	7	48
ONGC	34	1	30	11	17	40	13	15	7	48
PDVSA(*)	35	1	30	54	40	31	13	15	7	48
PEMEX(*)	36	33	37	19	28	23	41	54	53	31
Pertamina(*)	37	11	50	51	15	17	40	7	13	48
Petrobras(*)	38	30	1	40	54	13	31	15	7	48
PETRONAS(*)	39	15	17	40	54	7	51	13	31	48
Pioneer	40	41	33	39	24	19	25	51	43	34
PTT(*)	41	14	17	7	13	40	22	48	51	50
Repsol	42	3	47	25	31	54	34	43	24	51
Rosneft(*)	43	4	1	30	40	17	13	15	7	48
Shell	44	19	3	24	43	47	54	34	31	51
Sinopec(*)	45	39	51	19	28	31	37	54	41	34
SK Energy	46	49	54	13	15	51	19	31	7	48
Socar(*)	47	30	50	17	22	40	15	13	7	48
Southwestern	48	33	10	38	34	3	24	25	43	51
Statoil(*)	49	3	51	46	48	37	23	41	54	31
Suncor	50	34	37	28	23	19	41	54	53	31
Tatneft	51	54	1	30	17	40	13	15	7	48
Total	52	19	24	48	47	43	34	51	54	31
Wintershall	53	48	9	6	21	24	29	36	50	22
Woodside	54	35	24	49	34	25	38	43	14	51

References

Abbott M. The Productivity and Efficiency of the Australian Electricity Supply Industry. Energy Economics. 2006, 28 (4):444–454.

Al-Obaidan A.M., and Scully G.W. Efficiency Differences between Private and State-Owned Enterprises in the International Petroleum Industry. Applied Economics. 1992, 24 (2):237–246.

Amsler C., Prokhorov A., and Schmidt P. Endogeneity in Stochastic Frontier Models. Journal of Econometrics. 2016, 190 (2):280–288.

Anselin L. Spatial Econometrics: Methods and Models: Springer Science & Business Media, 2013.

Artis M.J., Miguelez E., and Moreno R. Agglomeration Economies and Regional Intangible Assets: An Empirical Investigation. Journal of Economic Geography. 2012, 12 (6):1167–1189.

Bernstein P.M., Montgomery W.D., and Tuladhar S.D. Potential for Reducing Carbon Emissions from Non-Annex B Countries through Changes in Technology. Energy Economics. 2006, 28 (5–6):742–762.

Bivand R. Regression Modeling with Spatial Dependence: An Application of Some Class Selection and Estimation Methods. Geographical Analysis. 1984, 16 (1):25–37.

Breusch T.S., and Pagan A.R. The Lagrange Multiplier Test and Its Applications to Model Specification in Econometrics. The Review of Economic Studies. 1980, 47 (1):239–253.

Buckland S.T., Burnham K.P., and Augustin N.H. Model Selection: An Integral Part of Inference. Biometrics. 1997, 53 (2):603–618.

Chen S., and Golley J. 'Green' Productivity Growth in China's Industrial Economy. Energy Economics. 2014, 44:89–98.

Detotto C., Pulina M., and Brida J.G. Assessing the Productivity of the Italian Hospitality Sector: A Post-Wdea Pooled-Truncated and Spatial Analysis. Journal of Productivity Analysis. 2014, 42 (2):103–121.

Du L., He Y., and Yan J. The Effects of Electricity Reforms on Productivity and Efficiency of China's Fossil-Fired Power Plants: An Empirical Analysis. Energy Economics. 2013, 40:804–812.

Eberhardt M., and Teal F. No Mangoes in the Tundra: Spatial Heterogeneity in Agricultural Productivity Analysis. Oxford Bulletin of Economics and Statistics. 2013, 75 (6):914–939.

Eller S.L., Hartley P.R., and Medlock K.B. Empirical Evidence on the Operational Efficiency of National Oil Companies. Empirical Economics. 2011, 40 (3):623–643.

Getmansky M., Girardi G., Hanley K.W., Nikolova S., and Pelizzon L. 2016. "Portfolio Similarity and Asset Liquidation in the Insurance Industry." Paper presented at Fourth Annual Conference on Financial Market Regulation.

Gong B. 2016. "Efficiency and Productivity Analysis of Multidivisional Firms." Dissertation, Rice University.

Gong B. Multi-Dimensional Interactions in the Oilfield Market: A Jackknife Model Averaging Approach of Spatial Productivity Analysis (Forthcoming). Energy Economics. 2017.

Gong B. Agricultural Reforms and Production in China Changes in Provincial Production Function and Productivity in 1978–2015. Journal of Development Economics. 2018a, 132:18–31.

Gong B. Different Behaviors in Natural Gas Production between National and Private Oil Companies: Economics-Driven or Environment-Driven?. Energy Policy. 2018b, 114 (3):145–152.

Gong B. The Impact of Public Expenditure and International Trade on Agricultural Productivity in China. Emerging Markets Finance and Trade. 2018c, 54 (15):3438–3453.

Gong B. The Shale Technical Revolution – Cheer or Fear? Impact Analysis on Efficiency in the Global Oilfield Service Market. Energy Policy. 2018d, 112 (1):162–172.

Hale T. International Sources of Political Order in the People's Republic of China: A Lacuna in the Fukuyama Framework. Journal of Chinese Governance. 2016, 1 (3):427–440.

Han J., Ryu D., and Sickles R. How to Measure Spillover Effects of Public Capital Stock: A Spatial Autoregressive Stochastic Frontier Model. In Spatial Econometrics: Qualitative and Limited Dependent Variables. Emerald Group Publishing Limited, pp. 259–294, 2016.

Hanley K.W., and Hoberg G. Litigation Risk, Strategic Disclosure and the Underpricing of Initial Public Offerings. Journal of Financial Economics. 2012, 103 (2):235–254.

Hartley P., and Medlock K.B. A Model of the Operation and Development of a National Oil Company. Energy Economics. 2008, 30 (5):2459–2485.

Hartley P.R., and Medlock III K.B. Changes in the Operational Efficiency of National Oil Companies. The Energy Journal. 2013, 34 (2):27–57.

Huang C., Yue X., Yang M., Su J., and Chen J. A Quantitative Study on the Diffusion of Public Policy in China: Evidence from the S&T Finance Sector. Journal of Chinese Governance. 2017, 2 (3):235–254.

Ike C.B., and Lee H. Measurement of the Efficiency and Productivity of National Oil Companies and Its Determinants. Geosystem Engineering. 2014, 17 (1):1–10.

LeSage J.P. An Introduction to Spatial Econometrics. Revue d'économie industrielle. 2008, (3):19–44.

LeSage J.P., and Pace R.K. Introduction to Spatial Econometrics (Statistics, Textbooks and Monographs): CRC Press, 2009.

Managi S., Opaluch J.J., Jin D., and Grigalunas T.A. Stochastic Frontier Analysis of Total Factor Productivity in the Offshore Oil and Gas Industry. Ecological Economics. 2006, 60 (1):204–215.

Managi S., Opaluch J.J., Jin D., and Grigalunas T.A. Technological Change and Depletion in Offshore Oil and Gas. Journal of Environmental Economics and Management. 2004, 47 (2):388–409.

Millo G., and Piras G. Splm: Spatial Panel Data Models in R. Journal of Statistical Software. 2012, 47 (1):1–38.

Moretz T. An Assessment of China's Ability to Regulate Its Iron and Steel Industries. Journal of Chinese Governance. 2018, 3 (1):101–121.

Ohene-Asare K., Turkson C., and Afful-Dadzie A. Multinational Operation, Ownership and Efficiency Differences in the International Oil Industry. Energy Economics. 2017, 68:303–312.

Ord K. Estimation Methods for Models of Spatial Interaction. Journal of the American Statistical Association. 1975, 70 (349):120–126.

Pesaran M.H. "General Diagnostic Tests for Cross Section Dependence in Panels." Institute for the Study of Labor (IZA). 2004.

Qiang L., and Tuohan W. Social Governance and the Qinghe Experiment. Journal of Chinese Governance. 2016, 1 (1):139–156.

Rahman F. Defeating or Delaying the Defaults: Bailout Strategy of the Chinese Government for Its State-Owned Enterprises on Their Bond Payments. Journal of Chinese Governance. 2018, 3 (1):86–100.

Ripley B.D. Spatial Statistics: Wiley Series in Probability and Mathematical Statistics. New York. 1981.

Sarafidis V., and Wansbeek T. Cross-Sectional Dependence in Panel Data Analysis. Econometric Reviews. 2012, 31 (5):483–531.

Sias R., Turtle H., and Zykaj B. Hedge Fund Crowds and Mispricing. Management Science. 2015, 62 (3):764–784.

Sueyoshi T., and Goto M. Data Envelopment Analysis for Environmental Assessment: Comparison between Public and Private Ownership in Petroleum Industry. European journal of operational research. 2012, 216 (3):668–678.

Thompson R.G., Dharmapala P., Rothenberg L.J., and Thrall R.M. Dea/Ar Efficiency and Profitability of 14 Major Oil Companies in U.S. Exploration and Production. Computers and Operations Research. 1996, 23 (4):357–373.

Tobler W. Cellular Geography. In Philosophy in Geography. Springer, pp. 379–386, 1979.

Wolf C. Does Ownership Matter? The Performance and Efficiency of State Oil Vs. Private Oil (1987–2006). Energy Policy. 2009, 37 (7):2642–2652.

Xiao H. Public Financial Management and the Campaign against Extravagant Position-Related Consumption in China. Journal of Chinese Governance. 2016, 1 (4):546–563.

Yang X., and Yan J. Top-Level Design, Reform Pressures, and Local Adaptations: An Interpretation of the Trajectory of Reform since the 18th Cpc Party Congress. Journal of Chinese Governance. 2018, 3 (1):25–48.

Zhu X. Dynamics of Central–Local Relations in China's Social Welfare System. Journal of Chinese Governance. 2016, 1 (2):251–268.

CPSIA information can be obtained
at www.ICGtesting.com
Printed in the USA
LVHW021117070620
657604LV00004B/256